FOUR CENTURIES AMERICANS

VAN FLEET/VAN VLIET/VAN VLEET

FAMILY HISTORY

1634–2001

James A. Van Fleet, Ph.D.

Eindelijk Wordt een Spruit een Boom

At last a sprig becomes a tree

De Boom Growit en Draagt Vrucht

And the tree grows and bears fruit

HERITAGE BOOKS
2010

HERITAGE BOOKS
AN IMPRINT OF HERITAGE BOOKS, INC.

Books, CDs, and more—Worldwide

For our listing of thousands of titles see our website
at
www.HeritageBooks.com

Published 2010 by
HERITAGE BOOKS, INC.
Publishing Division
100 Railroad Ave. #104
Westminster, Maryland 21157

International Standard Book Numbers
Paperbound: 978-0-7884-8479-7
Clothbound: 978-0-7884-2247-8

DEDICATION

To the memory of Seventeenth Century Dutch New Netherland colonists Adrian Gerritsen Van Vliet and Dirck Jans Van der Vliedt, ancient cousins and progenitors of today's American Van Fleet/Van Vliet family.

CONTENTS

ACKNOWLEDGEMENTS

This commentary is the result of extraordinary effort, persistence and countless hours of research among many dusty files or worn books, as well as in front of computers viewing data files and e-mails, by dozens of people. I must state clearly that most of the pages of this book reflect their work, and accordingly I recognize them all as its true authors.

Some of these writers and researchers are named in no specific order, but all are equally applauded for their work promoting lines of the Van Fleet/Van Vliet family history.

Nonetheless, I must begin my thanks with my late father, George Nelson Van Fleet, esquire, for his activities on behalf of the Holland Society and for recording for posterity information and sources on our Dutch ancestry; and my dear cousin Dr. Medora Van Fleet for her untiring efforts to highlight the Van Fleet family history in Florida and elsewhere.

Additionally, the following persons made great contributions to this publication through research and/or writings: Colonel George Craig Van Fleet, Kentucky branch; Ms. Vernita Van Fleet, Illinois branch; Mrs. Louise Elizabeth Johnson Spiess, diverse branches; Mrs. Edna Marie Hobbs, diverse branches; George Allan Van Fleet, esquire, Texas branch; Mr. Keith E. Horner, New York and Ontario branches; Mrs. Elizabeth P. Kujawski, New York, Pennsylvania and Ohio branches; Mr. Scott Van Fleet, Utah branch; Mr. And Mrs. Jack and Nancy Soper, Michigan branch; Mrs. Edith Kuhn, New York branch; Ms. Miral Haubner, New York branch; Mr. Fred Sisser III, New Jersey branch; and Mr. Allison Van Vliet Dunn, Vermont branch. This list is not exhaustive, and I ask forgiveness from the many others whose names are not cited.

i

A special acknowledgement is owed to the late Reverend Mr. William Lewis, Lackawanna Historical Society, who prepared a superb history of the Van Fleet family in Luzerne and Lackawanna Counties, Pennsylvania, through his interest in local church records and early pioneering families in Northeastern Pennsylvania.

In that vein, the work of the Church of Jesus Christ of Latter Day Saints, or the Mormon Church, is recognized for its much appreciated and invaluable role in family history preservation for this country and others around the world.

Mention should be made of the historical societies that labor long and hard throughout our states' counties and in state capitals and archives. Special recognition goes to the Minisink Valley Historical Society and the Ontario, Orange, and Onondaga County Historical Societies, New York; the Lackawanna and Luzerne County Historical Societies, Pennsylvania; the Marion and Lucas County Historical Societies, Ohio; and the state historical societies in New York, Ohio, California, Colorado, Pennsylvania, Kentucky and Florida.

Lastly, very emphatic recognition must be given to the Holland Society of New York, to which every Van Fleet and Van Vliet descendant of Adrian Gerritsen Van Vliet and Dirck Van der Vliet in the male line ought to belong.

A similar sentiment should be expressed for the Sons of the American Revolution, the Society of Colonial Wars and for many the Huguenot Society, not to overlook the relationship that all should have with the local historical societies cited above, and in everyone's home county. Across America, they labor long and hard to preserve our history and heritage.

Female family members should use the information presented in this commentary for support for membership where appropriate in the Colonial Dames and Daughters of the American Revolution, as well as Dutch-related organizations.

At the risk of preaching to many who are already converted, it is our collective obligation to preserve the past for the present and future generations of our American family.

If you could see your ancestors
All standing in a row,
Would you be proud of them
Or would you really want to know?

Strange discoveries are often made
In climbing the family tree,
Occasionally one is found in line
Who shocks the progeny.

If you could see your ancestors
All standing in a row,
Perhaps there might be one or two
You wouldn't want to know.

Now turn the question right about
And take another view.
When you shall meet your ancestors,
Will they be proud of you?

Anon.

PREFACE

I doubt that many people are born to do genealogical research, even those like myself who have a fondness for history. In school, history was a fascination for me, easily yielding the highest grades throughout my elementary and secondary preparation. After more years of law, doctoral studies in economics and administration, and non-degree courses, I still seek refuge in reading history.

But as a youth when my late father began talking about family history, my eyelids shut. He seemed to turn history into a series of dates read from a tombstone rather than reflect the action-packed events I saw in books. Only as a favor to him when I followed up on some research issues while attending college, did I realize that much meat could be placed on the bare bones under those dated stones. So it was four decades ago that at first hesitantly and then eagerly, I developed an addiction to family history.

The pursuit was not even over the years. Living and traveling abroad were not conducive to family history as a steady activity, not to mention an absence from the best sources of information for an American in the days before computers. Proximity to United States libraries and research centers was the *sine qua non* for this work. With frequent delays, one that lasted a full decade, I returned to the sizable but motley collection of materials from diverse sources, augmented by those gathered by my Dad, in the spring of 1999.

Looking at this as the three hundred and sixth eighth year of a Van Vliet/Van Fleet presence in America, I thought it timely to finally publish these materials as a family history, insofar as the notes, papers and borrowed research could take us.

I have enjoyed this project, because it carries us all beyond the present into a collectively owned past to look as best we can at profiles that in no small measure reflect in us as we are today. I believe that much as the genetic sciences have demonstrated biologically, we are psychologically the products of our ancestors. I can see traits in many of the people discussed in this commentary that are well defined in family members alive today, including myself.

These traits are for the good or perhaps for the questionable, but we owe it to ourselves and for future generations to commit to paper what we know of our history, somewhat like the Spanish king's instructions, to be "painted with warts and all."

But is that the "message" of this product? It is one of several. I want readers to have an appreciation for the flow of American history vis-à-vis Van Fleet/Van Vliet/Van Vleet family members who preceded us as they came into the uncertain world that this land represented in the 1600s, and then sense what their children and children's children experienced through the generations when they became the pioneers in territories and states of the evolving American Union.

And too, I want readers to appreciate what this family has contributed to the weaving of the American fabric, through countless efforts from school teaching to the ministry; from the practice of law to clearing and farming the land; from fighting America's wars as privates and generals and everything in between to governing towns, cities and states; from editing newspapers and writing books, to caring for the ill and infirm. All this, as paupers and millionaires; craftsmen and doctors; merchants and soldiers.

Perhaps this family is not remarkable in ways different from thousands of others, but it does merit our best effort to make a record of who it is, where it came from, what it has done, if for no other reason than to give us knowledge of our roots and a sense of direction as to where we should and – God willing – will go in the coming centuries.

In all of the research and correspondence preparing this book, I have found no other publication that has focused to any degree on the Van Fleets, et al, in America, save one slim privately printed paper that looked only at one descendant of Adrian Gerritsen Van Vliet.

Since the task of this publication is to provide material on Adrian Gerritsen and his distant kinsman Dirck Van der Vliet as our family founders, their children, grandchildren and descendants to contemporary times reflecting whatever information is available, this book establishes a framework for other researchers and long-lost cousins to build yet more knowledge of the family through their own research.

For the coming centuries, it is my hope that each family descendant will make such research a project of high priority within their families. In contacts with so many other Van Fleets, et al, around the country, this writer has found it sad that much of our collective family history was "lost" or at least left undiscovered for the scores now seeking more information on the roots of the Van Fleets/Van Vliets in America.

If this book serves to establish a base of knowledge, information and interest on the Van Fleet/Van Vliet heritage, then the effort to write it will have been a most worthwhile pastime.

James A. Van Fleet

3

AN INTRODUCTION

TO OUR HERITAGE

THE AMERICAN HERITAGE AND ITS DUTCH ROOTS: WHY WE MATTERED

The closing decades of the Twentieth Century marked the two hundredth anniversary of the founding dates and documents for our Republic: the Declaration of Independence; the Constitution; and the Bill of Rights. Americans had much to be proud of and cause to have celebrated these events, for those are the basic instruments upon which our Federal Government is still based. Ours was one of the first nations founded on written philosophical concepts and political ideals, principals that have stood the test of time.

The lofty goal of our founding fathers – to create a single nation out of thirteen very different colonies – was not achieved with ease. Perhaps that task could not have been achieved at all had not their history lent a special character to the peoples of America as her numbers grew, particularly in the 1700s. That character was formed out of the accumulated experiences of the previous one hundred and seventy-odd years, from the founding of the colonies of Virginia, Plymouth and New Netherland, and then the newer settlements that followed along the Atlantic Coast from Georgia to Nova Scotia.

Although the smallest of the three major colonies in 1664, New Netherland was destined to have a profound and lasting impact on America's formation through its ties to Europe's mainland and as a New World magnet for diversity. More than any other colony, New Netherland gave rise to a multicultural society in the truest sense on American shores, welcoming peoples from many countries, religions, regional and racial backgrounds.

5

While often begrudgingly tolerant of dissent and difference, this colony nonetheless saw the widest sweep of languages and nationalities gathered in any one place in the Americas. It accommodated such differences and epitomized the "one out of many" concept, that developed from the Dutch colony's social mores, political and business practices, even after the English came to dominate a renamed New York.

The very name "United States" traces its origins to the "United Provinces (or States) of the Netherlands," the name given to the republic after securing independence from Spain. Having fought its own war of independence in the centuries before the United States, much of its rationale – not to overlook the founding ideals for the Dutch form and philosophy of government and civil society – lent themselves well to America when its turn came to secure independence in the late 1700s.

From the naming of the country to its currency and market economy; to the founding in 1614 of what became the five American states of New York, New Jersey, Connecticut, Pennsylvania and Delaware; to the revered traditions of Thanksgiving and Christmas' Santa Claus; to the wording and basic concepts of (a declaration of) independence and form for a federal government, not to overlook the principles contained in our Bill of Rights; to the roles of entrepreneurship, commercial endeavor and the dignity of work; the Dutch imprint on America is writ large.

A mere 10,000 inhabitants by generous account at the time of capitulation to the English in 1664, the New Netherland world lives on today forming a core for much of the political, cultural and social heritage of the United States of America.

6

This commentary is about just one American family of Holland Dutch descent, the lines of Adrian Gerritsen Van Vliet of Utrecht Province and of Dirck Van der Vliet of Rylevelt, North Holland Province. While their heirs in the modern Van Fleet/Van Vliet/Van Vleet/Vliet family are not necessarily of the standing of many others of Dutch descent like the Roosevelts, Tafts and Vanderbilts, it may be though of as typical of those who contributed to America in countless ways in many places across the land. It is the story of an American family that has prospered and contributed now well into the fourth century on this country's shores through all of its branches.

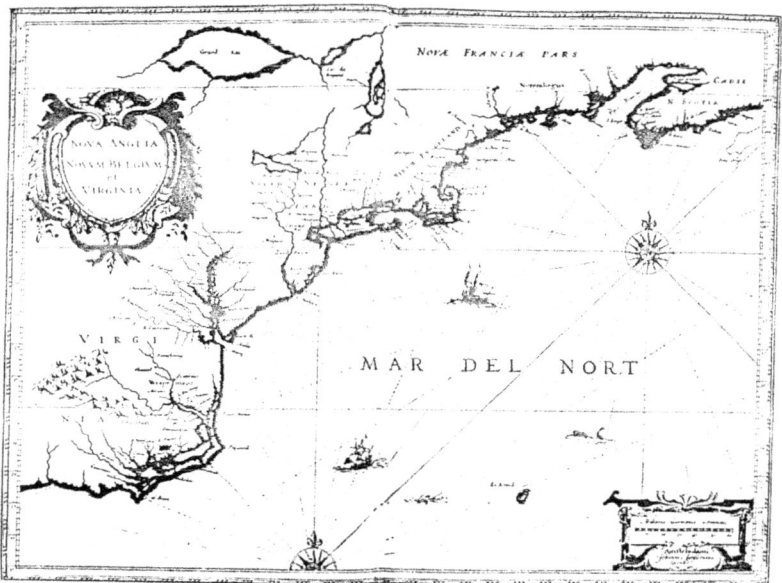

New Netherland

PART I.

EUROPEAN ORIGINS OF THE

VAN FLEET/VAN VLIET FAMILY

HISTORICAL BACKGROUND ON ORIGINS: THE VAN FLEET/VAN VLIET FAMILY AND NAME

In the swampy northern European lowlands of the present-day Netherlands, pre-Roman tribes occupied territories singularly unattractive for the Empire's colonization. Villages of native Celtic Belgae and Frisians farmed small plots of arable land in the region, never far from the invading waters of multiple rivers and the North Sea. Along with fishing and hunting, these early Celto-Germanic peoples eked out an existence in micro plot farming on land marginal by the standards of any advanced civilization of the day.

But in time, the northerly and northeasterly advance of the Roman Empire demanded control of those marshy lands, principally because the various rivers that emptied from present-day Germany into the North Sea passed through them. In fact, those areas control the headwaters of the Great Rhine estuary system, today the mightiest shipping area not just in Europe, but in the world. Even two millennia ago at the dawn of Europe's Christian Age, the strategic importance of this immense river system was well understood, and the broader question of control of the Germanic tribes east of the Rhine and its tributaries demanded that Rome come to rule and to militarily occupy the land.

In the years of their empire's expansion, the Romans brought the local populations to heel and established numerous fortified locales on waterways leading into the interior of the continent, Arnheim, Dordrecht and Utrecht (Trajectum ad Rhenum, or Rhine Ford) among them.

9

At the site of the present-day small City of Worden on the Old Rhine, the Romans created a minor fortification and satellite settlement protected by a mostly natural but partly man-made moat, called Castelum Luarentum.

It was a somewhat important garrison for the Old Rhine area, and a defense against the not wholly subdued Frisians, not to overlook the fierce Germanic tribes further inland. In the truest sense, it was a vanguard post situated at the very edge of the Roman Empire, and so it would remain for centuries under Rome.

When Rome itself fell in the late 400s and Europe was awash in the invading Germanic tribes from the east, Castelum Laurentum – Woerden – survived as a community, albeit small in size and undoubtedly diminished in importance.

Its inhabitants accommodated – or in time became part of – the new arrivals: Saxons and then Franks, and more than a few Vikings who settled, having begun their raids around 700. Indeed, the rulers of the medieval "County of Holland" received lands only in 922 under Dirk I, whose ancestry was Viking.

By the close of the first millennium of the Christian era, the population of Woerden, like much of what came to be known as the Netherlands, essentially had the "gene and blood" composition that it has today; that is, Frisian, Saxon, and Frank "branches," with other and ancient Celtic and Germanic roots.

These early Celtic and Germanic dimensions of the Netherlands are an important aspect of this mix, because their ancient and widespread traditions go far toward explaining the origins of the special and ennobled classes in all the lands they came to dominate.

According to historian Hans Delbruck, among others, even the Romans came to accept the local methods of identifying leaders in northern Europe, who they in turn used for their military rule and civil administration. Then as the Roman legions became more Germanized through the use of mercenaries in ensuing centuries, other lands they controlled were inculcated with this tradition of leadership selection.

Specifically, the most physically and mentally able male was elected (or selected) by the peoples in the clan or village to be their spokesman, protector and defender for whatever purposes and whenever needed.

This ancient practice that predates Roman rule was continued long after the collapse of their western empire, and likely became increasingly important as chaos followed in the centuries after the mid-400s.

But the role of "elected minor administrator" for Roman law or military control that was typical during this era became more one of "elected protector and defender" to maintain order thereafter, since the Roman legions were no longer around to fulfill that function. Thus, by a point in the 500s to 700s, the individual as an "armed protector" and overseer emerges in Europe for the elected champions of the people.

It is evident then how a system of championship evolved into middle ages knighthood, emerging out of its nascent forms in the Roman era through the dark ages and into full bloom in the medieval period. Indeed, this system explains the evolution of much of the higher nobility itself, when viewed against the developing system of fiefdoms, particularly after the reign of the Christian emperor Charlemagne.

As events unfolded, the cost of arming protectors fell to the local people whom these knights were defending. There was no larger jurisdiction, let alone the defunct Roman Empire, to absorb such costs. It has been noted by many historians that several communities often had to ban together to accept these expenses for their protector, due to the small size of many villages and the high cost of horses, retinue and armor. Consequently, the influence of a defender often extended over a territory rather than just a single village.

In addition to the investment in such individuals as well as their training, knowledge and formal education (as far as it went), it was logical that their place would be special in society at all levels.

In time, this class emerged no longer as an elected/selected group: it became an inevitable selection of these persons because they were not just the obvious candidates, but in reality the only possible choices for leadership. Election fell by the wayside and this class became hereditary, and imbued with authority to select other knights. It thereafter constituted a basic building block of the nobility, giving rise to – or at least reinforcing – the system of social order in the feudal age of Europe, and in many instances to the structure of the nobility itself.

After 800 when the Frankish King Charlemagne was crowned "Emperor of Germany" and ruler of what came to be called the Holy Roman Empire, the region of present-day Netherlands was controlled by numerous and often at odds noble families. The line of Viking-descended Dirk I ruled the County of Holland, whose name derived from "holt-land" or "marsh land."

12

Adjacent to Dirk's holdings was the Bishopric (or Diocese) of Utrecht, which was Christianized thanks to Wilfred of York (634 to 710), an English monk, who preached to the Frisians in the 678 to 679 period.

By the mid-medieval period of the 1000s and 1100s when the Bishopric of Utrecht and the County of Holland were considered distant parts of the vast Holy Roman Empire that stretched from central Italy to Prague, westward to the Rhine and north to the Baltic Sea, the region around Woerden – an area of jurisdiction under the Utrecht bishop – was endowed with a knight-defender.

Specifically, by the recorded date of 1131, Herman I van Woerden was confirmed by the bishop as "ridder" (or knight) and "Lord of Woerden."

From that date forward, his family line would serve not only as Lords of Woerden (Heren van Woerden) but for other areas as well in the feudal lands of the western Diocese of Utrecht, known as the "Vlietpolder" or simply as "the Vliet."

In something of an aside, it is useful to comment on the concept of "polders" and the meaning of "vliet" in particular, in the context of this narrative. The "holt-land" (or Holland, as it came to be known) was reported by the Roman historian Pliny as a low lying region (Nederland, in the local language) broken by "mounds" or dykes, upon which people built their homes. The resulting outlined lower plots of land in time were drained and dried after several "washings" with fresh water to ensure that saline free earth was left for cultivation.

13

The origins of this land reclamation practice are lost in time, but by 1150 the system was mastered, and thus "polders" – literally stake fields, since they were outlined and anchored by stakes driven into the ground before soil was piled atop forming dykes – or reclaimed lowlands expanded the "netherlanden" territory dramatically over the ensuring centuries.

The middle ages configuration of the region involved reclaimed marsh lands in a long and broad swath from areas around present-day Amsterdam through the western reaches of Utrecht Province, and on into the southwest Netherlands.

This is precisely the area that includes Woerden and its surrounding towns, a land with some fairly fast flowing waters or "vliets" (from which the English word "fleet" is derived). Called "Vlietpolder" or simply "Vliet" was a way of identifying a very specific region with a distinct characteristic, but one which as the reader shall see, soon came to be associated specifically with the family whose lordship over the land gave rise to their surname.

Crest of Vliet Region of Netherlands

Polders or Reclaimed Lands of Netherlands
(All of the Vliet Region including Woerden)

NORTH SEA

NOORD ZEE

DRENTHE

OVERIJSSEL

GELDERLAND

UTRECHT

DUITSLAND
GERMANY

NOORD · BRABANT

LIMBURG

BELGIË
BELGIUM

● provincial capital	● other important town	—— provincial border	Randstad urban conurbation	Land below sea level

15

The Van Woerden Van Vliet Family

Little is known of the first Herman, but the name itself is significant. It is considered to be a Germanic form of the Latin-based name Arminius, the great German hero who defeated the Roman advance into Germania in the First Century (also known in German legend as Siegfried, as in Wagner's opera).

Beyond this, there are a few related facts worth noting. In 1160 Woerden officially was recognized as a town under the Bishop-Count of Utrecht Godfried van Reenan, the bishop then ruling as both a nobleman and clergyman.

By that point in time when the Crusaders were fashioning the heraldic crests that became stylish among European nobility, the "Van Woerden Van Vliet" coat of arms probably came into being. Its simple basic design, reflecting the earliest origins in the art of heraldry, however, might be traced to the mid-100s as shown on a still-standing building that bears the image in stone in the Vliet polder town of Oudewater.

It is known that Herman I had at least two children, the first a son and his heir named Herman II (born about 1165), and the second named Godescalc (a form of Godfried).

This second son is believed to have given rise to several notable families in Lowlands history, including the "van der Haer" and possibly the van Hamme and van Enghe families.

The beautiful and famous Castle de Haar near Utrecht is adorned with Herman I's family crest, in late Nineteenth Century style (when the castle was reconstructed on Fourteenth Century ruins), reflecting descent from this knight via the van der Haar family.

16

Herman II van Woerden had a son and heir who was named in succession Herman III (sometime in the 1200s), in addition to sons Frederic (who probably was Frederic van Merloo) and Alber(echt?). Herman III in turn sired Herman IV and Gerard van Hermalen. Hermalen, a town in Utrecht Province, is located quite close to Woerden as well as to the Oudewater community in the Vliet area, as reflected on the map of Utrecht's political divisions.

Gerard van Hermalen in turn likely gave rise to the families Van de Poll and Van Hermalen, that are still found in the Netherlands today. The proximity of Hermalen to Woerden is strong testimony to the regional nature of the family's stewardship for the bishop of Utrecht's western provincial holdings under the Van Woerdens.

Herman IV van Woerden was the father of Herman V van Woerden (born 1252), as well as two daughters, one who married Both van der Eem, and the second who married Chris(brecht) (van?) Bokel. He had two additional sons, Spanyard (born 1260) and Rothard (died 1295) about whom there is little information that can be relayed here.

In turn, Herman V van Woerden was the father of four sons, two of whom have primary importance for purposes of this narrative. The first son in importance in Dutch history and his heir was Herman VI van Woerden (born by at least the late 1250s) and the second of pivotal importance for this commentary, Gerard (or Gerrit) van den Vliet. The other two sons were Johannes and Engelbert (born 1272), but nothing is known about them.

Herman VI van Woerden was heir and Lord of Woerden and other lands of the Vliet. From 1268 to 1279, he was a squire (knape) and then a nobleman-knight under Floris V van Holland (from 1280 onward).

17

Specifically, from 1288 to 1296, he was a knight and ruler of lands of the Vlietpolder under his liege; that is, from 1280 onward under the Count of Holland Floris V, who had taken away possession of areas of western Utrecht from the bishop-count. It can be implied that if knighthood was conferred in 1280 (Woerden fell in 1279), Herman was at least twenty-one years of age at the time and more likely several years older, Floris then being twenty-six, and was closely allied to the count.

Herman was married to Elizabeth van Anstel (who died young in 1292, possibly in childbirth), sister of Gilsbert van Amstel of Ijsselstein, another noted lord and knight of Utrecht (and later of Holland under Floris). Historical records indicate that just one child was born of the union of Herman and Elizabeth; that is, a daughter Clementia. Ultimately shemarried Hubert van Beusichhem, Lord of Culemborg (a town in Gelderland).

Herman VI van Woerden and Gilsbert van Amstel served their feudal lord Floris V from 1280 onward. By that year Amsteland and Woerden had been acquired by the Count of Holland, along with Waterland, by force of arms from the bishop-count of Utrecht. That, of course, necessitated transfer of allegiance to Floris as holder of their fiefdoms.

Although there is evidence that they served Floris well in the following years, it might be suggested that this takeover really marked the beginning of their discontent that matured in an event reflecting one of the most important stories in Dutch history that came to unfold in the summer of 1296. Additional support for this thesis lies in Davies' notation that Floris "...undertook to curb arbitrary rule by his bailiffs" which could have been common under a weaker bishop-count than under the powerful Count of Holland.

18

Floris V ws the son of the (very briefly) Holy Roman Emperor Willem (Willem) van Holland. He acceded to the title of count at the age of two, when his father William died in a winter accident, falling fully armored through thin river ice. When at majority age he assumed control of his lands, by all accounts he ruled Holland brilliantly for the times, as one of the most enlightened nobles of Europe.

Beloved by the people for his evenhandedness in taxation and issues of justice, Floris is remembered in Holland for the development of administrative districts, the construction of dykes, drainage systems, free roads as well as other public works that were used by all, vastly enhancing the physical and economic well being of the masses. Indeed, among the oft-used names of respect and endearment for Floris V, one from the Dutch translates as "God of the Common Man."

It is useful here to make several additional comments about the times and places mentioned in this narrative, beyond it being the end of the era of Marco Polo in Asia as well as of St. Francis of Assisi in Europe, and was in fact contemporaneous with the founding of Beijing in China, the development of the Ottoman Empire in the Middle East and the lives of Ghengis Khan and St. Thomas of Aquinas.

In the first instance, one must remember that most of Europe in this period lacked recognizable national communities. There was no "France," "Germany" or "Netherlands" as we know them today, only territorial holdings of competing noble houses that in many instances included scattered lands in several of today's European states.

Moreover, language was very regional. Less than half present-day France spoke French, and Dutch as we know it was spoken only in Flanders, not in either Utrecht or the County of Holland.

19

In the second instance, the Counties of Holland and Utrecht, like others of the three hundred that constituted the Holy Roman Empire, did not have a strong "national" character of single dominating culture, let alone single language. As late as the mid-1200s, the County of Holland was still absorbing and assimilating diverse Frisian, Frankish and Saxon elements and cultures, according to Davies.

In the third instance and again according to Davies, "social conditions in Holland did not conform to the standard structures of the 'age of feudalism.'" In fact, feudal institutions there were weak. Although its nobles were well integrated "into the practices and mores of knighthood and land ownership, they were not subordinated in any systematic way to feudal superiors." Their relationship was much looser to their superiors than the conditions of vassalage would dictate as found in such comparable settings as German and French lands.

Against this background, the commentary continues on Floris V. He was essentially a political animal, reflected by his seizure of border lands from the always near bankrupt and militarily much weaker bishop-count of Utrecht, his struggle to take over Zeeland (in which Holland ultimately succeeded), and his involvement with major warring European rulers of the day. He was a builder but a survivor above all, and engaged in every necessary action to ensure the House of Holland would continue long after him.

This period in history was, of course, one involving ongoing French and English interests on the continent that ultimately led to the Hundred Years' War, and is sometimes referred to as the "First Hundred Years' War."

For several centuries until the mid-1400s, these seminal events pitted France, a not yet great or united country, against the England of the (Norman descended) Plantagenets, who ruled large parts of present-day France and claimed their own monarchs to be the true kings of France.

In this conflict in the late 1200s, Floris V sided with Edward I of England. This is the same Edward who was occupied fighting the Scots, in part under the famed William Wallace, known commonly as "Braveheart."

Floris had a valid claim through his grandmother to the Scottish throne in 1292, but Edward was not to honor it. Seeking greater control if not outright rule over Scotland, this "Edward Long Shanks" had only recently subdued Wales (and had given the world the first "Prince of Wales," later the ill-fated Edward II). In 1292 he chose a compliant John Baliol to rule Scotland as Edward's vassal, a role Floris would not likely have accepted quite so eagerly.

Ever the conniver and cruel military campaigner aside, Edward was also an innovative and clever ruler who promoted national economic development in part through trade in wheat, wool and cloth (mainly woolens and linens) and fishing rights for the Dutch off the East Anglia coast between Holland and England. In so doing, he greatly enhanced the base of wealth for both realms.

However, by early 1296, Edward I was alienated from his erstwhile ally Floris V. Certainly this occurred in part because Edward did not support Floris' Scottish claims, but more so because Edward began to trade wool with Flanders, becoming close to that country's (or county's) ruler, Guy de Dampierre.

21

That was seen as treachery by Floris, since the Dampierres of Flanders were his chief rivals and hence enemies, despite the fact that Guy was his cousin. Consequently, Floris abandoned Edward's cause and allied himself with Philip IV of France, Edward's arch-enemy, largely at the urging of his cousin and staunch French ally John (Jean) of Avesnes, Count of Hainaut (and remarkably the brother of Guy de Dampierre, both being sons and heirs of Margaret of Flanders, or Zwarte Griet – "Black Meg").

Edward, who had been so close as to have had Floris' only son under tutorage and his personal protection in England, sought to persuade Floris to change his mind again. Pursuant to this, he enlisted the aid of several of Floris' nobles, including Gerard van Vlezen, van Amstel and van Woerden. The plan was to take Floris prisoner and to send him to England, where Edward would convince him to again support his cause and claims in France.

The plot was hatched in early summer 1296, when Floris was taken prisoner while on a falcon hunt with these nobles. He was removed to the castle at Muiden in (North) Holland (built on land formerly in the possession of the bishop-count of Utrecht), which he had erected in 1280 as a military outpost for his recently extended holdings.

News of his capture spread rapidly, and as soon as he was incarcerated many farmers – his ardent supporters – began surrounding the lightly defended castle. On 27 June 1296, the fifth day of his imprisonment, his noble jailers attempted to break out of the growing encirclement and to remove Floris to a portage point, where he could be taken to England.

Floris V of Holland

As history and Dutch writers relate, within a mere breath of freedom being gained with the clamorous aid of his farmer-supporters, Floris was murdered by his three kidnapping nobles and erstwhile friends, who would rather have seen him dead than liberated. He was stabbed and according to some records, hacked to death.

Holland's "Rhyming Chronicle," the "Rijmkronik van Melis Stoke" relates:

> *Tgraefscap ende dat jonghe kynt*
> *Daer wonder of ghesciede sint.*

"So ended the countship of the young man (who) was the wonder of history."

Naturally, these assassins became outcasts of the people, but importantly not of much of the nobility – and likely silent supporters for this act – who were better positioned to punish the errant knights. However, demands for the banishment were met, and historic records point to the termination of their titles and privileges in the same year of 1296.

Ultimately the assassins were killed themselves, but van Woerden for example lived on until 1304, and van Amstel until some time later. Herman VI was probably around forty-five to fifty years of age at the time of his death. In the interim, he was exiled from his home and castle in Woerden, and after 1299 was replaced by Wolfert van Borselen as lord of Woerden. Exactly where he spent his years in exile is not known with certainty, but it was possibly in Flanders but more likely – at least for a time – in Utrecht, under the protection of the bishop.

The Castle at Woerden from a 1600s Engraving

Bishop-Count Willem van Mechelen of Utrecht intervened following this infamous event, retook (for a while) some lands Floris had seized from Utrecht, and razed the Holland count's castle at Muiden at the site on the river controlling the bishop's own access routes from Utrecht to the open sea. But his hold was not to last.

Floris' heirs retook Muiden and all other short-lived gains of Bishop-Count van Mechelen, and rebuilt the castle at Muiden that stands to this day as one of Holland's finest medieval landmarks.

By 1299 when Floris' son died an early death still in his teens, Floris' cousin John II (Jean) of Hainaut joined his realm with that of Holland and (by then) Zeeland, and ruled until the successions of the Houses of Burgundy, Wittlesbach and (Spanish) Hapsburg gained control.

Netherlands history was indeed changed dramatically through this Thirteenth Century royal assassination, with Holland and what was to become the country of the Netherlands falling into the hands of non-Dutch rulers for centuries to come.

WOERDEN

25

HOUSE OF VAN VLIET

Although this family history focuses on the Van W Woerden of Vliet antecedents for today's Van Vliets/Van Fleets/Van Vleets, the story of the Americans bearing those names more than likely trace their origins to the "House of Herman," and so the story continues in a most interesting vein.

Herman VI's brother Gerrit (or Gerard), who played no role in the conspiracy to capture or in the assassination of Floris V, was reconciled with the heirs of the murdered count. They allowed Gerard, also a knight and nobleman, to reclaim some of the lands that were under his older brother's ownership, but not Woerden itself.

Thus it was that in the last years of the 1200s, Gerard built a castle near present-day Oudewater, that was called "Huis te Vliet." This means "House of Vliet," and reflects the Netherlands' historical records that aver that Gerard, who died in 1314, established "the Van Vliet family."

This family has been known variously as "Van den Vliet," "Van Vliet" and "Van der Vliet" and for a time at least during Gerard's life and likely for some generations thereafter (as noted by Van Reitstap) as "Van Woerden Van Vliet," reflecting the meaning of this ancient family's origins; that is, as lords of Woerden in the Vliet of the Netherlands.

The Van Vliet/Van Fleet/Van Vleet family in America that derives from Adrian Gerritsen Van Vliet and from Dirck Van der Vliet who came to colonial America, likely can trace their origins to these 1200s and 1300s persons and events in the Netherlands.

26

Castle Huis te Vliet

The castle Huis te Vliet was owned by the Van Vliet (the most familiar Dutch form of the surname, and the *only* one used in Dutch records to describe castle ownership) family for several more centuries.

In 1497 just some five years after Columbus' travels, the then owner Jan van Vliet – the way in which his name is cited in historic records – requested that prisoners kept there be removed, possibly due to either the decrepit condition of the castle itself or to changes it might have been undergoing as a manor house.

In any event, the Van Vliet family owned the stronghold another one hundred and twenty-seven years until 1624, according to information from Oudewater. It is also noted in Dutch records, however, that by 1647 this castle was in ruins, with no explanation as to how or when such a condition came about.

Castle Huis te Vliet Ruins

It is quite possible that the sad fate of the castle could have befallen the structure as early as 1575, when the Spanish monarch's forces destroyed Oudewater as an object lesson to those Dutch who preferred to be rid of him, in the early days of their revolt against their Spanish masters.

Today, all that remains of the castle is a thirty foot high section of the north side of the castle keep, and parts of the moat that functioned in its entirely until late 1770. In recent years, the remains of the bailey or outer wall and courtyard were unearthed.

Oudewater Crest   *Ancient Emblem*

There is an idealized outline of what Castle Huis te Vliet may have looked like, emblazoned on the crest of the City of Oudewater. The design was taken from an ancient engraving showing the main keep behind high walls with two jutting towers on either side of the façade.

Heraldry of the Van Vliet Family

In the HISTORY OF DUTCHESS COUNTY that was published in the late Nineteenth Century, early families of the Hudson Valley were explored with commentary on their European roots. Adrian Gerritsen Van Vliet, who was first identified with his full family name in 1663, was described as being of an ancient Netherlands family, and according to the Dutch heraldry of Van Reitstap and as cited in this HISTORY, the coat of arms of the Van Vliets was described in detail.

Van Reitstap contains entires for Van Woerden and for Van Vliet as individual surnames, but it also notes that the original family surname for both was Van Woerden Van Vliet. It goes on to describe the identical family crests under both names, with the same notation that this is, in fact, one and the same family.

Under each, there is a description of the ancient family armorial bearings affiliated with the House of Herman. The crest consists of a red field with three silver losanges – diamond-like devices – with two on top of a third. This color scheme is noted as later changing, to become one with a gold field with red losanges.

Van Woerden Van Vliet

(Noted as the full name until the mid-Fourteenth Century, or the mid-1300s).

"d'or a tois losanges de gules: Casque cournonee: Crest, une tete et col du chien braque de gules; ou, une pate de lion, de gules, les ongles en haut sortant d'une cuve de gules."

29

This description is the "modern" one; that is, the post mid-1300s one of a gold crest with three red losanges (or diamonds), placed two on top of a third. There is a coronet denoting nobility. The shield is mounted with either the head of a hunting dog or a lion's head with a raised claw, atop the coronet.

Although the rationale for this device is unknown, generally the simplicity of the crest reflects its ancient origins in early heraldry. The three-fold placement might represent the Holy Trinity (Floris used three similarly placed leaves) and may reflect participation in one of the Crusades (a distinct possibility for several of the Hermans, given their timing).

Red was often used as a symbol for the blood of Christ, a device employed by the Crusaders, while silver (represented as white) is for purity. Gold is a color frequently reserved as symbolic for Christ, inasmuch as it reflects the highest nobility and the gift of the Magi.

In concluding comments about the Van Vliet family and its likely origins, it can be reiterated that those who came to America beginning in 1634 are descendants of Gerard Van Woerden Van Vliet's "House of Van Vliet," as well as descendants from the older Van Woerden Van Vliet line dating back to the first Herman, and through him to his Celto-Germanic, Saxon and Frankish ancestors in the distant past of northern Europe.

The background of this family is indeed as Van Reitstap stated: ancient, historic and from a modern perspective, utterly fascinating in the Dutch context, and equally if not more so in viewing it through the centuries in an American setting.

The Van Vliet/Van Fleet Coat of Arms

PART II.

THE NEW AMERICAN HOMELAND:

NEW YORK, NEW JERSEY AND

PENNSYLVANIA

A COMMENTARY ON COMING TO AMERICA:
THE HISTORICAL BACKGROUND

In historical perspective, North America was the object of European exploration, colonization and settlement for many reasons. Although Latin America and the Caribbean had been settled much earlier by the Spanish and Portuguese, their principal goals were the famous "Glory, God and Gold," not permanent residence in new lands with substantial numbers of people. Raw exploitation characterized the Iberian experience in the Americas, with the aim of gaining wealth and fame to live comfortably back in the mother country.

It is true that the initial reasons for the discovery and conquest of the Americas were tied to the control of trade routes, but power in Europe was the end game, and one well understood by all Old World monarchies.

For example, England saw that overseas colonies could generate the wealth that gave Spain the ability to mount the history's greatest Armada in 1588. But luck and cleverness won the day for England against a potential invader, and gave Queen Elizabeth room to plan a takeover of some of the Iberian Americas for her own realm and coffers.

For its part, the Netherlands confronted Spain in another arena. As part of the Spanish Hapsburg Empire in the 1500s, the Netherlanders came under the heavy administrative hand of a king for whom the Dutch had no love.

Worse yet was the ineptitude and insensitivity of Spanish viceroys in the Netherlands. They failed to understand or to come to terms with the Dutch mercantile mentality, non-conformity in politics and in religion, among other factors, leading to the rebellion of the northern provinces after 1566.

The rebellion that ultimately brought about the formation of the Dutch Republic was financed by the wealth generated by an increasingly able and ambitious sea-going trading peoples, who viewed all the known world as their ken. It was open to any and all men who had the creativity to seize opportunities as they arose, and to enjoy the profits to be derived from the "empire" of international trade.

The lure of wealth to be gained from trade was understood by the English, though not so well as among the Dutch. But transactions in fact propelled both nations in the Seventeenth Century to set sail from English and Dutch ports to explore North America for the glory of gold to be garnered from trade rather than from the mines. Importantly, neither country had much interest in conversions for Christianity, the Spanish preoccupation in the previous century in the Americas.

In 1607, the Virginia Company succeeded in establishing the first permanent Enlish settlement on American shores, replacing the failed experiment of Sir Walter Raleigh two decades earlier at Roanoke. In 1609, the Englishman Henry Hudson sailed for North America under Dutch sponsorship to seek and explore trade routes to Asia through an alleged Northwest Passage.

Although the Halve Maen (Half Moon) never did sail the waters of that elusive passage, it took Dutch interests to the shores of what is present-day Hudson's Bay, into the mouths of the Connecticut, Delaware and Hudson Rivers, as well as along Long Island, Rhode Island and Manhattan Island. Dutch settlement followed, adding to the English in Virginia, but more importantly it provided yet another European state's presence in the Americas.

34

In another vein, the Plymouth Colony was founded in 1620 for other than economic reasons. The Pilgrims' religious freedom was the guiding principle, one for which these English men and women first sought refuge in Holland before proceeding to the New World to establish a community of their own.

Then as events unfolded in England during the 1600s, the political unrest and religious persecution, not to overlook economic dislocation, saw a steady stream of new colonists set sail for North America, and the creation of many more colonies to accommodate them.

There was a gradual realization that these European ventures in North America, where such were established for investment purposes, would not be profitable immediately. Indeed, this realization brought about adjustments and changes in thinking effecting colonization policies for both the English and the Dutch.

In the latter case, by 1624 the few hearty souls who were in New Netherland engaged in fur trading were joined by a contingent of Protestant Walloon families, who settled in or near the newly established village of New Amsterdam at the tip of Manhattan Island.

Four years later in 1628, the population of all New Netherland was still just some three hundred persons, with perhaps two hundred and seventy living in New Amsterdam alone. A similar number lived to the north in the Plymouth – later the Massachusetts – Colony.

Only the Virginia colony began developing a population sufficiently large enough by 1628 to sustain something resembling life in a rural English setting, with around 4,000 inhabitants reported in that year.   35

In point of fact, from the beginning of the Seventeenth Century at Jamestown and later at Plymouth and New Amsterdam, the populations of the northern European colonies in America expanded only slowly, through immigration and natural growth. Such progress was hampered by more than the occasional setback from disease, famine and hostilities with the Indian population.

Among the major European countries establishing colonies in North America – the French, Dutch and English – only the English were completely successful in populating their settlements. The political, economic and religious factors at play in the British Isles at the time provided the impetus for immigration. Moreover, the practice of sending convicts into exile in an overseas possession was begun around this time by British authorities.

In contrast, more economically favorable – and certainly more stable domestic – conditions in a homeland of some one and a half million persons proved to be major obstacles to any large scale movements from the Netherlands to its relatively unappealing North American colony, particularly in contrast to its more promising ones in the Caribbean, Brazil (New Holland), Africa and the Far East.

In order to address the issue of populating New Netherland, in the 1628 to 1629 time frame under the leadership of West Indies Company stockholder Killiean Van Rensselaer, a patroon system was introduced. Under this scheme individuals would receive large tracts of land in New Netherland with the provision that they recruit colonists for their grants, who would settle permanently. They were to establish the bases of a civil society in North America as it was known in Europe.

Although patroonships were granted to various individuals, all efforts to attract sufficient numbers of persons to make proposed settlement viable, failed completely except at Rensselaerswyck. Due to considerable investment in his venture, Van Rensselaer attracted farmers and skilled and unskilled workmen to his patroonship between 1630 and 1644.

In that time frame, passenger lists from some fifteen of the many sailings from the Netherlands were reported, giving some idea of the numbers who likely came to Rensselaerswyck. Nonetheless, as late as 1660 that community consisted of only about forty houses and some two hundred inhabitants. According to one authority writing on the subject, Van Rensselaer's estates never contained more than three hundred people at any given time.

In an effort to alter this situation, the Dutch colonies on the Hudson River offered free land, tools and supplies as well as freedom from taxation, to attract settlers from the mid-Seventeenth Century onward. The previous incentives offered to individual patrons to recruit colonists for New Netherland were widely seen as failed efforts, in no small way a consequence of the generally favorable economic conditions in the home country during what is described as the Netherlands' "Golden Age."

In an otherwise booming Dutch economy in the 1600s, only Gelderland and Utrecht appear to have lagged behind, in the former case because of effects of the Thirty Years' War and in the latter because of changing technology. Rink wrote that "after 1620, the rising popularity of the so-called 'new draperies' (a light woven linen cloth) disrupted the Utrecht-based heavy linen industry, causing an exodus of skilled linen workers to other areas."

The position that Utrecht had enjoyed vis-à-vis Gouda, Delft and Haarlem was lost, and particularly to Leiden. It was faced with the prospect of being drained of "every able worker" seeking opportunities elsewhere.

Consequently, when the call went out for colonists in New Netherland, far more responses were heard from Utrecht than from any other province in the Dutch homeland. Rink continued, stating that "...so effective (were) forces in encouraging inhabitants of Utrecht...to emigrate that the inland province contributed more colonists...than South Holland and North Holland combined." This fact is astounding when one considers that the largest concentration of Dutch citizens in the country was in those two provinces.

Occasionally male orphans in the twelve to seventeen year age bracket were brought to settle in New Netherland, but Governor Peter Stuyvesant's corrspondence reflected the view that such efforts were unsuccessful.

Van Rensselaer focused his attention on contracting young men, and his records clearly demonstrate that most of the recruits for his patroonship were single males with an average age of nineteen (that is, youths in their teens to early twenties).

It is important to note that as many as half of the New Netherland colonists may have been of other than Dutch origin, with thousands coming from French-speaking Europe (and virtually all of them being fleeing Protestants), Scandinavia, German states (mainly Lutherans) and England. In a sense it is not surprising that one found so many non-Dutch in the West Indies Company colony, because this population movement tendency reflected what was happening in the Netherlands itself.

Rink noted "so popular had the United Provinces become as a center for refugees that a 1631 tax assessment in...Amsterdam revealed that of the 685 wealthiest individuals (at least) 160 were Flemish or Walloon...30 German, and numerous Italian, English and Scandinavian...on the list." The reader is reminded as well that the 1620 Pilgrims did not come from lives in England, but rather from Holland after many years of self-imposed exile there.

Despite earlier problems in populating the land, the last eight years of the New Netherland colony saw considerable activity in the settlement of new families. Many ships were sailing the North Atlantic trade route. On 11 March 1662, fifty-eight people left Amsterdam for America aboard the Purmerlande Kerke and the Vergulde Arent. Other sailings that year included De Hoop with seventy-two, De Vos with forty-four and De Trouw on 24 March, with twenty-eight passengers, all ships that were frequently used in New Netherland-Holland trade.

Although no census data for the mid-Seventeenth Century exist, estimates of the European North American population have been made based on various sources. According to Van Zant, in 1664 the English-controlled New England colonies (including Massachusetts) had about 50,000 inhabitants, Virginia around 40,000, and New Netherland some 10,000. Wabeke estimated that both Virginia and New England had closer to 30,000 each in 1664, but that New Netherland had 10,000 (if not the 9,000 that Rink cited). Van Zant's figures take into account census-like materials from 1698, when both Virginia and the New England colonies had some 60,000 inhabitants each and New York had around 20,000.

In concluding these comments about the early history of the New Netherland colony, it is appropriate to ask some questions about the people who chose to live out the rest of their lives far from their mother country, in small villages and isolated settlements scattered along the Hudson River, its numerous tributaries and in the valleys more distant yet from anything resembling a "civilized" population center.

Who came to America, and why? What were their families like? What were their religious beliefs and backgrounds? What socio-economic status did they enjoy? And finally, what about their politics and allied philosophies?

De Trouw
Ship Type
Of 1600s

Seventeenth Century Dutch Sailing Ships: Pirates, Privateers and Settlers in America

Existing records of New Netherland reflect sailings by a relatively small fleet of ships over the several decades of Dutch control, with some vessels being cited in a specific time frame such as the 1650s and 1660s. Three ships falling into this category are DeTrouw, DeHoop and the Eendracht.

In earlier research, while thinking nothing remarkable of this trio – roughly Faith, Hope and Charity – in the context of the times, what was amazing for this commentator to read was an article in the Fort Myers NEWS PRESS in fall 2001, discussing three Dutch privateers with the same names, that operated in 1628 against the Spanish in Florida's waters.

Specifically, the article described these privateers in the context of the Tampa Bay region, and noted that a Spanish ship, the San Juan Bautista (Saint John the Baptist), was captured by the Eendracht and that that Dutch ship was later hopelessly grounded on a sandbar at the mouth of the Calousahatchee River at present-day Fort Myers. Abandoned and left for future underweater archeologists to find in the 1990s, the ship's name was carried over to the captured Spanish vessel, and the trio of ships sailed on in history.

Were these the same three ships that sailed to and from New Netherland in the decades to come? A naval historian at a 2001 Holland Society of New York conference thought not, assuming the worst for the nature of shipbuilding and the lack of longevity of ships at the time. He postulated that a newer group of ships might have been given the same names – a common practice, particularly for the same owner.

Of special interest then is the fact that the ship in question was, according to the newspaper article, captained by a Jan Janzoon (sic), decidedly a patronymic, not a surname. Is this sufficiently close to the late 1650s-early 1660s DeTrouw Captain Jan Jansen Bestevaer's name to give rise to further questions?

Perhaps this is the case – and perhaps not. But furthermore, it should be noted that these ships, if newly and qualitatively constructed in the last years of the 1620s for the rigors of privateering, would have a projected life expectancy of about some thirty years, bringing them into the late 1650s or possibly early 1660s.

Since there were no further sailings of settlers from Holland following the English takeover of New Netherland in 1664, is it possible that these early transports for the Dutch were put to that use late in their expected service lives, for the tamer activity of moving settlers and goods to the New World than (pirate) privateering against the Spanish in the Caribbean?

A Commentary on Two Early Settlements

The New Netherland's first family-oriented colonists who sought to form permanent communities arrived in 1624. They were Protestant Walloons fleeing the excesses of the viceroy of the Spanish Netherlands. They developed the first agricultural base for the colony, although they came to an area that had seen many Europeans come and go on a short-term basis, invariably connected with the fur trade further up the Husdon River.

With the advent of the patron system, particularly at Rensselaerswyck, an influx of single young men dominated the demographics of New Netherland. These individuals came to the colony on contract from individuals such as Van Rensselaer, usually for specified periods of time. Upon completion of the contract, many if not most then returned to their Holland homeland or continued on to other Dutch outposts around the world. A few continued to work on for a while in this West Indies colony or otherwise to settle permanently in America.

Indisputably though, records from the 1630s and 1640s indicate clearly that there was a serious gender imbalance in the colony that made staying on in America somewhat unattractive, and the gradual arrival of families immigrating to New Netherland did little to redress that situation in the short run.

Moreover, Rink pointed out that the overriding need for agricultural labor may have discouraged the immigration from Holland of families with daughters, knowing what hardships awaited them in the new colony.

Rink stated:

That the migration was dominated by single young men should not make us forget that for nearly a third of these people the decision to migrate to New Netherland constituted the beginning of a new life as members of transplanted households. For the single men...New Netherland may well have represented a rite of passage to adulthood, an adventurous sacrifice of the amenities of civilization for the brief experience of life in the wilderness. For the families it...meant much more.

Certainly for some, a decision to leave Holland was based on a desire to start anew, the case for religious rufugees in particular, while for others the attraction lay in the opportunity to strike it rich in the fur trade or perhaps even to discover precious metals that could be turned to riches and a comfortable life back home. The latter case was the self-devised trap into which the Spanish fell, not to overlook some English in Virginia.

For the most part, however, the purposes for which so many came to New Netherland – to settle and to farm in permanent communities – never left their minds. In time, New Netherland not only developed a stable core population, but also a reasonable reputation for tolerance and commercial opportunity that would draw family migration in the later years of the colony's existence.

It is evident from early records that despite being founded on the fur trade the colony's mainstay was agriculture. Van Rensselaer's records of early settlers classified persons according to jobs, and some 38 percent of such individuals were in agriculturally-related activities (perhaps too modest a figure).

44

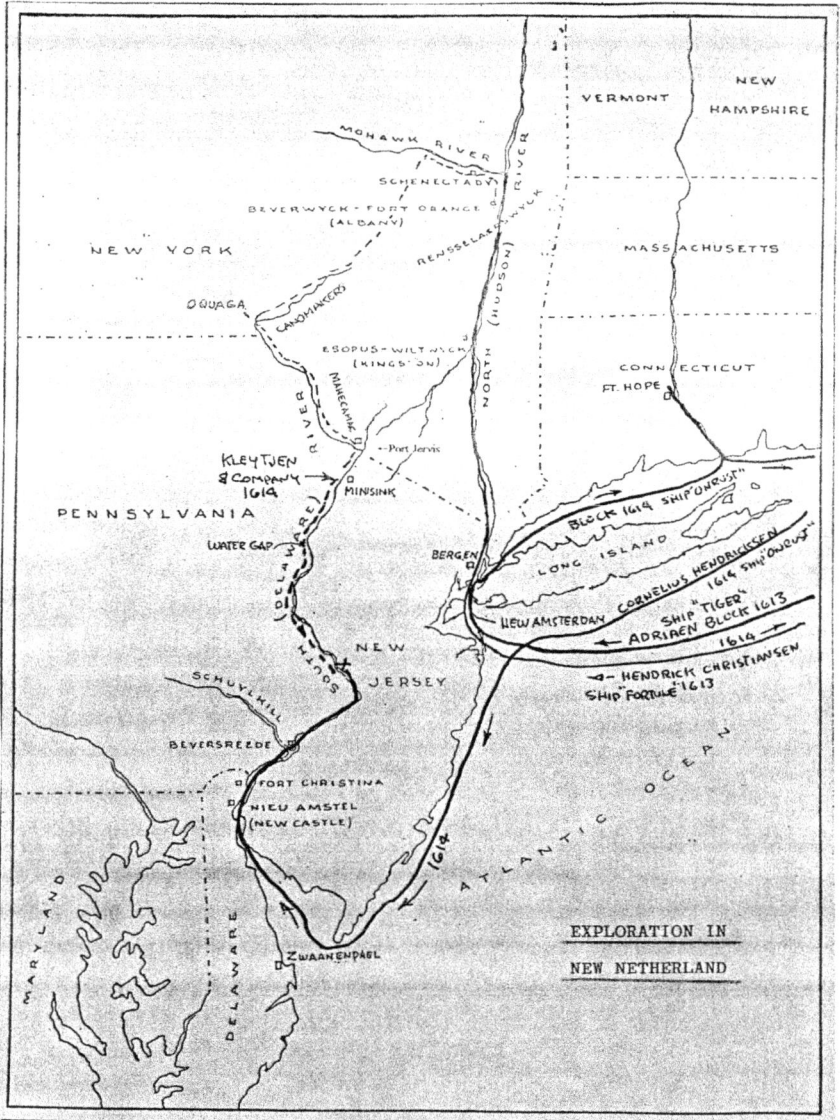

VERMONT

NEW HAMPSHIRE

MOHAWK RIVER

SCHENECTADY

BEVERWYCK · FORT ORANGE
(ALBANY)

NEW YORK

MASSACHUSETTS

OQUAGA

CANAJOHARIE

ESOPUS · WILTWYCK
(KINGSTON)

CONNECTICUT

FT. HOPE

MANECHING

RENSSELAERSWYCK

NORTH (HUDSON) RIVER

Port Jervis

KLEYTJEN
& COMPANY
1614

MINSINK

PENNSYLVANIA

WATER GAP

BLOCK 1614 SHIP "ONRUST"

DELAWARE RIVER

BERGEN

LONG ISLAND

CORNELIUS HENDRICKSEN 1616 SHIP "ONRUST"

NEW AMSTERDAM

SHIP "TIGER"
ADRIAEN BLOCK 1613

SCHUYLKILL

SOUTH RIVER

NEW
JERSEY

1614

HENDRICK CHRISTIANSEN
SHIP FORTUNE 1613

BEVERSREEDE

FORT CHRISTINA

NIEU AMSTEL
(NEW CASTLE)

MARYLAND

DELAWARE

1614

ATLANTIC OCEAN

ZWAANENDAEL

EXPLORATION IN

NEW NETHERLAND

45

Clearly, Van Rensselaer was intent upon making his holdings a self-sufficient agricultural enterprise. In 1638 he wrote:

I do not care to suffer in my colony those who have an eye mainly on the fur trade.... Those who make purely a business of it, I do not care to have...as my principal object is directed toward farming and things connected therewith.

The patron was true to his word, for some 60 percent or more of the colonists in one study of his holdings came to farm the land. Van Rensselaer paid them well to do so, with salaries ranging far higher in his colony than could be earned in comparable work in the Dutch homeland.

Records for the New Netherland colony were sparse between 1645 and the mid-1650s, due to losses at sea, fires and other disasters that took their toll on what are now historical documents. However, from 1657 through to the end of the Dutch colonial period in 1664, a wealth of documentation exists that among other things, points out that the difficulties that New Netherland had in populating its territory were overcome.

As noted, the growth was dramatic between 1645 and 1664, increasing the population nearly four-fold in just two decades. More importantly, this growth was accomplished in no small part by family immigration of "young and vigorous" parents and children, whose permanency in the colony was unquestioned and whose family and personal values were to add to the stability of this New World society that they helped to build.

Although New Amsterdam was the largest and most important of the Dutch communities, the early years – that is, the first two generations – in Van Vliet family history focused on other Hudson Valley areas that are now examined in some detail.

46

Rensselaerswyck

The patroonship of Kilian Van Rensselaer was a product of West Indies Company policy adopted in 1628 and 1629 to populate its territories. Manorial estates were to be developed in the New World with leasehold farms for settlers. From 1630 onward, Van Rensselaer's Hudson Valley properties in the general area of present-day Albany were colonized by scores of persons, unlike many other patroonships that were similarly established.

Ships' records note some fourteen sailings from Holland to his patroonship at Rensselaerswyck between 1630 and 1644, with a total of one hundred seventy-four immigrants. That number is only a representation of the movement of peoples coming to the colony in that time frame, given the absence of more complete records. However, it is adequate to arrive at some conclusions about the settlement, but more importantly about population movements in general.

In fact, many if not most persons coming to Rensselaerswyck did so to pursue employment contracts in agriculture and related activities. Many who stayed out their contract period – and most did not – returned to the Netherlands or went elsewhere in the expanding Dutch Empire. Some stayed on and built lives for themselves in America, and ultimately for the families they were able to establish.

Individuals who came to Rensselaerswyck represented many skills and trades, but in fact they complemented the bulk of the population which was made up of farmers. These persons came mainly from the Netherlands but there were others amongst them including Germans, French Huguenots and English.

It has been noted in many histories that as many as half of the New Netherland colonists may have been from European homelands other than Holland, and that some were blacks – a few free and other slaves. However, identifying countries of origin is often troublesome for New Netherland, given the proclivity to "Hollandize" surnames.

Within the Dutch community, the single largest percentage came from Utrecht and then to a lesser degree from Gelderland. Most arrivals were males, and given the fact that so many were young adults, as one commentator stated this population in large part could hardly be considered as adults.

Rensselaerswyck ceased to be a patroonship in the fashion in which it was originally envisaged; that is, as a manorial estate entirely in the hands of the Van Rensselaer family. Economic, demographic and political realities prevailed in the abandonment of this scheme.

The lands of the western side of the Hudson River eventually gave way to permanent settlements, most notably to Albany and Schenectady (the former known by various names, including Fort Orange, Orange and Beverwyck). The area became a focus of growth from the late Dutch colonial period onward, and under the English Albany flourished and became the capital of the Province (then the state) of New York.

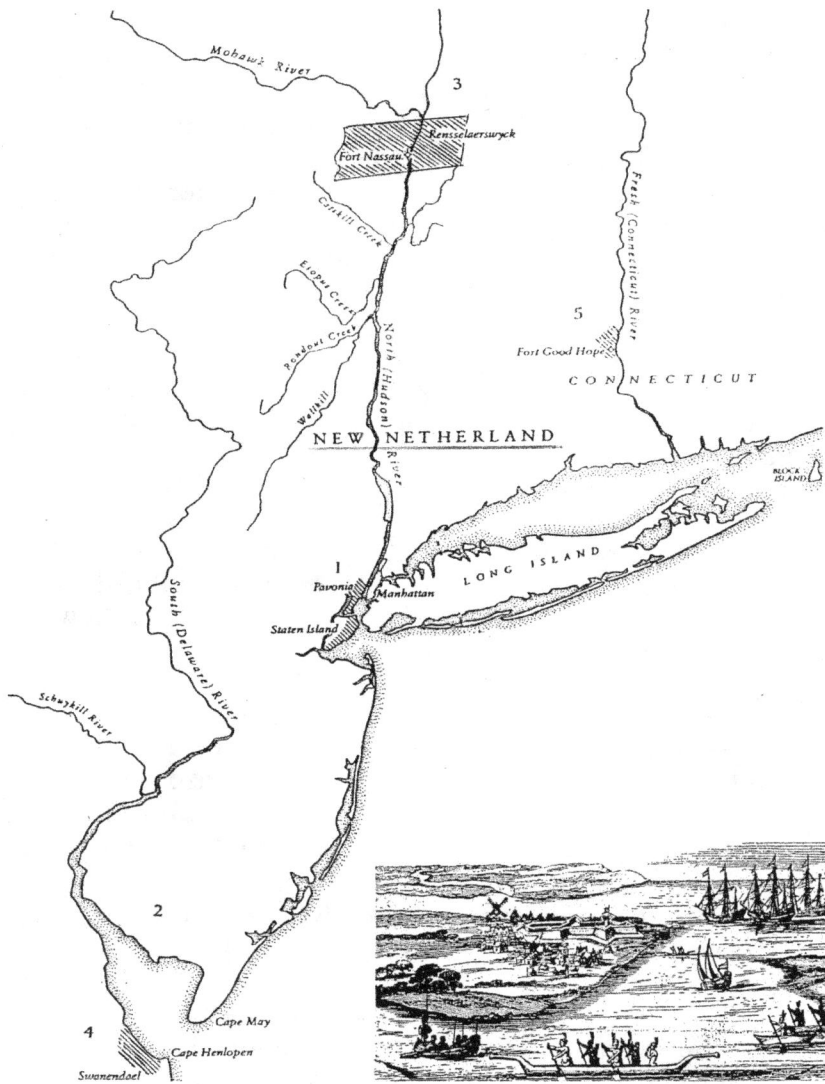

Mohawk River

3

Fort Nassau   Rensselaerswyck

Catskill Creek

Esopus Creek

Rondout Creek

North (Hudson) River

Wallkill

Fresh (Connecticut) River

5

Fort Good Hope

CONNECTICUT

NEW NETHERLAND

BLOCK ISLAND

LONG ISLAND

1

Pavonia   Manhattan

Staten Island

South (Delaware) River

Schuylkill River

2

Cape May

4

Cape Henlopen

Swanendael

49

Wiltwyck

A settlement called Esopus (allegedly for the Dutch form of Aesop) was established near Esopus Creek in 1652 by Thomas Chambers, an English contract worker at Rensselaerswyck from the 1640s onward. According to DeJong. The community took the name of the nearby Esopus Indians, who had granted Chambers the right to settle there. The colony was located some fifty miles south of Fort Orange or present-day Albany, and about a hundred miles north of New Amsterdam (New York).

The region is characterized by rich soil and is well-watered. It can be visualized as an area of undulating land, with a somewhat more temperate climate than in Albany just a short distance away. Identified from its beginnings as an agricultural settlement, Esopus attracted permanent settlers from the Rensselaerswyck patroonship, and ultimately more than a few from Europe.

In August 1657, the Reverends Johannes Megapolensis and Samuel Drisius of New Amsterdam wrote that the region around Esopus was "exceedingly fine country" and that the "Dutch families settled there...(were) doing very well...."

Three years later in 1660, Esopus received its own minister, the Reverend (Dominie) Hermanus Blom. His presence was a reflection of the community's growing status. As importantly, in 1661 the village was granted a charter from Governor General Peter Stuyvesant, and was formally constituted as Wiltwyck. This means, roughly speaking, "wild area settlement."

The town's name, with a certain panache, was nonetheless short-lived. After 20 August 1664, New Netherland fell under the control of the English, and the community was renamed Kingston.

Wabeke noted that by 1658, Esopus had between sixty and seventy settlers, while other sources, largely confirming this estimate, state that thirty of them were adult males. However, by 1661 when its charter as Wiltwyck was granted, there were sixty-seven taxpayers recorded, and presumably that number roughly corresponded to the heads of family count.

Other sources indicated that in 1661, Wiltwyck had "fifteen farmers who cultivated about one thousand one hundred acres," and the community included "twenty families of laborers and artisans," implying a small number of heads of families.

As noted, from its beginnings Wiltwqyck was intended to be anagricultural settlement, as the acreage under cultivation and the number of farmers would indicate (cultivating an average of nearly seventy-four acres each).

In substantiation of the point made about the origins of Rensselaerswyck's contract farmers, Wabeke noted that most of Wiltwyck's people came from the farming provinces of Utrecht and Gelderland. Wabeke also cited the disruptions of the European conflicts such as the Thirty Years' War and continued Dutch struggles with the Spanish as reasons to relocate. Interestingly, Reverend Megapolensis originally came from the town of Woerden, ancestral home of the Van Vliet family and culturally if not politically at that time considered part of the Province of Utrecht.

The physical layout of the Wiltwyck community is not described in precise detail in historical records, but it is noted that in 1661 there were forty-five houses (implying there were forty-five families) there and a crudely constructed church, as well as a small fort.

Diorama of the Kingston stockade and church, 1680. Courtesy Old Dutch Church, Kingston, N.Y.

Wiltwyck

Contrary to popular belief, log cabin home construction techniques had not yet been adapted to this part of the New World (presumably the Nordic influence was not yet felt), so most structures were made of stone, mud and wattle, as well as crude slats. The protective stockade or fort that was built following the First Esopus War in the late 1650s gave rise to the first formal street layout, around which most of these houses were built.

Indeed, the present-day Old Dutch Reformed Church of Kingston occupies the same general area on which its predecessor churches stood, in what is still called the "Stockade" area of the city. However, there were yet other structures closer to the navigable Esopus Creek in that section then and still called "Rondout." This name probably derives from the Dutch for a protected or palisade-like enclosure.

It is acknowledged that away from the immediate surroundings of Wiltwyck – virtually outside the line of sight of the village – there were no settlers. However, this changed in 1661 when another community called Nieuwe Dorp – meaning New Village – was established a few miles to the southwest. Since the site of the New Village was contested by the Indians but built anyway, a strain in relations developed. In the Second Esopus War of 1663 to 1664, Nieuwe Dorp was completely destroyed by the Esopus, and not rebuilt until 1669 under the English (and then as a renamed Hurley). It is alleged that the objection to the location of this village laid in its being constructed upon sacred Indian burial ground.

The population of Wiltwyck, small as it was, was remarkably heterogeneous, much like that which was developing in New Amsterdam. The Netherlands was singular among European countries in permitting freedom of religious conscience and a high level of freedom of political thought. Consequently, many peoples fleeing persecution found their way to the Netherlands, and from there in many cases to the Dutch settlements along the Hudson River.

Indeed, Wiltwyck was described as every bit as cosmopolitan as New Amsterdam by many sources. There were numerous French Protestants or Huguenots, German Lutherans, English of various religions, and even some Roman Catholics of diverse nationalities, among the majority (Reformed Church) Dutch.

Although the Dutch were numerically the largest single group, their influence was not necessarily dominant in political, economic, cultural and arguably even religious matters. It is widely acknowledged that in this intermingling of nationalities and backgrounds in a peaceful and open fashion with a high level for (and tradition of) tolerance, the New Netherland colony provided the first and foremost model for a "melting pot" assimilationist environment among the many peoples of North America. The ideals that set forth this tolerance and openness, not to overlook the ability and willingness to borrow and absorb from the many, created the very basis for this country's successful social and political experiment and existing system, still our national characteristics.

If the experiences of European conflicts that gave rise to horrors elsewhere in the Old World, as well as to flight to the Netherlands, those events were still fresh in the minds of some Seventeenth Century colonists as they disembarked in America. But perhaps such events prepared them for what dangers might lie ahead to life and limb, kith and kin, in New Netherland frontier communities.

In June 1663, an Esopus Indian (and allied tribes) attack known as the Second Esopus War was launched against Wiltwyck. Indians entering the small settlement for the ostensible purpose of trading pelts and other goods casually began moving throughout the village: then the war began.

54

On a pre-arranged signal from one of their leaders, the Indians started attacking and killing men, women and children indiscriminately, as part of their process of knocking over structures and setting fire to everything. One observer wrote:

Wiltwyck...survive(d) the Indian raid on June 7, in which twelve houses were burned, eighteen people killed, and nine more taken prisoner; the recently started "New Village," however, was entirely destroyed, with the loss of three men and thirty-five prisoners. Fortunately during the military expedition under Captain Cregier and at the following peace all the captives were recovered.

Other sources cite the raid as being even more horrendous. In all, Reverend Blom stated that twenty-four men, women and children were killed and that forty-five women and children (and possibly one adult male) were carried off, after which only "an effective" sixty-nine men were left to protect Wiltwyck. Reverend Blom described the scene as one of smoking ruins, with stone houses toppled in and virtually all structures lost.

Adrian Gerritsen Van Vliet, his wife Agatha Spruyt and their five children were in Wiltwyck at the time of the raid. One of their children, daughter Machteld, thought to be their youngest, was one of the prisoners taken by the Esopus. But like all others held by the Indians, she was recovered unharmed. As history notes not a single European was molested in any fashion by the Esopus during their months-long captivity.

Captain Cregier's rescue mission made use of many Wiltwyck adult males, enlisting them in service against the Indians. Adrian Gerritsen was one in the Cregier Expedition, and in a curious note discussed later, that was the basis for a lawsuit he filed much later for unpaid services.

Little time remained for Holland's control between mid-1663 and the English takeover of the colony after August 1664. The small population of the settlement barely rebounded, even with the return of the captives. When the Dutch relinquished authority in Wiltwyck, it was reported that between two hundred and two hundred and fifty "souls" (quoting the Reverend Blom) were counted in the settlement. All were cited as free men and women, again a reflection of their "yeoman" status as farmers and related tradesmen.

In 1664, some four hundred and fifty troops of the English Crown and allied militia from English colonies took New Netherland almost without a struggle, save for some minor incidents in Long Island settlements. Title to the Dutch colony was granted by Charles II to his brother James, Duke of York, the year earlier, utterly ignoring the legitimacy of Dutch claims to the region. In his honor, the colony was named New York, and was called "the Duke's Own Province," in recognition of his proprietorship over the whole of the land.

The imposition of English rule in New York was initially benevolent under Royal Governor Richard Nicolls, a Scotsman in the service of the Duke of York. However, there were strains that developed over the years in conflicts between English law and Dutch law and customs, juxtaposed against the burgers of New Amsterdam's so-called "terms of surrender" of the colony.

Friction in many ways was inevitable but uneven. The transition was smoothest in the recently named City of New York (in reality, a mere town) and on Long Island, less harmonious in Albany and environs, and resisted in substantial measure in other communities along the Hudson River.

In fact, these more remote communities, encompassing those of the Esopus River Valley including Kingston, culturally tended to resist English encroachments. This fact belies the often-described peaceful transition, and shows that the Dutch social foundations laid between 1624 and 1664 were more ingrained and inured to change than imagined.

The population of the Kingston region began growing and by 1669 New Village was rebuilt as Hurley, honoring Royal Governor Francis Lovelace, Baron of Hurley, Ireland.

In the 1669 to 1669 period, another nearby community was created, called Marbletown. Two overseers were named for Hurley and Marbletown by English authorities, Frederick Hussey, a soldier who likely arrived to an English community (likely on Long Island) somewhere near the Dutch colony in 1663; and John Biggs, whose daughter Mary was later to marry Frederick Van Vliet, son of Jan Van Vliet.

In another connection, Adrian Gerritsen Van Vliet's son Jan married Judith Hussey, establishing a close Van Vliet relationship in the power structures of these two communities, to add to an even closer connection with Wiltwyck's founder Thomas Chambers, as related in the following chapters.

Growth proceeded with some rapidity in the region in general, reflected by the fact that even in Marbletown, newest of the three Esopus River Valley communities, by 1670 there were already thirty-one landholders in the newly-created Marbletown alone, including of course Thomas Chambers, John Biggs and Frederick Hussey and his recently-acquired relatives of Dutch ancestry, the Van Vliets.

ADRIAN GERRITSEN VAN VLIET
(c. 1614 – c. 1689)

On 24 March 1662, the ship De Trouw (The Faith) sailed from Amsterdam under the command of Captain Jan Jansen Bestevaer, destined yet again for the Dutch North American colony of New Netherland. De Trouw carried twenty-eight passengers on this sailing, most of whom were males. The majority of the adult passengers were noted in the ship's log as farmers, including three "farm boys," but several others were wives and children.

Among these were various persons whose origin was the Province of Utrecht, one of the seven stalwarts that originally formed the Dutch Union. Included on the ship's list was Adrian Gerritsen Van Vliet as head of a household that included his wife Agatha Spruyt whom he married in 1647 (or more likely in 1649) and five children. These were:

01. Gerrit Adrianse Van Vliet, born in 1649 and died 1723;
02. Jan Adrianse Van Vliet, born 1650;
03. Dirck Adrianse Van Vliet, born 1651;
04. Geertruyd Van Vliet, probably born 1654; and
05. Machteld Van Vliet, probably born in 1655.

The children's ages were recorded as thirteen, twelve, eleven, eight and seven, without further indication as to which child matched which age.

The Nineteenth Century book the HISTORY OF DUTCHESS COUNTY, among other sources, described Adrian Gerritsen Van Vliet "as being of an ancient family." Dutchess County noted the family armorial bearings, cited by Van Reitstap, and related in the first section of this commentary as essentially the crest of the City of Woerden in the Dutch region of the Vliet.

Woerden is the ancestral home of the Van Vliets. It is located today in the Province of Utrecht, as it was until 1279. Its current population is around 26,000, but it has been classified as a city since 1372, and existed in one form or another since at least Roman times.

As noted in the section on the Van Vliet/Van Fleet name and origins, the family traces its descent to the House of Herman Van Woerden. The last nobleman to hold the title of "Lord of Woerden" was Herman VI, a co-conspirator in the murder of Floris V, Count of Holland. Because of his role in this event, he was banished from Woerden.

Where his family went is something of a question mark, but his heirs did seek refuge at least for a while in the Diocese of Utrecht, just some nine miles distant from their original home. As for Herman VI, ultimately he was slain as were his fellow knight-conspirators Gijsbrecht van Amstel and Gerard van Velzen.

Was the City of Utrecht Adrian Gerritsen Van Vliet's home, some three centuries later? It is improbable as such, because he clearly was noted in history as a farmer. But living near Utrecht he would likely have been identified with that locale. Interestingly there is a connection between that fact and later records relating to this New Netherland settler. Specifically, there had been references to possibly two "Adrian Gerritsens" noted in early Dutch materials, sometimes with no other (sur)names noted, and at times, with either "Van Vliet" or "Van Papendorp" added.

When this writer was living at Ramstein Air Force Base, Germany, in the late 1980s, he chanced to visit another American base near Utrecht. He scoured all maps to locate "Papendorp" because as the word implies, this village (dorp) would be listed.

59

No such place could be found. Moreover, no inquiries met with any encouragement. It did not now exist, if it ever did. Then, in passing over a main street in the City of Utrecht, jumping off a signpost ahead were the words "Papendorp Industrial District."

The mystery was solved and decidedly so, for the writer was also able to obtain an original Seventeenth Century rendering of Utrecht with its ancient walls outlined and with surrounding farmlands delineated. Papendorp had been a polder immediately outside Utrecht and in the very shadow of the city walls, replete with farms, windmills, a small church and other buildings on a carefully planned and drained parcel of agricultural land.

What is the importance of this? As Frederick Bogert wrote in DE HALVE MAEN on the confusion of surnames, places of origin and actual last names were often confused, among other difficulties in early Dutch records. That problem came back to haunt this commentator in reviewing many documents dealing with Adrian Gerritsen Van Vliet. Was this man, in fact, also Adrian Gerritsen Van Papendorp? With that question left unanswered for the moment, the narration on this branch of the Van Fleet/Van Vliet family in America continues.

Dutchess County records make reference to Agatha Jans Spruyt as being "of Kriekenbeck and Opstal" in the Province of Utrecht. She was described as also "being of an ancient family," whose armorial bearings are described as well in Van Reitstap, simply as a medium blue shield with three fleur-de-lis in silver, two over one. In 2001 a Dutch genealogist stated that it was historically common to see marital unions between Spruyts and Van Vliets, ancient allied families of Utrecht.

60

The ship De Trouw arrived in New Amsterdam on 13 June 1662, and in celebration of that successful Atlantic crossing six pounds of gunpowder were discharged. Continuing its active involvement in trans-oceanic trade, neither the ship nor the Van Vliet family remained long in New Amsterdam. After paying respects to the Governor General – a tradition that continues to this day whereby foreign visitors call on the Mayor of New York – the family proceeded to Wiltwyck some one hundred miles up the "North River" (Hudson). Thereafter, the Van Vliets were reported as citizens of that settlement for some years to come. In fact, they are often referred to in history books as "1662 settlers at Kingston."

Upon their arrival, it is assumed that the Van Vliets set about establishing a household within the fortified area for this sizable family, and initiated farming activities in the vicinity of the settlement. Aside from the mundane activities of everyday life and the terrifying events of the Second Esopus War, life in Wiltwyck for them probably was only somewhat more notable than for other families of similar status; that is, freeholder agriculturalists of likely better than average means.

This statement is based on information from many early Dutch records that note that throughout the 1660s and 1670s, Adrian Gerritsen appeared in court, sometimes for suits brought by him and at other times as a defendant. Properly referenced on those occasions substantiate the assertion about his status.

One Twentieth Century historian noted that the peoples of New Netherland were very litigious, perhaps setting the tone for what has become (sadly) yet another modern American national characteristic.

61

Wilcoxen noted "the impressive...litigious nature of the citizens...took their neighbors into court frequently and for reasons that often seem ridiculous." Van Rensselaer noted this tendency as well and wrote in exasperation that "they stir one another up." Contemporary accounts create a suspicion that the inhabitants of the colony sued each other more as a diversion than for any real redress of wrongs.

Nonetheless, these court proceedings give a glimpse into life in Seventeenth Century Dutch America. In virtually every instance, the sums of money, quantity of goods and nature of personal possessions were such that one could conclude that the Van Vliets were reasonably well blessed with material wealth, and – again according to court records – in an economic position adequate to hire people for services, to sub-contract work and to contract themselves out for more remunerative activities.

Adrian Gerritsen was listed as a patentee and freeholder in Ulster County in 1664 (the second year and the latest date in which he used "Van Vliet" as a surname) and again in 1680, with the latter date referring to lands located in Rochester (now Stone Ridge) along the Old Mine Road.

It was reported as well that he held several parcels of land in Albany in 1675 records, implying that not only did his land wealth go beyond holdings in the immediate Kingston area, but raising questions as to how and when he acquired such titles some fifty miles away.

It should be noted that quite a few Kingston-based people, including Thomas Chambers and others related in this commentary in coming chapters, also held land titles to parcels in the general vicinity of Albany.

Exactly where Van Vliet's land was located in the Kingston area is a question, although there are references to it being at Preewenheck, a site unidentified today. A clue may lie in the fact that Governor Stuyvesant held two farms privately somewhere between Hurley and Kingston, which were tilled under contract by Adrian Gerritsen and Juriaen Westphael (later Westfall). Logically, Van Vliet's farm was located in the immediate vicinity. The contract, incidentally, was the subject of arguments and some litigation between Stuyvesant and Van Vliet in the 1660s.

Adrian Gerritsen and his family relocated several times, specifically to Rochester and to Marbletown. These moves always involved land, although records are incomplete as to what was acquired and how much was sold, for the most part. However, on 25 March 1680, he received forty-six morgans (each being equal to 2.1 acres) at Rochester, which is located a few miles southwest of Kingston.

On 27 April 1667, Van Vliet was among others signing a document produced by the English authorities that called for an explanation or "reasons" for being in (bearing) arms. At that time, Kingston and other former Dutch settlements were under a somewhat troublesome occupation by English soldiers, who picked fights with local denizens and even stole from them at will.

The period in question saw great stresses in what was otherwise a relatively peaceful transition from a Dutch colony to an English possession. This change that was accepted by most settlers in New York and Long Island, apparently without much or any opposition, was resented by many in the Esopus River Valley and brought more than a few persons to the brink of revolt against their new masters.

Adrian Gerritsen, who had once been detained for (in effect) stating that the English King Charles II could "only fight shit" was supposedly only a farmer, so arms in his possession should not have posed a threat to the peace and good order of the community. Or should they?

Although Adrian Gerritsen's family was victimized by the events of the Second Esopus War, that conflict was long over by the time he was called upon to cite reasons for being in arms.

But if anything, firearms of the period were dangers unto themselves. One interesting footnote – as later related more fully – in this family's history is that of son Dirck who lost his left leg at a New Year's party in 1678, due to an accidental shooting by Gysbert Krom. The records note that his wound healed in time, and on 5 April 1685 he married and thereafter had a large family.

The Van Vliets were apparently active in religious and community affairs, a conclusion based on church records that cite Agatha Spruyt as a frequent witness at baptisms, and Adrian Gerritsen being described in some detail as one of fifteen electors of two delegates on 31 March 1664, to represent Wiltwyck at a New Netherland General Assembly in New Amsterdam.

This notation is important in that being an elector was in and of itself a position of prominence in the community. Sylvester described this as the first popular election in New Netherland by the first voters in what was later to become Ulster County. However, what is more important in the context of this commentary is the fact that the two selected – Gysbert Van Imborch and Thomas Chambers – tie Van Vliet into a relationship with the latter that helps explain many curious notations reflecting a much earlier presence in the colony than 1662.

By the second decade of the Van Vliet family in America, the political situation began to change from the toleration that marked the Dutch period, through the relatively gentile English transition particularly under Governor Nicolls, into an era with an environment of distrust and uncertainty. This occurred when Charles II died without legitimate issue, leaving his Catholic brother the Duke of York on the throne as James II, in 1685. Such a succession ultimately precipitated open war in Protestant Great Britain, and the reverberations of this matter were felt in the American colonies, with a demand for the citizenry to pledge allegiance to one side or the other.

On 1 September 1689, adult males in Ulster County were called upon to swear allegiance to the new British monarchs William and Mary. Adrian Gerritsen's sons Gerrit and Jan Van Vliet did so, along with some one hundred and eighty-nine other adult males in the county.

However, neither he nor his son Dirck did so on that date. Some sources indicated that Jan had actually taken a loyalty oath in 1687 (an impossibility, at least to these monarchs), and that Adrian Gerritsen did so in 1690 (there being no record of such), which is what another researcher cited as the probable year of his death.

Only four persons from Ulster County's males refused to swear allegiance to the new monarchs in 1689. Thirty in all, including Adrian Gerritsen and his son Gerrit Van Vliet, simply did not appear initially for whatever reasons, from among the male population of the community. One web-generated genealogical source (Kindred Konnections) reported the reason for Adrian Gerritsen's absence as being his death in late 1689.

The issue of allegiance is an interesting footnote to history, in that the period in question that was called "The Glorious Revolution" in England brought about many political changes that found their way into the United States Constitution and the Bill of Rights, from Dutch-inspired concepts. But for the moment, this event marked the removal by Parliament of Catholic James II in favor of the Protestant Mary and her husband Prince William of Orange-Nassau.

William, as ruler of the United Provinces of the Netherlands, effectively brought full circle the rivalry between the Dutch and the English, that in the 1600s led to two Anglo-Dutch Wars. Their struggle for North American colonies not to overlook trade rivalries ended, and too in at least some sense, for the Dutch of New York there may have been some solace in this new monarchy.

Given the incomplete records for this early period in New York history, it is difficult to know if Adrian Gerritsen ever swore allegiance to William and Mary in written form, but in all likelihood his sympathies were with them.

Despite his difficult nature at times as indicated by Seventeenth Century court records, Van Vliet was a man of substance and status. His relatively extensive property listings in official records; his role (and his wife's church involvement) in community affairs; his service as an officer in diverse military capacities; and his (and his family's) involvement with persons of primary social and political importance in these areas, all lead to such a conclusion.

But there is more to the story of Adrian Gerritsen Van Vliet, which is now presented for the consideration of the reader.

Extensive but not exhaustive ship lists of passengers to the Dutch colony were kept from the 1650s onward, but there are persons in New Netherland whose arrivals are not noted. Consequently, it is of particular importance to relate that Van Rensselaer's papers state that Adrian Gerritsen was "present" at his patroonship in 1634.

Certainly we know that Adrian Gerritsen came with his family in 1662, a well-documented fact, but the evidence points to his arrival *for the first time* much earlier.

O'Callahan noted in his works that at Fort Orange on 6 September 1659, Adrian Gerritsen offered to go voluntarily as one of ten deputies for purposes of peaceful intervention with the Mohawks.

Similarly with reference to Indians, on a later date in the 1674 to 1675 period, Adrian Gerritsen is noted as "commissary for lands" given by the Indian chief 'Schermerhoorn' (as called by the Dutch) to Jan Bronk. *These notations are made in conjunction with his and Thomas Chambers' commissions as militia officers.*

Between these dates, one should also remember that when Adrian Gerritsen's daughter Machteld was taken hostage by the Esopus in the 1663 Second Esopus War, he was called to arms to pursue the Indians and to punish them for the massacre at Wiltwyck.

Is this service explained by his familiarity with the Indians and the countryside, as earlier experiences would reflect? How can we explain this service if he was merely an able-bodied male in a village then short of men, where as "only" a farmer unfamiliar with arms or the environment, he might have been better suited to stay within the stockade to defend it and its inhabitants against further attack?

The Esous War was concluded in 1664 and thereafter in the only entry of its type in court records, Adrian Gerritsen sued for compensation for his services in the expedition against the Indians. Although his hostage daughter was rescued unharmed, that was not reward enough. What was it about his services that would reflect some "special value" worthy of payment, even through a lawsuit?

To reiterate the record that is so well documented by O'Callahan, it was reported that on 28 April 1667, Adrian Gerritsen had to give reasons for being in arms. Perhaps his prowess with arms would explain such an odd notation, one imposed on very few other Dutchmen (if any, since this was the sole entry of this type). Could he have been a potential threat to the English, something they would scarcely have seen in a mere farmer?

It is well documented that Adrian Gerrtisen Van Vliet resided in Marbletown, and quite possibly died there. Marbletown is indeed a key connection to Thomas Chambers, being where he chose to build his baronial manor house and live as "Lord of Fox Hall." It is also the site where Chambers died, on 8 April 1694, perhaps some five years after his colleague Adrian Gerritsen.

Thomas Chambers, the 1652 founder of the Esopus settlement, was a one of the most prominent citizens of the province. Adrian Gerrtisen obviously had a keen appreciation of his importance, and Chambers' status thus reflected in him as well. Again, the reader must remember that Van Vliet was one of the electors that attempted to send Chambers to New Amsterdam in 1664 to the General Assembly. This is just one dimension of a relationship that dated back even further to their days in Rensselaerswyck.

Resettlement from Rennselaerswyck

"... a typical case being that of Thomas Chambers, who leased a farm from 1647 to 1654, thence moving to Esopus (Kingston), where he had bought his own land on June 5, 1652."

A FRACTIOUS PEOPLE, Patricia U. Bonomi, Columbia University Press, New York, 1977, page 199.

These facts explain why Adrian Gerritsen, like Chambers and others, had several parcels of land in Albany in the immediate vicinity of the patroonship. Moreover, Van Vliet traded some of his land specifically at Rensselaerswyck for land in Kingston, according to a notation in the NEW YORK HISTORICAL MANUSCRIPTS (Kingston Papers, Volume II 1664-1675). Then later, with these two individuals living in Wiltwyck. and later still in Marbletown, as well as serving as militia officers, we are provided with further and convincing proof of an association with roots in a time prior to Van Vliet's sole reported arrival in America in 1662.

Two other issues need to be addressed here. In the first instance, Van Vliet's principal occupation was farming. But in fact, from his arrival in New Netherland he was a landholder. How did he get title to land, and when? Moreover, from his beginnings in Esopus, he apparently held the confidence of the Governor General to till his lands under contract, implying great responsibility vis-à-vis the financial interests of a well known fastidious absentee landowner.

Could it be that Adrian Gerritsen's New Wrold farming skills were already known and tested? Was that testing at Rensselaerswyck? Was the choice of a permanent location Chambers' exclusively farming Wiltwyck not coincidence but part of a well planned return for Van Vliet with his family to resume for himself and them a new life in America?

In the second instance his probable death in 1689 or possibly 1690; the time span of the birth of his children; the year he was listed on Rensselaerswyck payrolls, clearly demonstrate that Adrian Gerritsen was in America as a young man of about twenty, before returning to Holland at least twice and returning in a later trip with a wife and family.

These facts must be borne in mind: many young –
around nineteen – farmers were contracted for by
Van Rensselaer; his business practices included
passage for his farm workers to come to his Hudson
Valley estates, granting many benefits and paying
high wages; and giving these farmers return trips to
the homeland at the conclusion of the contract
period, if they did not opt to remain in America.

Various historians writing in books and in DE
HALVE MAEN have noted multiple crossings by
persons associated with the Dutch colony were
much more common than one might imagine, given
the perils of cross-Atlantic travel in the Seventeenth
Century. But were these voyages more dangerous
than what the New World represented?

Adrian Gerritsen likely would have made three
journeys, one in or before 1634 when "Adrian
Gerritsen" was noted on the Rensselaerswyck
payroll; a second after the birth of five children
between (say) 1655 and 1662; and a third with his
family in 1662. He could well have married in
Holland and sired five children between 1649 and
1655 (a remarkably short period given common two
year spacing), and have been in America later for a
while, returning again in (say 1661 or) 1662.

No records preclude this possibility nor contradict
its construction. Unfortunately those that exist do
not prove such events occurred; that is, reflecting
three voyages for Adrian Gerritsen Van Vliet. But
two are clearly shown in the existing records
explaining his presence in 1634 and in 1662.

Logic does dictate, however, that in so sparsely
populated an area as this colony, the presence of
two "Adrian Gerritsens" is unlikely, particularly
when available information implies overlaps of
people, places and times, indicating there in fact
was just one.

But what about the Papendorp confusion? It is only coincidental that this name should be that of a likely place of origin for a farming Van Vliet family from Utrecht? Why does this name cease to be cited in records virtually as soon as Adrian Gerritsen begins using the Van Vliet surname? Why does "Van Papendorp" disappear completely in Dutch and English colonial records as a surname?

One can only conclude with almost complete certainty that in this small Dutch world, there was only one Adrian Gerritsen in 1634 through 1662, and of course thereafter. Most Americans of the Van Fleet/Van Vliet/Van Vleet lines can, in fact, trace their origins to 1634 through this sole Adrian Gerritsen.

It is not known where Adrian Gerritsen died or lies buried, but it was possibly in Marbletown or more remotely in Albany, the former community being where this Van Vliet lived for many years in America.

Publications on tombstone inscriptions found in Ulster County burial grounds do not list him or his wife Agatha Spruyt, but since marked graves, many with wood or other temporary material memorials, were the rule rather than the exception in rural areas prior to the mid-1700s, that fact is not surprising.

The Van Vliet Daughters

Although this commentary focuses on the male line of Adrian Gerritsen Van Vliet, it is important to add several notes on his two daughters Gertruyd and Machteld. Both married well and established distinguished lines in America, but these are not traced in this publication.

72

Gertruyd Van Vliet was born in Utecht Province in 1654. In adulthood, she married Gysbert Willemse Crom (or Krom) in Marbletown where her family was living. He was the owner of a large estate there, according to NEW YORK HISTORICAL MANUSCRIPTS (Kingston Papers). He was also the brother of Floris Willemse Crom of Flatbush, Long Island, patentee of the Crom Patent at Haverstraw, and a man of wealth.

Crom was the unfortunate person who accidentally shot Gertruyd's brother Dirck on New Year's Eve in 1678. That caused him to loose his left leg, thereafter suffering the nickname "Dirk Wooden Leg."

Machteld Van Vliet was born in Utrecht Province in 1655, the youngest of the Van Vliet children (about seven) when she arrived in New Netherland. She was held captive by the Esopus Indians in 1663, and was released the following year after many months following a punitive expedition that included her father secured the release of all the hostages.

Machteld married first Barent Van Borsum, son of Egbert Van Borsum of New York City. She was widowed at an early age, and then married Jan Jacobson Stol, as noted in the commentary on her father, who likely was a personal friend of Adrian Gerritsen. He was the son of Jacob Jansen Stol and his wife Gertruyd Doesburg, he being a magistrate at Esopus.

Adrian Gerritsen Van Vliet:
A Pioneer And Adventurer Among the Indians

COLONIAL HISTORY OF STATE OF NEW YORK by Broadhead and O'Callahan, 1861, contains many references to Adrian Gerritsen Van Vliet in a way supportive of the assertion that he was a well-known and presumably respected "Indian specialist." These references relate to his military prowess as well as ability to interact with the Indians, representing the European settlers' interests.

01. *In Volume 13, page 88, "at Ft. Orange (Albany), August 13, 1658, Adrian Gerritsen and five others (appeared) with 16 Maquas (Mohawk) Indians and one Frenchman." Page 92 provides further information on this incident with the date 8 October 1658, and it is tied directly to Esopus.*

02. *On 12 October 1658, Adrian Gerritsen Van Vliet is appointed an overseer for the defense of the village.*

03. *On page 110 at Fort Orange on 6 September 1659, Adrian Gerritsen offered to go voluntarily as one of ten deputies for purposes of peaceful intervention with the Mohawks.*

04. *On page 246, Adrian Gerritsen's daughter is noted as having been taken prisoner by the Esopus in the summer 1663 raid. He later sues for payment for his services.*

05. *On page 413 and 414, Adrian Gerritsen is required by English authorities to "give reasons for being in arms," on 28 April 1667.*

06. *In Volume II on page 627, it was stated that "Adrian Gerritsen, for militia officers, ensign (Hurley and Marbletown)," on 6 October 1673.*

07. On page 482, in 1674-75, Adrian Gerritsen is "commissary for lands given by the Indian chief "Schermerhoorn" (as called by the Dutch) to Jan Bronk. The official was Jan Provoost, secretary (a family member in the later Van Vliet marriage). This Jan Bronk's farm is what is presently called "the" Bronx, New York.

08. In 1674-75 as well, Thomas Chambers is noted as the captain of Kingston's and Marbletown's militia, serving with Adrian Gerritsen.

09. Lastly, Fox Hall is erected and elevated by English authorities as a baronial manor house for Thomas Chambers in Marbletown, Van Vliets' long time associate from Rensselaerswyck, Kingston (formerly Esopus or Wiltwyck) and Marbletown.

Peter Stuyvesant

ANCESTRAL CHARTS:
MALE CHILDREN AND GRANDCHILDREN OF

ADRIAN GERRITSEN VAN VLIET

01. GERRIT	02. JAN	03. DIRCK
born 1649	born 1650	born 1651

Cornelia 1681	Archie 1686	Arie 1686
Agatha 1683	Arie 1687 (d.)	Hilltje 1688
Teunis 1685 (d.)	Frederick 1691	Andries 1691
Lysbeth 1687	Jan Jr. 1694	Aegjen 1694
Jenntje 1692	Arie 1697	Cornelia 1695
Geertjen 1694	William 1699	Gerrit 1697
Neetje 1697	Deborah 1701	Rachel 1699
Adrian 1699	Geertje 1704	Dirck 1701
Teunis 1702	Anna 1711	Caterina 1702

(d.) indicates the child died young

GERRIT VAN VLIET'S Grandchildren by Sons:

01. *Adrian* 1699	02. *Teunis* 1702
Pieternelle	Gerrit 1735
Francina	Nelly 1737
Garret	Evert 1739
Petrus 1737	Arie 1741
Teunis 1740	Teunis Jr. 1745

JAN VAN VLIET'S Grandchildren by Sons:

01. *Frederick* 1691

John Van Fleet 1719
Mary Van Fleet 1721
Judik Van Fleet 1723
Willem 1725 (d.)
William Van Fleet 1727
Thomas Van Fleet 1729
Frederick Jr. 1731
Abraham Van Fleet 1733
Rachel Van Fleet 1737
Leah Van Fleet 1735

02. *Jan Junior* 1694

Samuel 1726
Benjamin 1728
Elizabeth 1730
Daniel Van Fleet 1733
Deborah 1736
Jacobus 1739
Marie Van Fleet 1743
Catherine Van Fleet '44
Scynta Van Fleet 1738
Marya Van Fleet 1747
EsyntjeVan Fleet '59

03. *William* 1699

Maria 1727
Debora 1729
Judik 1730
Jannekin 1733
Abraham 1738
Lydia 1741
Catrina 1743

Notes:

(01) Names listed with "Van Fleet" as a surname are for persons who cited themselves as such while all others used the "Van Vliet" surname.

(02) Naming patterns are repeated among siblings, with some Dutch sapellings retained while others are English forms.

(03) Note that "Van Fleet" is utilized by cousins Frederick in New Jersey and several (but not all of) Jan Junior's children in New York about the same 1740s to 1760s time frame.

The 1635 Fort Orange depiction below illustrates what the Dutch fortification would have looked like to Adrian Gerritsen Van Vliet, who arrived in America by at least 1634.

The schematic outline of Kingston in 1695 shown below is not much different from what it looked like to the Van Vliet family in the previous decades.

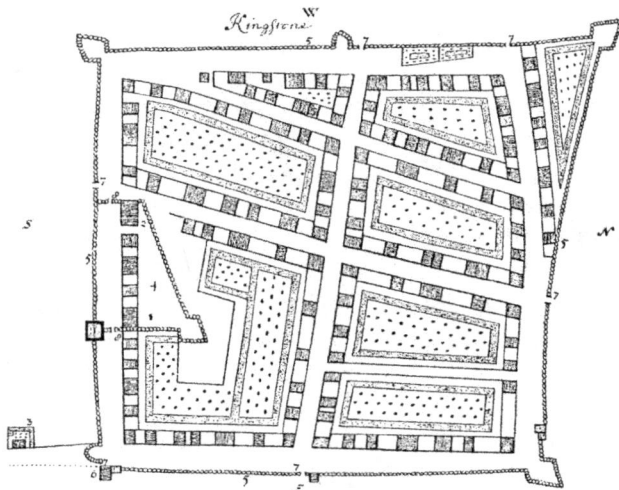

GERRIT ADRIANSEN VAN VLIET (1649 – 1723)

Gerrit Van Vliet was the eldest of Adrian Gerritsen Van Vliet's five children, being named for his grandfather, and was thirteen years of age when he came to America aboard De Trouw with his parents and siblings. He lived with them for a period of time in Kingston, but later in life relocated to the east side of the Hudson River near present-day Poughkeepsie in Dutchess County, New York.

The sole notation about Gerrit in his younger days in the DOCUMENTARY HISTORY OF NEW YORK states that on 1 September 1689 "Gerrit van ffliett" and "John van ffliett," sons of Adrian Gerritsen Van Vliet, took the oath of allegiance at Kingston.

Sometime in 1680 in Kingston, he married Pieternelle Swart, at age thirty-one. Between 1681 and 1702, they had nine children.

These were:

01. Cornelia Van Vliet, born 28 August 1681, married Andries Davidson (possibly of the Leah Decker Davids family line);

02. Agatha Van Vliet, born about 1683, named for her grandmother, married Marcus Van Bommel of Poughkeepsie on 21 June 1725;

03. Teunis Van Vliet, born 19 July 1685 and died young;

04. Lysbeth (Elizabeth) Van Vliet, born 2 October 1687, married Nathaniel Davenport;

05. Jannetje Van Vliet, born 30 October 1692, married Louis DeBois of the original families of New Palz;

06. Geertje Van Vliet, baptized 11 November 1694, married Christoffel Van Bommel, brother of Marcus, who served as the first judge of Poughkeepsie, Dutchess County;

07. Neeltje Van Vliet, born 21 February 1697, married Johannes Ter Box of Fishkill;

08. Arie (Adrian) Gerritse Van Vliet, named for his grandfather and in a sense his father, born 26 March 1699 and died June 1778; and

09. Teunis Van Vliet (again), born 14 June 1702, and married Sara Van Wagenen.

This family "who moved from Esopus to Fishkill before 1714 (actually, in 1709). When his home was included in the first census of Dutchess," established a long line of Van Vliets still residing in the area with the surname spelled the same way. At the time of their move to Fishkill, this Dutchess County area had only four hundred and forty-five residents, including a notation of some twenty-nine slaves.

It is interesting to note that one somewhat more contemporary Van Vliet family member (John) was a close "local boy" friend and confident of Franklin Delano Roosevelt, when the former President could "be himself" at his Hyde Park home in Dutchess County, completely away from his aides and more importantly from the public eye.

In Helen Wilkinson's DUTCH HOUSES IN THE HUDSON VALLEY BEFORE 1776, there are pictures of the original Gerrit Van Vliet homestead. In fact, mention or photos appear in at least two such publications from the 1920s and 1930s about the Hudson Valley's early history.

According to information conveyed by this commentator's father many years ago, he stated he had met some Gerrit Adriansen descendants from Dutchess County and that they were pleased to report that the family still had an ancestral bible, printed sometime in the early 1700s in Dordrecht, Holland.

In the distinguished family line from Gerrit, his son Adrian Van Vliet who was baptized 26 March 1699 married Janneke Cloet (or Knoet) of a French Huguenot background. Adrian died 27 September 1769, but he and Janneke had a sizable family. Their children were:

01. Peiternelle Van Vliet, who married Isaac Van Banseloten;
02. Francina Van Vliet, who married Petrus Low;
03. Garret Van Vliet, who apparently died young (note the changed spelling);
04. Teunis Van Vliet, born 7 October 1740 and married Lemmentje Romeyn;
05. Frederick Van Vliet; and
06. Petrus Van Vliet, born 1 January 1737 and married Johanna Van Wormer in Fishkill.

In turn, Petrus and Johanna Van Vliet had eleven children, who were:

01. Engeltje Van Vliet, baptized 6 April 1766, died 18 May 1851, and who married first John Cromwell and second Captain Peter Bogardus;
02. Jennacke Van Vliet, born 26 July 1765, married Jeremiah Myers;
03. Johannes Van Vliet, born 25 September 1770, died 25 October 1847, married Elizabeth Cromwell, sister of John;
04. Arie Van Vliet, born 20 July 1773, married first Levina Cromwell (same family as above) and second Louisa Bogardus, sister of Peter;
05. Petrus Van Vliet, born 31 October 1775, died 18 September 1835 and married Sarah Hough (and had fifteen children);
06. Garret Van Vliet, born 1777 and died 1843 unmarried;

07. Alida Van Vliet, born 25 February 1780 and married William Higbee, living in Vermont;

08. Fransyitje Van Vliet (sic), born August 1782, married Jacob Bartley and lived first in Vermont and then removed to Canada;

09. Teunis Van Vliet, lived in Vermont and then Canada, but later moved west;

10. Frederick Van Vliet, born 1787 and died 1838, married Polly _____ and had ten children, lived in Westfield, New York; and

11. Christian Van Vliet, born January 1790, married first Rachel Hough, sister of Sarah, and second Maria Cromwell whom he wed on 11 January 1825 in Fishkill, another sister of the Cromwell family mentioned above.

Christian Van Vliet also lived in Vermont. By his wife Rachel Hough, he had five children, including Isaac, Rachel and Delia Ann. His two other sons were Lieutenant Frederick Van Vliet who served in the Mexican War, and (ultimately Major General) Gerrit Stewart Van Vliet.

Known principally and simply as Stewart Van Vliet, this son from the second generation American line of Gerrit Van Vliet was born in 1815.

Van Vliet graduated from West Point in 1840, in the same class with his friend and former roommate William Tecumseh Sherman. He too saw action during the Mexican War, and then later served ultimately as a Major General in the American Civil War. Van Vliet retired from the United States Army Quartermaster Corps and died in 1901 in Washington, D.C.

The subject of a monograph by his descendant Allison Van Vliet Dunn in the 1970s, he is profiled as well in a chapter in this commentary.

JAN ADRIANSEN VAN VLIET (1650 - 1722)

Adrian Gerritsen's son Jan (John) who was born in 1650 was – like his parents – from the Province of Utrecht. Nothing is known of his childhood or early life, save for the fact that he came to America at twelve years of age.

At age thrity-four shortly after their first bans were announced on 4 October 1684, Jan married Judith Hussey, a native-born Kingstonian. She was the daughter of Frederick Hussey, an Englishman, former soldier, large landholder and an overseer for Hurley and Marbletown. Her mother Margaret was of a Dutch background, having married Frederick in America. Judith was baptized and reared in the Dutch Reformed church.

Frederick Hussey was an erstwhile soldier whose position under English rule provided considerable prominence. Hussey was well known not only in his capacity as an overseer in two communities, but as a large landholder, once the English Crown was in power. South of Kingston there is a hill named for this family, but their other lands were located more to the southwest of that community.

Judith was baptized on 9 October 1667. She was much younger than Jan, who as noted was in his thirties at the time of their marriage. In March 1685, Jan and Judith bought "Mombackus," a corner lot in Kingston, paying two hundred and fifty schepels of wheat to Jan Jacobson Stol, the same person who married Jan's sister Machteld.

In 1690 Jan and Judith moved to Marbletown some seven miles to the southwest of Kingston, a community established as English in the 1668 to 1669 period. It was there that Frdierck Hussey was an overseer and where Jan's father had been a militia ensign and landowner.

Later in life – specifically in 1712 – they relocated again to Rochester (now Stone Ridge) further into the center of Ulster County. It is noteworthy that the earlier locales coincide with similar movements of Jan's father and mother, and that the relocation to Marbletown likely coincides with Adrian Gerritsen's death in that (or the previous) year.

One record indicates that Jan and Judith had ten children, while others report nine born over the twenty-five year period following their marriage.

These children were:

01. Archi Van Vliet, born 31 January 1686;
02. Arie (Adrian) Van Vliet, born 4 December 1687;
03. Frederick Van Fleet, whose birthdate was sometime in 1690 or 1691, and who married Marbletown's other overseer's daughter Mary Biggs in November 1718;
04. Jan Jansen Van Vliet Junior, born 16 November 1694, an early settler of the Minisink Valley;
05. Ari Van Vliet, born 31 January 1697;
06. William Van Fleet, born 4 June 1699;
07. Debora Van Fleet, born 12 October 1701;
08. Geertje Van Fleet, born 3 September 1704; and
09. Anna Van Fleet, born 24 June 1711.

Jan's son Frederick Van Fleet removed to present-day New Jersey around 1725 and established a family branch with his children by Mary Biggs Van Fleet.

This family has gained note in many fields of endeavor throughout the subsequent generations. As a sidenote here, since Frederick later spelled his name "Van Fleet," this notation is made above for all those who adopted (later in life) that same spelling.

84

Frederick (who died at age ninety-five) and his wife had ten children, and possibly three more. Those known are as follows:

01. John Van Fleet, born 1719;
02. Mary Van Fleet, born 1721;
03. Judith Van Fleet, born 1723;
04. Willem (William) Van Fleet, born 1725 married Mary Autien;
05. Thomas Van Fleet, born 1729, married Margaret Wyckoff and died 1812;
06. Frederick Van Fleet Junior, born 1731 married Rebecca DuBois;
07. Abraham Van Fleet, born 1733 and died 1813;
08. Rachel Van Fleet, born 1737; and
09. Leah Van Fleet, born 1735.

Jan Van Vliet was a farmer and landowner like his father and father-in-law. Aside from this obvious statement and the fact that he must have enjoyed considerable status within the community, little is known of him. The sole entry in records of any type relate to a will in which money owed him by Jan were to be paid to another.

Judith Hussey Van Vliet died in Readington, New Jersey, where he son Frederick was located, but the date of her death is not noted. Jan's death, however, is recorded in a family bible as 1722.

In a final note, records of early settlers are confusing for many reasons, not the least of which is spelling. Rules for same were not formulated for many years to come. During Jan's lifetime, the surname had many variations, but importantly it was through his line – mainly through son Frederick and grandson Daniel – that the form "Van Fleet" became fixed and accepted by many, but not all, in the New Jersey and Minisink Valley, New York, areas.

DIRCK ADRIANSEN VAN VLIET (1651 - 1744)

Dirck Van Vliet was the youngest of the three sons of Adrian Gerrtisen Van Vliet and Agatha Spruyt. He was born in 1651, and came to Wiltwyck as an eleven year old, growing up in that community and moving later to the eastern side of the Hudson Valley – specifically, to Fishkill, where his brother Gerrit had located in 1709. Some of the descendants of Dirck through his son Dirck Junior reestablished themselves near the present-day community of Stroudsburg, Pennsylvania, across from the central New Jersey area on the Delaware River. Details of this move are related in another chapter of this commentary.

Dirck Van Vliet married Anna Andries (or Andriessen or Andrise) on 23 April 1685. She was born in Holland and had come to America in the ship DeTrouw on an earlier sailing with her family, sometime in the year 1659. That family settled in Wiltwyck, and in 1663 during the Second Esopus War, Anna's father was mortally wounded during the fighting. Specifically, he suffered his wounds during the fight to free the hostages carried off by the Esopus Indians, which included Dirck's younger sister Machteld.

Dirck, who was thirty-four at the time of his marriage, and Anna Van Vliet had nine children born between 1686 and 1702. Records of baptisms are noted in the Kingston Dutch Reformed Church. These children were:

01.   Arie (Adrian) Van Vliet, born 11 July 1686, with baptismal witnesses being brother Jan Van Vliet and their mother Agatha Spruyt;

02.   Hilletje (or Elletje) Van Vliet, baptized 1 January 1688, married Gysbert Peel on 3 May 1712;

03. Adries Van Vliet, born 5 November 1693 (or 1691), died unmarried in 1722;

04. Agatha Van Vliet, named for her grandmother, born or baptized in 1693, married Teunis Swart of Albany on 15 November 1715;

05. Cornelia Van Vliet, born 7 June 1695, married Matthew Edward Thompson;

06. Gerrit Van Vliet, named for his uncle, born 27 June 1697, married Judith Van Neste;

07. Rachel Van Vliet, born 7 May 1699, married a cousin of sister Agatha's husband by the same name, Teunis Swart;

08. Dirck Van Vliet Junior, born 1 January 1701, and whose line is reported elsewhere in this commentary; and

09. Catarina Van Vliet, born 12 November 1702.

Although Dutchess County records indicate that Dirck Van Vliet and family remained there, particularly around Fishkill, it is believed that after his son Dirck Junior was established in New Jersey around Somerset County, he may have gone on to the Stroudsburg, Pennsylvania, area. The New Jersey move occurred perhaps in the 1720s and the final move in the fourth decade of the 1700s, when he and Anna were in thelast years of their lives.

While Dirck Van Vliet ws obviously an attentive husband once married, judging by the number of children he and Anna had, there is an amusing and well documented story about his philanderings prior to the vows.

According to two descendants, on 17 October 1687, Hendrick Schoonover brought his wife Debora Christoffels Davids before a justice of the peace in Ulster County, to testify in a deposition (Book AA, page 66, Ulster County Clerk's Office) about the paternity of one Niclaas.

Debora stated that Hendrick was not the father, but rather "Dirrick Wootin Legg" – that strange name being translated as "Wooden Leg" – was the real father of this child.

And who was Dirck Wooden Leg? None other than Dirck Van Vliet. As related earlier, Dirck's left leg was accidentally "shot off" by Gysbert Krom (or Crom) in a roudy New Year's celebration in 1678. More likely, the wound necessitated amputation, and the practice of the day was – as had been the case with Peter Stuyvesant – to have a wooden peg leg attached for ambulatory purposes.

The deposition went on to state that when she became pregnant, Dirck would not marry her, and instead married another woman – to wit, Anna, daughter of the late Andries and Hillitje Hendricks Barentsen.

The child that Debora bore was born in 1685, the same year that Dirck began his union with Anna – somewhat on the rebound(?) – siring the many children noted above over the following years of their marriage.

However, there is a bit of irony in this gossipy story. Over the years there were many inter-marriages among the Schoonover, Krom, Davids (Davis) and Van Vliet (Van Fleet) families, one notable wedding taking place between Debora's granddaughter Rebekka (sic), who married a Krom who in turn was the grandson of – none other than Dirck Van Vliet!

When Dirck Van Vliet died, he was buried in Stroudsburg, according to Twentieth Century Van Vliet family records. Nonetheless, along with his brother Garrit, the Van Vliets – who retained that spelling – became well established in Dutchess County where descendants live today.

88

INTERNAL MIGRATION AND RESETTLEMENT IN EARLY AMERICA

Here are the founders of a mighty nation,
Here are the pioneers who won the soil.
As generation followed generation,
With ax and plow and with backbreaking toil.

Judge D.D. Banta

As the numbers of children and grandchildren born into families like the Van Vliets swelled the population, and occasional comments are made about inheritance patterns, it becomes obvious that the quest for new good quality, readily available free or inexpensive land was a recurring demand for early settlers. Indeed, that was the single most important theme that was destined to mark the next century and a half in American history at least until the close of the frontier in the earely 1900s.

We were an agricultural nation, and land for new generations of farmers was a necessity. It propelled our ancestors to move ever westward, when such could be found in abundance. When authorities hindered this progress, people rebelled. Indeed, the American Revolution itself was very much a struggle for the control of one's own destiny to move into western lands unfettered by legal prohibitions.

Lands in Ulster and Orange Counties, not to mention all those others lying further to the east, had long since been staked out as farms and planted with orchards. Now the movement had to be further inland, crossing the mountains to dangerous distant places like the Minisink River and then beyond the Delaware River into the Indian territories of Pennsylvania in the east, and the Mohawk River Valley of the northwest.

A Sketch of Deerpark, New York

When the state legislature set Rockland County apart from Orange County in 1798, it provided some lands for Orange from Ulster County's jurisdiction. An early settler in this area set off his small holding with a brush fence, and thereafter his neighbors jokingly called it his "Deerpark."

However, the name did in fact become synonymous with this area, and today Deerpark has six hamlets. These are: Cahoonzie, where an Indian sub-group of the Delawares once lived; Cuddebackville, named for Colonel William Cuddeback of Revolutionary War fame; Godeffroy, named so in 1878 for his estate there; Huguenot, once called "Sindeaquan" by the Indians and "Peenpack" by the earliest European settlers, was named for the French religious feeedom seekers; Rio, called "Quarry Hill" for the bluestone once mined there; and Sparrowbush, named for Henry Sparrow who had timber holdings in the area.

The Delaware, Neversink and Mongaup Rivers and the Basha Kill have influenced the development of the town.   Today, however, they are used for recreational purposes.

William Tietsoort was the first inhabitant of the area, arriving in 1690 when the Indians asked him to Jacob Codebeck (sic), Thomas, Anthony and Bernardus Swartwout, Jan Tyse, Peter Gumaer and David Jamison.

Because of lax boundaries the "Border War" was fought among local residents, each wanting the best lands.   In 1773 the present New York and New Jersey boundary was approved by England, resolving an issue that had cut the town in become a blacksmith for their tool-making requirements. Others followed through a patent for 1,200 acres granted in 1697 to two.

90

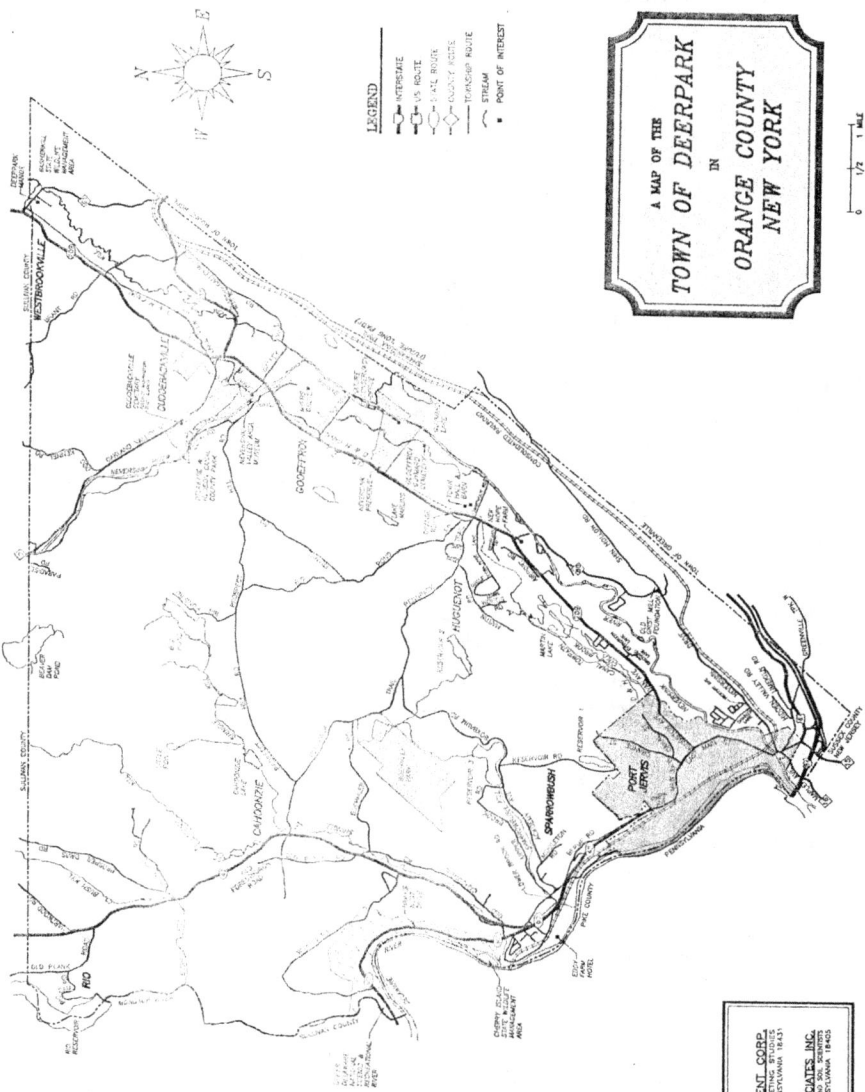

JAN JANSEN VAN VLIET JUNIOR (1694 – 1775)

The story of third generation American Jan Janse Van Vliet Junior begins with comments about his maternal family origins. His father, Jan Van Vliet, was born in the Netherlands, as noted, and came to America with his parents as a youth, probably at age twelve. Growing up in the environs of the Hudson Valley in Wiltwyck/Kingston, and then likely in Marbletown, it was logical that he would marry a woman from the small community of Dutch or French Protestant families residing in the (by then) English colony of New York.

Jan Junior's spouse came from the Swartwout family, one of the most distinguished in early Ulster and Orange County history. His wife's grandfather was Roeloff Swartwout, who came from Amsterdam in 1655. He married a widow senior to him two years later, she having already borne five children. They had five more over the coming years, including sons named Thomas, Anthony and Bernardus.

Roeloff Swartwout was commissioned sheriff, the chief legal officer and magistrate for Wiltwyck, on 31 May 1661, at the young age of twenty-seven. This was done against the "better judgement" of many in the Dutch colony. Citing his youth and lack of experience, persons such as Governor Peter Stuyvesant claimed that Roeloff Swartwout was not well-suited for the position, which commanded a high level of prominence and authority within the community.

Despite objections, Roeloff Swartwout held the position of sheriff (or magistrate) – though not without continuing controversy – for a period of time, and continuously maintained his role as one of the notables of the Dutch, and later the English colony.

92

In 1690, the Swartwout sons Thomas, Anthony and Bernardus, together with another Dutchman named Jans Tys, an Englishman called David Jamison and two French Huguenots Peter Gimaer (sic) and Jacob Codebec (sic) obtained by grant and patent extensive Orange County lands formerly owned by Chief Penhausen, and consisting of the area corresponding to the border of Ulster County in the east and Pennsylvania's present border in the west.

Although these men had title to these vast lands, in fact they were not the first settlers of the region. That historic distinction goes to another Dutchman named William Tietsoort, who had arrived in the region just shortly before as a refugee from the Schenectady Massacre during King William's War. But the region had been explored even earlier in the first years of Dutch colonization, inasmuch as it formed part of the general Old Mine Road (in reality a trail, and one which had other names over the years) connection to copper mines located further south in present-day New Jersey's Minisink area.

For this commentary the region in question is generally referred to as Deer Park, a somewhat loosely defined area that extends to present-day Port Jervis along that famed New York State Route 209 – the Old Mine Road – into the very heart of the Minisink Valley of a two state (new York and New Jersey) area.

It was there that Jesyntjen (a variation on the more common spelling) was born, in a place called Peenpack. This Dutch derived word means low, flat land, and specifically refers to one side of the Neversink River. The place in general includes present-day Cuddebackville and Huguenot, mere dots of communities in the Minisink Valley along the Old Mine Road.

The Minisink Valley
c. 1650 - c. 1783

Destruction of Schenectady by the French and Indians, February 8, 1690.

Jesyntjen (later at the time of her marriage, called Ezyntjen) Swartwout was baptized on 13 August 1699. As stated, her grandfather was Roeloff, her father was Thomas Swartwout, and her mother was Lysbeth Gardinier, the daughter of a French Huguenot settler with antecedents in the Kingston area.

With marriage bans having been registered on 21 February 1725, on 11 March 1725 Jan Van Vliet Junior and Ezyntjen Swartwout were united in marriage at the (now) First Dutch Reformed Church in Kingston. Presumably, she was not quite twenty-six years of age at the time she married Jan Junior, who was thirty, fairly advanced ages for the first marriages for both at that point in history.

On her marriage day, Ezyntjen was given the portion of her father's land that she had inherited, although records are not specific as to the locale of this bequest other than it being logically within the patent area. However, thereafter – specifically beginning on 7 July 1728 – Jan Van Vliet Junior was listed in New York Historical Manuscripts as one of six freeholders in Maghaghkemeck (sic) in Orange County, and later is noted as an "ancient" (or initial) owner in "the Lower Neighborhood," another name for the general Deerk Park and Peenpack/Minisink region near Port Jervis. Of note, the other five owners were cited as Jacob Kuddeback (sic), Samuel Swartwout, Bernardus Swartwout Junior, Peter Gomar (sic) and Harme Van Emwegen in New York historical manuscripts.

Jan Van Vliet Junior was born 16 November 1694 in Marbletown, where his grandfathers Frederick Hussey had been overseer for the English, and Adrian Gerritsen Van Vliet had been an agriculturalist and an officer of the militia in close association with Hussey and Englishman Thomas Chambers.

Aside from the logical pursuits as an agriculturalist and frontiersman, little is known of Jan Junior's formative years, save for one interesting notation that as a youth in 1712 (at age eighteen) he was a bounty hunter for wolves, receiving one guinea per pelt.

It is apparent that although Jan Van Vliet Junior and his wife Ezyntjen held lands in the Minisink area, they did not locate there immediately, explaining in part why they were married in Kingston and not closer to that newly settled region. In fact, one source stated that it was not until some time in 1733 (probably after the birth of Daniel), that they and the first three or so of their children, having been living in Marbletown, moved into the Minisink.

Relocation to such a remote area must have posed special difficulties. Indeed, this was a very sparsely settled area. As late as 1738, the Minisink had just ninety-eight males above the age of ten years, some two hundred and twenty females and children, as well as twenty-one blacks (whose status is not cited), for a total population of three hundred and thirty-nine persons out of Orange County's total of 2,830 in that year. In comparison, Ulster County had nearly twice that population, some 5,270 inhabitants.

Despite these paltry numbers for the Minisink Valley, the region was beginning to grow, reflected by the fact that Dutch Reformed Church activities included establishing churches there (ultimately three congregations). Interestingly, records for both Deer Park and the Minisink Dutch Reformed churches make reference to the Van Vliet family repeatedly, as noted in the MINISINK VALLEY REFORMED DUTCH CHURCH RECORDS 1716-1830.

THE SWARTWOUT CHRONICLES state that Ezyntjen "...united with the church in Maghaghkemeck on October 16, 1748." Jan Van Vliet Junior, "...her husband, a freeholder of Maghaghkemeck...was appointed on March 7, 1742, by the consistories of the churches of Minissinck (sic) and Maghaghkemeck, one of the collectors of money" to aid and to "build up the Low Dutch churches (High Dutch usually referred to Germans and Lutherans) in the provinces of New York and New Jersey."

On 28 September 1762, Jan Junior was elected an Elder of the Church in the place of Philip Swartwout, who presumably had died. So near to the end of his life, this act appears to have been something of a capstone for Jan Van Vliet's Junior's long career promoting the Dutch Reformed Church interests in the region, where this faith still enjoys great vibrancy.

Most of Jan Van Vliet Junior's children were born in the general Minisink region in the ill-defined area of New York and New Jersey, after he and Ezyntjen relocated to that frontier land. In all, they had a total of nine children born between 1726 and probably 1746.

These were:

01. Samuel Van Vliet, baptized 8 May 1726;
02. Benjamin Van Vliet, baptized 28 January 1728;
03. Elizabeth Van Vliet, dates of birth and baptism unknown;
04. Daniel Van Fleet, born 4 February 1733;
05. Debora Van Fleet, baptized in the Minisink 18 May 1736;
06. Jacobus (James) Van Vliet, baptized 30 October 1739;

97

07. Maria (or Marie) Van Fleet, baptized 14 April 1743 (Gumaer's HISTORY OF DEER PARK states 23 October 1743);

08. Catherina Van Fleet, baptized 23 April 1744; and

09. Marya Van Fleet, baptized 21 June 1747 (Gumaer claims Mahackamack church records cite 10 May 1747).

Most of these children reached adulthood, and married prominently into local families, but none so important as the descendants of the community's co-founder, Jacob Codebec (sic).

This man was born Jacques Caudebec, as will be related later. As a young man he found his way by a circuitous route from France to Maryland and then ultimately to the Dutch and French Protestant communities along the Hudson, and finally to the interior of the New York colony along the Old Mine Road. With his name anglicized to "Cuddeback," this family was and remains one of the most noted in Orange County.

Jan Van Vliet Junior's daughters Jesyntje (also Esyntje, or Jane) married James Cuddeback. Daughter Catherina (or Catherine) married Benjamin Cuddeback, and thereafter lived on his of his father's estate, the remaining half being occupied by brother Abraham Cuddeback and his then-wife Esther Gumaer (who probably died young).

Quite likely, daughter Maria Van Vliet later married this same Abraham Cuddeback, a man who served as a captain in the American Revolution and who was the individual whose military service included supervision for at least some Van Vliet/Van Fleet family members also serving in the American Revolutionary armed forces.

Lastly, son Daniel Van Fleet – the surname having been anglicized by his adult years – married Sarah Cuddeback, a granddaughter of Jacques. These lines and other family connections are related in CAUDEBEC IN AMERICA, Gumaer's HISTORY and the SWARTWOUT CHRONICLES.

Jan Junior became a widower in the mid-1750s, and at a remarkable sixty-three years of age, on 19 May 1757, he remarried. His second wife was a widow of yet another prominent family, one Leah Decker Davids (or Davis). She had been married to Solomon Davids, a lineal descendant of Christoffel Davids originally of Albany and of the Esopus/Wiltwyck/Kingston area, precisely the same as Jan Junior's grandfather, Adrian Gerritsen Van Vliet.

Solomon and Leah had been married around 1733, and thereafter had ten children whose births were duly recorded in church records at Machakemech (sic) and earlier at Kingston, some eight children in the first instance and two – obviously the oldest – in the latter case. These children were all born between 1735 and 1752.

As a note explaining the close knit relationships that existed and on which families depended in the American frontier communities, the eldest of Jan Junior's children, Samuel, was a witness to the baptism of several of the children borne by Leah Decker and her first husband, Solomon Davids.

The marriage of Jan Junior and Leah, so late in life for both but particularly for a woman whose child-bearing years were essentially over, produced an additional child. There is no error in this birth inasmuch as Jan and Leah are noted in church records as the parents. These records are very specific and complete, documenting what might be termed something of a "senior citizen birth."

99

A daughter named Esyntje was born on 28 January 1759, more than twenty months after this marriage. Jan was sixty-five at the time, and Leah was likely at least forty-two, based on a reported birth date for her in 1717.

This daughter Esyntje (named for his first wife) by his second marriage is cited in CAUDEBEC IN AMERICA, is the one who later married James Cuddeback and had a son whose name was Gerardus Swartwout Cuddeback, and interesting tie-in to Jan's first wife's family. This child was baptized on 6 September 1781, when his mother was twenty-two years of age.

There is speculation among some researchers that a second child was born to this couple in July 1764. The complete lack of birth and/or baptism documentation (when all other children are noted by this church official father) for this birth, as well as the advanced age of Leah at that time (forty-seven) makes this highly improbable, at best.

As in the case of his father, Jan Van Vliet Senior, one can only speculate about Jan Junior's lifelong pursuits. As stated, he was a sizable landowner and presumably derived income from agricultural pursuits and other products of the land. Undoubtedly, he was very prominent in the community, an assumption supported by many facts, not the least being his family's marriages, relationships with prominent figures in the community, the church and his position therein, and ultimately in politics.

Jan Van Vliet Junior was an early signer of the Articles of Association, and was affiliated with the Committee of Safety in the Minisink region, both precursor associations leading to the citizen uprising known in this country as the American Revolution, and in Great Britain as "the American War."

100

These facts are recorded in many sources, and the Daughters of the American Revolution (D.A.R.) and the Sons of the American Revolution (S.A.R.) classify him as a "Patriot," meaning one who provided personal services and succor to the American Cause.

Of special note reflecting Jan Van Vliet Junior's and his family's support for the American Revolution is the record of those who served in its military campaigns. His son Daniel Van Fleet and grandson Daniel Van Fleet Junior, served with the Second Ulster Regiment. His grandson Abraham Van Fleet served (1778 – 1781) as a corporal in the First Ulster Regiment. His youngest grandchild, Joshua Van Fleet, also saw service with the New York Troops, despite his being a young teenager (fifteen at enlistment) at the time.

These and numerous others of the Van Vliet/Van Fleet family from New York and New Jersey served in the American Revolution, as did so many from related families. But it should be noted as well that there were a few Van Vliets from the more immediate confines of the Hudson Valley, who saw fit to serve the Crown as Tories.

Jan Van Vliet Junior himself did not live to see the fighting that would literally take place in his Minisink back yard. Although the first shots of the Revolution at Lexington and Concord occurred during his lifetime, he died in the Minisink Valley where many of his descendants live to this day, sometime in July 1775. He was buried near present-day Port Jervis, New York.

Orange County documents note that Jan Junior's older children (and perhaps just James, or Jacobus, who married Margaret Palmatier) inherited his farm.

101

Jan Junior's grandchildren Michael and Solomon Van Fleet continued to work this property – allegedly the original William Tietsoort place – well into the mid-1800s and as late as 1846, according to the SWARTWOUT CHRONICLES, in 1889 their nephew Solomon Van Fleet had possession of the property.

Eager's HISTORY OF ORANGE COUNTY (1846 – 47) named Daniel Junior; Jacobus (or James); Jacobus Junior; Michael; Solomon; John; and (another) James Van Fleet as living in the general Port Jervis/Deer Park region in the early to mid-1800s. The surname used by these persons was primarily Van Vliet, although there are Van Fleets there as well.

As a final note, the farmhouse that was occupied by Jan Junior and his family, and then by James and his family, figured prominently in the July 1779 events of the Indian and Tory invasion of the Minisink. The Van Fleet home was burned to the ground by Chief Joseph Brandt and his Indians, as well as by the Loyalists on the twenty-second of that month. Local histories state that only a few yards of cloth and a glass vinegar bottle survived the conflagration, but despite their attempts to murder all of the local American population, the Van Fleet and allied families survived the devastation to rebuild again in a land they had claimed as their own.

The Indian raids led by Joseph Brandt in July 1779 were devastating for the Minisink Valley, as they had been for the Wyoming Valley in 1778.

When the Jan Van Vliet home was burned during the Minisink battles of July 1779, a second home was built shortly thereafter by his heir, James Van Fleet (pictured below).

The Old Mine Road

ANCESTRAL CHART FOR MALE CHILDREN OF JAN VAN VLIET JUNIOR (Birth/Baptism Dates)

A. CHILDREN OF **BENJAMIN VAN VLIET** (1728)
01. Samuel Van Vliet (born 1759)
02. Annatje Van Vliet (1764)
03. Cornelius Van Vliet (1766)

B. CHILDREN OF **DANIEL VAN FLEET** (1733)
01. Solomon Van Fleet (1754)
02. Daniel Van Fleet Junior (1756)
03. Jesyntje Van Fleet (1759)
04. Sarah Van Fleet (1759)
05. Abraham Van Fleet (1760)
06. William Van Fleet (1762)
07. Mordechai (or other) Van Fleet (died young)
08. Thomas Van Fleet (1764)
09. Joshua Van Fleet (1764)
10. Jacomyntje Van Fleet (date?)

C. CHILDREN OF **JACOBUS VAN VLIET** (1733)
01. John Van Vliet (1771)
02. Solomon Van Vliet (1773, died young)
03. Lydia Van Vliet (1776)
04. Eunice Van Vliet (1778)
05. Syntche Van Vliet (1780)
06. Michael Van Vliet (1783)
07. Elizabeth Van Vliet (1785)
08. Thomas Van Vliet (1788)
09. Solomon Van Vliet (1791)
10. Clara Van Vliet (1794)
11. Jacobus Van Vliet (1800, died young)

DANIEL VAN FLEET SENIOR (1733 - c. 1810)

In 1641, the Dutch-sponsored settlers in the Hudson Valley heard rumors of gold in the hills to the west, in the general vicinity of the Neversink River. The Dutch West Indies Company ordered the investigation of this possibility on 31 August 1645, and by December 1646, many ore samples had been extracted from the region.

Although no gold was found, some copper was mined from the 1600s onward, with the Dutch and later the English following what in effect the Indians had been doing for some time.

Given the geography of the region, the logical trail followed by the Indians was similarly used by the Europeans. This trail passed through Ulster County to the Minisink region, forming a natural roadway for any settlers moving in a general westward direction, and because of its ultimate destination at the holes containing copper ore, in time it was called the Old Mine Road. An expert on the history of the region commented that "...the trail ran from the Hudson, via Marbletown, Rochester, Wawarsing, Wurtsborough, Port Jervis and the Delaware nearly to the Water Gap."

As stated in the commentaries on Jan Van Vliet Junior, a third generation American, the first settler to the region of the Minisink was a blacksmith by the name of William Tietsoort, a refugee from the aftermath of the Schnectady Massacre of 1690, called King William's War. Tietsoort made friends with the Indians, from whom he obtained land outside present-day Port Jervis in Deer Park. According to Booth's 1975 HISTORY OF ORANGE COUNTY, this very site later was known as "the Van Fleet Homestead."

Others followed Teitsoort into the Minisink region, including members of the Swartwout, Gumaer, Jamison and Cuddeback families. Indeed, one of the original (and probably the largest) grantees of land obtained from the Indians was Jacob Codebec (sic).

This man was born Jacques Caudebec, a French name derived from the Norse "kalt" and "bek," meaning "cold rivulet." His birthplace most probably was the town of the same name – Caudebec – a provincial capital on the Normandy Coast on the banks of the Seine River in France.

According to CAUDEBEC IN AMERICA, Jacques was born into a wealthy and prominent family, which – unfortunately for them at the time – was also Protestant. As a Huguenot, following the Revocation of the Edict of Nantes in 1685 and like untold thousands of others, Jacques Caudebec was forced to flee France to save his life.

Caudebec escaped with a friend Peter Gumaer either to England but ultimately to Holland, and then proceeded to Maryland in America. In 1690, he appeared in Kingston before continuing on in a westward direction, finally to the remote Kingston region.

The Caudebec name was ultimately anglicized to Cuddeback, but it was not yet as such that he received the grants from the Indians and patents from the New York governor, for lands in the greater Deer Park area. Thereafter, Jacques Caudebec is credited as the founder of one of the first settlements in this part of Orange County.

On 21 October 1695, Caudebec was married to Margaret Provost of Kingston, daughter of Benjamin Provost, a Huguenot settler. The marriage was in the Dutch Reformed Church, noted in history books (perhaps erroneously) as in New York City.

Jacques and Margaret had nine children, including a son named William, who was born 21 June 1704. He was baptized at the same Kingston church where his parents were married, which undoubtedly was in fact, in Kingston, New York.

Son William Cuddeback – the surname by which the family generally came to be known – inherited his father's properties, and became very prominent in Orange County. Like his father who lived to be around one hundred years of age, he was long-lived. On 8 April 1732, he married Jacomyntjen Elting of New Paltz, and in the following years they had six chi,dren. Their daughter Sarah Cuddeback was born 4 May 1737.

Daniel Van Fleet was born 4 February 1733, the same year that his parents Jan Van Vliet Junior and Jesyntjen Swartwout relocated to the Minisink region from Marbletown, bringing the three of their first children. Consequently, Daniel Van Fleet grew up in the woods and newly cleared farms of this area, very much on the cusp of the American frontier.

On 8 December 1752, Daniel Van Fleet married Sarah Cuddeback, when she was just fifteen and he was nineteen. The ceremony was performed by the Reverend Johannes Casparus Fryenmoet in the Dutch Reformed Church. The pastor's name is important to keep in mind, in view of later religious difficulties that beset the Minisink region, as this commentary will later review.

Gumaer's HISTORY OF DEER PARK states that Daniel Van Fleet "owned the farm heretofore sold by Samuel Cuddeback and William Donaldson to Ezekiel P. Gumaer and brothers (nearly one half mile south of Port Clinton)." In 1919, this property was called the Godeffrey Farm, according to Gumaer and the Cuddeback family papers and 1881 HISTORY OF ORANGE COUNTY.

At this point in time, there is a small community between Huguenot and Cuddebackville on the Old Mine Road (Route 209) called Godeffrey, and a Nineteenth Century mansion bearing that name, built in the late 1800s. It is known, according to the HISTORY OF ORANGE COUNTY and other sources, that Michael and Solomon Van Fleet owned the farm in 1846, and as late as 1889 it was farmed by their nephew Solomon Van Fleet.

While other information states that Daniel and Sarah Van Fleet lived at Machachkemeck, this notation does not necessarily conflict with Gumaer, et al, inasmuch as the references are all essentially to the same general area. It is important to know that Daniel Van Fleet was primarily a farmer like other members of his family, and that this was once considered excellent farming land.

Daniel and Sarah Cuddeback Van Fleet had at least eight children, and quite possibly more than that. Different sources cite variations of the precise numbers born to them, as the following chart reflects. Among those known to be their children are:

01. Daniel Van Fleet Junior, born 1756 and died 19 May 1840;
02. Solomon Van Fleet, born or baptized in 1754;
03. Sarah Van Fleet, born 1759;
04. William Van Fleet, baptized around 1762;
05. Thomas Van Fleet, probably baptized around 1764;
06. Magerie Van Fleet, baptized 31 August 1768 (and possibly this was a misspelling of Mordachai, reflecting notations in Gumaer's HISTORY OF DEER PARK and Mahakamack (sic) church records; or this child possibly was Joshua);

109

07.   Jacomyntje Van Fleet, born in the 1760's; and

08.   Abraham Van Fleet, born in Deer Park on 15 January 1760, baptized on 15 (or 1) October 1768, with witnesses Abraham Cuddeback and Hester Cuddeback, and died in Pittston, Pennsylvania, in 1837.

Excluding Daniel Van Fleet Junior, all of these children are recorded in the family history, CAUDEBEC IN AMERICA, although only some are cited in other sources.

Why are their disparities? While all of the births and/or baptisms for his father's family, Jan Van Vliet Junior, were well recorded in Dutch Reformed Church records, those of Daniel's family are somewhat confusing to researchers. What is the explanation for this, which logic dictates would be the opposite, being recorded at later dates?

In fact, the problem may well lie within a great and bitter controversy that raged within the Dutch Reformed Church during the period of time in which the Daniel Van Fleet children were being born. The controversy arose from the legitimacy of American born and trained clergy who were schooled entirely in America (the "Coetus Party"), versus clergy who were prepared for the ministry in Holland (the "Conferentie Party").

Importantly, MINISINK VALLEY REFORMED DUTCH CHURCH RECORDS 1716 – 1830 tends to confirm this suspicion about the lack of detailed information relating to this Van Fleet family births. It notes that Fryenmoet, who had married Daniel and his wife, "...was ordained in the spring of the year 1741 by Rev. Peter Henry Dorsius..." and thereafter began his ministering in the Minisink area. The book continues to say "the validity of his ordination by Dorsius was soon questioned."

110

The Classis of Amsterdam questioned the ordinations of Fryenmoet and of John Goetschius. Church records were altered to – in effect – annul or to at least question their legitimacy and that of their actions.

Additionally, in photocopies of the Reformed Church records published in the second half of the Twentieth Century, a notation was made that from 1760 to 1771, the manuscript "is so poor that in many instances the copying is mere guesswork."

Church records from this period are interesting in that they show the vitriolic nature of this religious dispute, but are tragic in that they alter history. Large sections of the original records are marked up as "in error."

Although one would expect Daniel to have followed his father Jan's leadership in this matter, there is more evidence to show that he did not, being loyal to Reverend Fryenmoet. In effect, the argument on theological fine points split families, and Daniel and Sarah Cuddeback Van Fleet were part of this problem that lasted for some years, until it dissipated around 1772.

For his part, Jan Van Vliet Junior never wavered in his support for the Amsterdam Classis faction, and for the congregation that he belonged to throughout his years in the Minisink, until his death in 1775.

There is a second issue that should be mentioned. There was yet another three-quarters of a century long boundary dispute between New York and New Jersey, that focused on the greater Minisink Valley region, and often disrupted families (especially the Swartwouts in New York) and certainly livelihoods. Whatever the reason, however, our records on Van Fleets are sadly incomplete, and one can only surmise as to causes.

There are several references to Daniel Van Fleet having served in the American Revolutionary War, despite his age (being born in 1733). Specifically, ULSTER COUNTY IN THE REVOLUTION, a compilation of records from various sources, states that he served with the Second Ulster Regiment. There is no doubt that the reference is to Daniel Senior, inasmuch as those same records note that his wife was Sarah Cuddeback. Furthermore, these records indicate that his sons Daniel Junior served as a sergeant with the Second Ulster Regiment, and Abraham with the First Ulster Regiment. His youngest son Joshua is noted in other records as having served with the New York Troops.

The 1790 Federal Census of the United States for Orange County reports two Van Fleets named Daniel, as well as two named James (one being James Junior), all noted as heads of families. One Daniel is listed with a less-than sixteen year old male and two females in the household, while the second is noted to have three males under age sixteen and five females, including the head of the household. The second listing is likely Daniel Junior, while the other is probably that for an older head of household; that is, Daniel Senior.

A census that definitively places Daniel Van Fleet Senior and Daniel Junior in Orange County in 1790 is important, because it was in the previous decade that several Van Fleets – specifically, Daniel Senior's sons Abraham and Joshua – were living in the Wyoming Valley of Pennsylvania, where they were recorded in the census of the same year. There is a possibility that Daniel Senior himself lived briefly in the Wyoming Valley, possibly as part of an ill-fated attempt to resettle the area, because in addition to these sons, his sister and brother-in-law, as well as many friends and neighbors, had moved into the region.

The book SUSQUEHANNA LAND COMPANY PAPERS make note of a "Daniel" with no surname, who could be this individual. There are no other single name notations, and the relevance of this "Daniel" lies in the fact that if he were living there in 1784 during a difficult time in Yankee-Pennamite relations, he would be the father referred to by Joshua Van Fleet, as related later in this commentary.

Daniel Van Fleet Junior relocated to Upstate New York where his future – and that of his children – became intertwined with Joshua's, as will be related, much as Abraham's and Joshua's lives (they had lived in close proximity earlier in Wilkes-Barre) were at one time.

Daniel Van Fleet Senior was living in the Town of Minisink in the 1792 to 1793 period "in District 13," according to Ruttenber's and Clark's 1881 HISTORY OF ORANGE COUNTY. Aside from the likelihood of his having farmed and fought in the Revolution, we do not know with any certainty what activities Daniel Senior pursued throughout his life.

There is a notation in Cuddeback records that Sarah died in 1807 at age seventy-five. Daniel is known to have lived into the earely 1800s, being recorded in the 1800 Federal Census. His name was not noted in 1810, however, and it is thus assumed that he died about that time, being buried in the Port Jervis area along with his wife.

THE DUTCH REFORMED CHURCH

The Protestant Reformation of the 1500s gave rise to the Netherlands' Calvinist religion called the Dutch Reformed Church (now known in America as the Reformed Church). It was the official faith of the Dutch West Indies Company, and its adherents in early America included most Hollanders, the majority of French Huguenots and more than a few English and Germans who had no alternative clergy for worship.

Like the Netherlands, the rule was one of tolerance in the American colony, so while not necessarily appreciated by the authorities or West Indies Company, persons of other persuasions could practice their own faiths, much unlike the rigid approach to religion in English colonies where one was persecuted, imprisoned and worse for non-conformity. Indeed, **the Dutch not only gave rise to freedom of religion in America, but to seperation of church and state as well.**

A superb example of tolerance is expressed in the Christian act of Dominie Megapolensis (whose origin was Woerden), whose work took him from Rensselaerswyck and environs to New Amsterdam. Like the Spanish, he made an effort to work among the Indians and to convert them, but obviously did not appreciate competition from other religions, most particularly Roman Catholics.

In the mid-1600s Father Isaac Jogues, a French Jesuit, was engaged is such missionary activities among the Iroquois. He was captured and was to be executed, but Megapolensis interceded and saved his life, then housed him in Albany, nursing him back to health (despite his personal disdain for Catholicism).

114

Later when Jogues returned to missionary activity, he was recaptured and killed before the Dutch dominie could intervene.

Van Vliets/Van Fleets were faithful members of the Dutch Refored faith, even when their marriages were to English or French descended persons. It was not until the very late Eighteenth Century and the early to mid-Nineteenth that this family became adherents of other religions, with the Episcopal and Presbyterian churches being most notable.

It is very important to understand that the Dutch Reformed Church was a pillar of society during and long after the Dutch colonial period, serving in many capacities, particularly in education. **The Dutch are responsible for introducing free public education in America,** for in fact this was a central role played out through the various congregations, that operated schooling for children and many adults, teaching reading, writing and "ciphers," among other subjects.

The growth of the church continued well after English rule, and the superbly kept records of this religion, maintained in many places including the Holland Society of New York, reflect the continuous building up of congregations throughout the New York and New Jersey areas, most with their attendant schools.

Machackemech Church, 1786.

115

DANIEL VAN FLEET JUNIOR (1756 – 1840)

Daniel Van Fleet Junior, son of Daniel and Sarah Cuddeback Van Fleet, was born in Goshen, not far from their farm in the Minisink region, in Orange County, in 1756. He was a fifth generation American. The earliest references to him are as a nineteen year old, when he was one of the signers of the Committee of Safety articles in 1775, like his grandfather Jan Van Vliet Junior.

During the American Revolutionary War, Daniel Junior served as a private, and more specifically as a carpenter, for which he filed papers claiming a pension in the 1800s. His service was at least in part under an uncle, Captain Abraham Cuddeback.

Daniel Junior's military time was fairly unremarkable, according to his pension application. He was "marched" from one fortification to another during his thirty-eight months with the New York Troops. He ended his service as a sergeant, and in fact did receive a pension in the years before his death.

At about age twenty, Daniel Van Fleet Junior married Martha Brown, the daughter of Jonathan Brown, a Minisink area resident of British antecedents. Daniel Junior's brother Abraham Van Fleet married Martha's sister, Sarah Brown. Daniel and Martha resided in Orange County until some time in the early 1800s, and then they relocated to Cayuga County, upstate New York, where yet others of the Van Fleet line (particularly from New Jewrsey) were settling.

Daniel Van Fleet Junior was a farmer and engaged in this activity for most of his life. He died in 1840, and is buried in Baldwinsville, not far from Syracuse, New York.

Over a twenty year period, Daniel and Martha Van Fleet had ten (or perhaps twelve) children.

These were:
01. Samuel Van Fleet, born June 1777 in the Minisink area, married Rachael Thacker;
02. William Van Fleet, born 29 October 1780 in Deer Park, later removed to Ohio;
03. Rebecca Van Fleet, baptized 18 August 1782 in Deer Park, married a Brink;
04. Charity Van Fleet, born 12 January 1783, married first a Brink, then a Wesyfall of the Minisink area;
05. Elizabeth Van Fleet, born 26 February 1786;
06. Mary Van Fleet, born 5 April 1788, married Alanson Story;
07. James Van Fleet, born 29 October 1790, married Leah Kuyendoll (sic) around 1816, and died at Scipio, Seneca County, Ohio in 1850;
08. Levi Van Fleet, born 26 March 1793, died 1850 in Fulton County, Ohio;
09. Catherine Van Fleet, born 27 February 1795, married Alanson Strong; and
10. Sarah Van Fleet, named for Daniel's mother, born 20 July 1797, married Solomon Van Auken.

It is of interest to note that the names Mary, James, Elizabeth and Rebecca were found among those of the children of his brother Abraham. Those of James and Mary are two of brother Joshua's children's names. Joshua, born in 1764, was also Daniel Junior's contemporary in upstate New York.

Although Daniel and Martha Van Fleet remained in upstate New York for the remainder of their lives, their children – like those of Joshua – relocated to Ohio beginning by the early 1830s. The 1840 Ohio state census lists sons Levi and William living in Seneca County in the township of Scipio.

117

Additionally, it is known that Levi's son James (who married Permelia Finch on 1 November 1853), grandson of Daniel Junior, was in Seneca County as well.

As noted, Daniel Van Fleet Junior's son James married Leah Kuyendoll (sic) sometime in 1816, she having been born in 1793. She was from a well-established Minisink area family that spelled the surname Cuykendall in the HISTORY OF THE MINISINK REGION. Quite likely, that is where they were married before moving to central New York and then on to Ohio.

James and Leah Van Fleet had children who included:

01. Alanson Van Fleet, born 1817 or 1819, in Wascord, Cayuga County;
02. James Van Fleet Junior, born in 1824;
03. Henry Van Fleet, born in 1826;
04. Mary E. Van Fleet, born in 1831; and
05. Martha Van Fleet, born in 1836, in Cayuga County, New York.

The location of Daniel Van Fleet Junior in New York state is important, vis-à-vis his brother Joshua's ultimate relocation to Manchester, Ontario County, after 1800. Although contemporaries, this juxtaposition gives rise to questions about continuous family contacts between two close relatives, living not more than forty miles apart.

But there is an additional issue involving their respective families and the founding days of the Church of Jesus Christ of Latter Day Saints, or the Mormon Church. Specifically, as is related in the chapter comments about Joshua Van Fleet, that Van Fleet knew Joseph Smith and his family who lived not seven miles from him.

While Joshua Van Fleet dismissed the Mormon faith's founder as a fraud, particularly after a meeting with Smith and his followers as witnessed by a grandson Alford White, Daniel Van Fleet Junior's grandson Alanson Van Fleet (and his son Elias) embraced the Mormon religion.

The story of Alanson and Elias Van Fleet is covered in a chapter on the former, but suffice it to state here that Daniel Van Fleet Junior's line gave rise to the considerable Mormon community in this family, found mainly in Utah today. Their descendants' lines are well traced in genealogies kept for the Latter Day Saints' church records.

The unusual names of Alanson and Alvah are introduced into the Van Fleet family through Daniel Junior in new York, and through Abraham's associations in Pennsylvania. These constitute names that have lived on through several generations in this commentator's immediate family.

Daniel Van Fleet Junior's son Levi, born in Goshen, Orange County on 25 March 1793, married Mary Ann Smith. They relocated to Cayuga County in 1810. He served in the War of 1812, and later yet removed to Ohio.

Levi Van Fleet died in 1850, and is buried in the Raker Cemetery some ten miles east of Wauseon. Although he was the father of numerous children, only son Henry Harrison Van Fleet is cited here, being born 11 February 1825 with death coming in 1904. Henry's only surviving son was Hubert Virgil Van Fleet.

In turn, Hubert Virgil Van Fleet married and had a son named for him and his father; that is, Henry Hubert Van Fleet. Coincidentally, this son was born in Henry County, Ohio on 8 August 1878, to his parents Hubert and Lozetta Bowers Van Fleet.

Not All Patriots: America's First Civil War

Despite what United States school students read in their history books, at the time of the American Revolution, the thirteen colonies were very divided. About a third of the colonists supported the Cause of Indepedence while another third preferred continued allegiance to the British Crown. The remaining third perhaps stood by indifferent or aghast at the carnage and destruction that the war wrought over its course.

The histories of New York and New Jersey counties often refer to those Tories who supported King George III. In general those who did so lived in the more populous areas of those colonies, in a more cosmopolitan setting. Others in the remote frontier regions tended to be overwhelmingly pro-independence, as was the case for settlers in the Minisink Valley.

Some of those who supported the Crown were Van Vliets, as noted particularly in Ulster and Dutchess County histories, but in neighboring New Jersey, at least one prominent Van Fleet family member was a Royalist.

Jack Van Fleet, a faithful corrspondent on the Canadian Van Fleet family history, was born 18 October 1910 in Bronte, Ontario and married Olivia Sharpe on 15 September 1934. He was the son of Walter Van Fleet, born 11 June 1877 and died in Bronte on 21 March 1963, who in turn was the son of Walter Huff Van Fleet, born in Wainfleet, Ontario, in 1806.

John's children were Elizabeth, Mary Ann (1830), John Junior (1835), Nelson (1837), Caroline (1845) and Robert (1849) Van Fleet. John Van Fleet Senior died in 1853.

120

John's father was Isaac Van Fleet who was born 23 July 1779 in Readington, New Jersey, married in 1805, and died in Niagara, Ontario in 1840.

In turn, he was the son of the "original" John Van Fleet, who was born in Readington 12 October 1751, married Eliza Hoff (or Huff) in 1772 and died 4 March 1831 in Canada. He was a Loyalist – later called a "United Empire Loyalist" – and the founder of the Van Fleet branch of Canada.

King George III seated on the Coronation Chair

A PORTRAIT OF A NEW JERSEY

The first European to sight lands of present-day New Jersey was Giovanni de Verranzano in 1524. Settlement, however, came only after the Dutch claimed New Netherland, incorporating the lands west of the Hudson River into their domain. They found the Delaware Indians of the Lenni-Lenape branch to be relatively peaceful, and relations between these peoples posed no problem for the newly arrived European settlers.

In a sense, the Dutch did not treat New Jersey as a separate colony, but rather as a continuation of their Dutch West Indies Company system of farms, towns and outposts established for diverse purposes. Indeed, the settlements of the Minisink Valley incorporated New Jersey lands, inasmuch as the Neversink River reached into that area south of the present border, and encompassed a general region running roughly parallel to the Delaware River, as well as to the Old Mine Road.

Consequently, the many Dutch, French Huguenot and English settlers of Hunterdon, Somerset and other counties in the more westerly and central portions of the province were in a sense "accidental" residents of New Jersey, after the English took over the Dutch colony in 1664. Title passed to Lord John Berkeley and to Sir George Carteret, who administered the lands as essentially two colonies.

It should be noted here that a definitive border between New York and New Jersey was not set until well into the 1700s, long after many colonists had settled in what they may have presumed to be New York territory. The disputes was often bitter between the two colonial governments, with resolution of the issue settled after much bloodshed.

122

New York and New Jersey Border Dispute Map

Following the movement of family before them, various Van Vliets and Van Fleets continued to locate and settle in the region, as indicated undaunted by the distinctions between New York and New Jersey jurisdictions. In this context and since their arrival often pre-dated the establishment of the province (later state), New Jersey came to them, rather than their coming to New Jersey.

Today, New Jersey – third of the original thirteen states to ratify the Constitution – ranks forty-fifth of the fifty states in size, with just 8,722 square miles of territory. Were the one hundred and thirty-odd miles along its northern border with New York a canal or a river, New Jersey would be an island, being now surrounded on three sides by water.

Despite its size, New Jersey – the erstwhile Dutch territory of Bergen – has figured greatly in American history, including its contributions during the American Revolutionary War. Over one hundred major and minor battles were fought on New Jersey soil during the struggle for national independence, including several involving Van Fleet and Van Vliet family members.

What Brought Van Fleets, Van Vliets and Van Der Vliedts to New Jersey?

New Jersey or Bergen as it was called under Dutch rule, had several settlements at the time of capitulation of the Hollanders to the English in 1664. Nonetheless, it was very sparsely settled, and it was not until the 1700s that substantial numbers of recently arrived immigrants and seasoned colonials with roots in nearby New York moved into the diverse parts of the province.

Among the earliest settlers to come to the English New Jersey colony from New York were Frederick Van Fleet and his cousin Gerrit Van Vliet. These are the first two of the Adrian Gerritsen Van Vliet line to locate in territory that came to be delineated as part of New Jersey. Frederick was a son of Jan Van Vliet Senior of Marbletown, New York, and a third generation member of the Van Fleet family in America.

Quite remarkably, around the time that Frederick relocated with his wife and children to New Jersey, first to Somerset County around 1725 and then to Hunterdon County around 1732, another family – unrelated in the immediate sense but of a similar surname and distant Dutch kinship – moved into the Somerset and Hunterdon County areas as well.

124

The historic record shows, they became known by the same surname over time, but that family was descended from Dirck Jans Van der Vliedt of Rylevelt, Holland. He was a soldier who arrived on The Spotted Cow with his wife Grietje Gerrits and two sons, aged six and nine, on 16 April 1663, about one year after Adrian Gerritsen Van Vliet returned to America with his wife Agatha and their five children. It is known, however, that Dirck was in fact reimmigrating, having come alone somewhat earlier as a soldier of the West Indies Company on a voyage of De Trouw.

Initially, Van der Vliedt settled in Midwout – later renamed Flatbush, Long Island – in 1663. Some years passed before his younger son Garret removed to New Jersey, and the family surname began to evolve from Van der Vliedt to "Van Vliedt" or "Van Vliet." Later still, the name was anglicized to "Van Fleet," although some dropped "Van der" and retained "Vliet" as a surname (the late former Mayor John Vliet Lindsay being a descendant of this line).

Perhaps this was the result of the close proximity to the established and much more numerous Van Fleet family members, the paucity of other Dutch speaking colonials able to pronounce his name, or the presence of a dominant English population more comfortable with an anglicized version, among other possible explanations.

But the inevitable happened; that is, the merging of these distinct, anciently and distantly related families seemingly into one occured, in representing the line of Van Fleets in New Jersey and then in many other states of the American Union as well as their familial descendants relocated ever westward in the nation.

Indeed, it is remarkably coincidental that the Van der Vliedt/Van Fleet line of Dirck Jans that was settled in New Jersey by his son Garret in the second generation, was moving into Pennsylvania by the fourth and on to Ohio in the fifth.

This is precisely the same migratory route to new lands as that followed by members of the Van Vliet/Van Fleet line of Adrian Gerritsen, with an occasional deviation to upstate New York. In each case, however, movement in the latter's family was just a few years earlier.

The following history of the Van Fleets in New Jersey is brief, and is reprinted for the most part from genealogical materials written by Fred Sisser III as well as from the research of Edith Kuhn on the Van Fleet family.

The New Utrecht, Long Island, church, built about 1700, followed in its design the early Calvinist churches erected in the rural Netherlands.

126

FREDERICK VAN FLEET (1691 – 1785)

Frederick Van Fleet was the fourth child born to Jan Van Vliet Senior and his wife Judith Hussey Van Vliet. A third generation American, his grandparents were Adrian Gerritsen and Agatha Spruit Van Vliet who had settled with their family in Wiltwyck in 1662. He was undoubtedly named for his maternal grandfather Frederick Hussey, an English soldier who later served as an official of the Crown and whose land holdings in the Esopus region were very extensive.

Frederick's parents were married after the first publication of their bans on 4 October 1684. They resided in the various communities of the Esopus Valley, including Rochester and Marbletown, in the latter case where his father-in-law was an overseer and where his grandfather had been an officer in the militia.

Of his youth little is known of Frederick, other than he was rewarded by the "supervisors in Kingston" with five pounds for going "five days to the Indians," a reference to the once feared Esopus. This type of action may explain why Frederick was noted as early as 1715 (at age twenty-four) as a sergeant of a foot company of militia, consisting of forty-seven men of Rochester under the command of Captain Johannes Vernooy in the Ulster Regiment of Colonel Jacob Rutsen Coll, according to a 1979 Hunterdon County Historical Society newsletter.

On 22 November 1718 in Kingston at age twenty-seven Frederick married Mary Biks (sic) (that is, Biggs) a daughter of Frederick Hussey's fellow overseer for the communities of Marbletown and Rochester. His name was John Biggs.

Mary Biggs was born in 1694 to John and Mary Hall Biggs, and was baptized in the Dutch Reformed Church at Kingston, despite her English antecedents. While residents of Ulster County, Frederick and Mary had four children, the eldest of whom was born in Hurley and the latter three in Marbletown.

These children were:

01. Jan Van Vlied (sic), baptized 9 August 1719;
02. Meery Van Vlied (sic), baptized 25 June 1721;
03. Judik Van Vlied (sic), baptized 17 February 1723; and
04. Wiljem Van Vlied (sic), baptized 9 May 1725 and died young.

At the turn of the Eighteenth Century there began a general movement of many inhabitants of Ulster County to the Province of East and West New Jersey, among them members of the Biggs, Crom and Cole families. They relocated primarily to present-day Hunterdon County in the central part of the state.

Included in this movement was Gerrit Van Vliet (born 1697 and died 1777), who is noted elsewhere in this commentary, and who was a first cousin of Frederick Van Vliet and who was also related in one fashion or another to others in the migratory group. Like them, travels took some via the Old Mine Road and Delaware region, while others moved from the Hudson Valley area.

The year 1725 has been attributed as the timing for the arrival of the Frederick Van Vliet family to that province. They came soon after the baptism of son William in May of that year. By 1727, another son had been born to them and baptized in Somerset, New Jersey. Then two others followed:

05. William Van Vliet, baptized 18 May 1727, married Mary Aten;

06. Thomas Van Vliet, baptized 18 June 1729, married Margaret Wycoff; and
07. Frederick Van Vliet, baptized 11 August 1731, married Rebecca DuBois.

Still later, three additional children were born to Frederick and Mary, to wit:

08. Abraham Van Vliet, born circa 1733, married Ann Low;
09. Leah Van Vliet, born around 1735, married James Emans; and
10. Rachel Van Vliet, born around 1737, married Garret Low, brother of Ann.

It is likely that Frederick and family, whose children were baptized in the Dutch Reformed Church on the Millstone River, lived in Somerset, but relocated to Hunterdon by around 1732. He is noted there in various business records, including in a mortgage for a two hundred and six acre "plantation" in 1749.

Described as a "yeoman" and a farmer, Frederick was also an active member of the community. He served as an overseer for roads, on grand juries and in other capacities over a forty year period. It is clear as well that he had debts, and on occasion is noted in court records with charges for same brought against him.

During his lifetime, the province witnessed the French and Indian War as well as the Revolutionary War. He signed documents of remonstrance against British interests, and in other ways was a supporter of the American Cause.

Frederick is believed to have died in 1785 well over the age of ninety. There is a will signed by him in which he left property already in the hands of his son Abraham to him. Other items were distributed, save for those with whom he had settled accounts prior to his death.

It is of interest to note that his will contained no provision for his wife, leading one to conclude that she predeceased him, possibly by many years, a distinct possibility given the absence of references to her after sometime in 1749.

By the end of his life Frederick was recording his name as Van Fleet. The anglicized version had come into use during his years in New Jersey by him and by the descendants of cousin Garrit Van Vliet, and somewhat contemporaneous to the use being adopted in the Minisink region by his relatives.

AN OLD DUTCH HOUSE

GERRIT VAN VLIET (1697 – 1777)

Gerrit Van Vliet, son of Dirck Adrianse Van Vliet and grandson of Adrian Gerritsen Van Vliet, was a third generation American and a first cousin of Frederick Van Fleet. Frederick was born a son of Jan, Dirck's brother.

Gerrit Van Vliet, like Frederick, relocated from the Esopus Valley precincts of New York to the New Jersey "frontier" of the western portions of that province early in the 1700s. In fact, Gerrit is believed to have preceeded Frederick Van Fleet to the Somerset and Hunterdon County areas.

Gerrit Van Vliet's large Dutch bible was in the possession of a descendant, David F. Mowen, in 1968 when another descendant and writer on Van Fleet genealogy, Frederick Sisser III, obtained a copy of the family record pages. Written in Dutch were Gerrit's date of birth, marriage and death, as well as other vital data including the birth dates of his eleven children.

Gerrit Van Vliet was born at "Kingston on the Esopus" on 27 June 1697, and was baptized there on 4 July 1697 in the Dutch Reformed Church. The family bible recorded that he married Judith Van Neste, the eldest daughter of Jeronimus and Neeltje Hendricks Van Neste, on 3 July 1719, at age twenty-two.

Gerrit and Judith then took up residence after a brief stay in Somerset County, in the general area of Reading Township, Hunterdon County, New Jersey, where they remained for the rest of their married life.

In 1727 Daniel Worms, a farmer from thef Albany, New York area sold "yeoman" (as described in the papers) Gerrit Van Vliet some farm land in New Jersey for some fifty pounds.

131

The thirty-five acres he purchased were on the northeasterly side of the Raritan River's South Branch in the Township of Amwell.

This initial farm parcel was augmented by seventy-five acres somewhat later in February 1731, and appears to have formed essentially the farming property that he held for the remainder of his life.

Garret Vanvlit (sic) of Reading Township made his last will and testament on 26 November 1767, leaving the use of his "plantation" or farm to his wife Judith. Sons Derick, Andris, Garret, William and Jeromas (sic) are named in the will, as are his daughters Hanauchy, Neilche and Jadak (sic).

Gerrit Van Vliet died some ten years later on 14 March 1777 at age eighty, followed by his wife Judith Van Neste Van Vliet on 16 September 1783.

During their long marriage, eleven children were born between 1722 and 1744.

These were:

01. Dirck Van Vliet, born 5 May 1722, married Rachel Van Keuren;
02. Jeronimus Van Vliet, born 13 Janauary 1725, married Annatje Schamp;
03. Annatje Van Vliet, born 9 November 1726;
04. Willem Van Vliet, born 5 April 1729 and died the same year;
05. Willem Van Vliet, born 16 August 1730, married Adriantje Wyckoff;
06. Gerrit Van Vliet, born 12 June 1732, died young;
07. Andries Van Vliet, born 6 January 1735, married Elizabeth Middagh;
08. Neeltje Van Vliet, born 14 June 1737;
09. Pieter Van Vliet, born 29 July 1739;
10. Gerrit Van Vliet, born 5 July 1741; and
11. Judick Van Vliet, born 14 January 1744.

WILLIAM VAN FLEET (1726 – 1798)

William Van Fleet, who always wrote his name that way, was the first male child born to Frederick and Mary Biggs Van Fleet. In all likelihood, he was born in Somerset County, New Jersey. Certainly his baptism took place there on 18 May 1727 at the Dutch Reformed Church on the Millstone River. Mary's sister Sarah Biggs and her husband Teunis Cole were witnesses at this event.

William Van Fleet, a fourth generation American descended from the Adrian Gerritsen Van Vliet line, married Mary Aten, whose older brother Dirck Aten had married William's older sister Judith Van Fleet. William and his two-fold brother-in-law Dirck Aten on 24 August 1748 secured the license for the marriage, inasmuch as both the groom and the bride-to-be were under the legal age to marry. Frederick Van Fleet gave a written paper in his own hand, reading: "Sir, I sand my son William vanfleet by the Consant of me and my wif for lisens." It was signed "Fradrick vanfleet."

Both William and Mary Van Fleet were members of the Dutch Reformed Church in Readington. They are recorded as donors to this congregation's building fund, which aided in its expansion.

They resided (ultimately) on a one hundred twenty-one acre farm given to him by his father Frederick, on 18 May 1762. This land was located on the Old York Road, next to his father's farm. He later added to this land, and eventually owned a sawmill that proved to be his principal livelihood later in life.

William and Mary had eleven children between 1749 and 1774, a period so long as to reflect a very early marriage for her.

These children were:

133

01. Mary Van Fleet, born 28 June 1749, married Michael Kenney;

02. John Van Fleet, born 12 October 1751, married Elizabeth Huff;

03. Judith Van Fleet, born 20 April 1753, married Abraham Brokaw;

04. William Van Fleet, born 13 March 1755, married Ann Huff;

05. Catherine Van Fleet, born 14 May 1757, never married;

06. Adrian Van Fleet, born 24 October 1759, married Elizabeth Switser;

07. Rachel Van Fleet, born 28 December 1761, married John Van Sickle;

08. Leah Van Fleet, born 26 June 1764, died April 1860 never having married;

09. Elizabeth Van Fleet, born 9 October 1766, married Peter Jennings;

10. Henry Van Fleet, born 24 July 1769, married Dorothy Turney; and

11. Rebecca Van Fleet, born 2 June 1774, married David Turney, Dorothy's brother.

Some five days before his death on 4 May 1798 at age seventy-two, William Van Fleet, describing himself as ill and weak, made his last will. He gave his youngest son Henry the farm on which he lived, three horses, various farming implements and a sleigh. The remainder of his possessions he asked be divided among his other children, all being named.

His estate, consistent with his yeoman status, consisted of many animals, farm implements and "green grain in the field." But there was no provision made for his wife, who in fact survived him by several years. Mary Aten Van Fleet died almost a decade later on 6 September 1808. She did, however, reside with Henry at the homestead.

THOMAS VAN FLEET (1729 - 1812)

Thomas Van Fleet, fifth child of Frederick and Mary Biggs Van Vliet (and later Van Fleet), was born 5 February 1729 in Somerset County, New Jersey, a fourth generation American.

Thomas married Margaret Wyckoff, who was born 24 January 1730. They lived on a farm about one mile from his father Frederick's farm. Thomas Van Fleet held some two hundred and twenty-eight acres, part of which was purchased in 1759 from Henry Stoll, and other acreage from the Aten family. His holding was probably a prosperous one, given tax records that report his chattels and that made note of the presence of one slave.

The farm produced a number of products, including wool that was dyed by contract and presumably spun to cloth, according to Thomas Van Fleet's specifications, as well as various grains that are reported in account ledgers as items for milling, with directions for same.

Thomas and Margaret Van Fleet were members of the Dutch Reformed Church of Readington, although earlier he had been baptized at the Dutch Reformed Church on the Millstone River. His wife became affiliated with the Readington Dutch Reformed Church in April 1785.

Between 1751 and 1768, some nine children were born to Thomas and Margaret, all but one surviving to adulthood.

These children were:

01.   Mary Van Fleet, born 22 April 1751, never married;
02.   Margaret Van Fleet, born 12 September 1753, married Adrian Hageman (Hagerman);
03.   Leah Van Fleet, born 20 December 1755, married a Frederick Van Fleet and then Bergun Huff;

135

04. Hannah Van Fleet, born 4 December 1757, married Joseph Hagaman (sic) (or Hagerman);

05. Judith Van Fleet, born 27 April 1760, married Isaac Hall;

06. John Van Fleet, born 19 May 1762, married Elizabeth Waldron and then Catherine Emans;

07. William Van Fleet, born 3 April 1764, married Agnes Mundy;

08. Elenor Van Fleet, born 20 May 1766, married Samuel Waldron; and

09. Elizabeth Van Fleet, born 5 July 1768, married Jerome Waldron, brother of Samuel.

Thomas Van Fleet – the manner in which he always signed his name – was involved in a court action regarding a debt, which ultimately was (in all likelihood) resolved by the New Jersey Supreme Court. Apparently, he had defaulted on a contract for a substantial amount of money.

Nonetheless, Thomas Van Fleet served in various public capacities, including as an elected overseer of the local roads. Similarly, he was an overseer for caring for the poor in the community, positions that reflect considerable public trust.

Margaret Van Fleet died in 1792, and was followed by her husband Thomas twenty years later in February 1812. Their son John Van Fleet, who was named executor of his father's will, remained on the family farm until his death at age ninety-three in 1855.

JOHN VAN FLEET (1809 – 1885)

Dirck Adrianse Van Vliet, son of Adrian Gerritsen Van Vliet, initiated a family move to locales other than the immediate Esopus River Valley. New Jersey proved to be a destination for several of his branch of the family, and it was there that Gerrit Van Vliet (born 1697 and died 1777) settled as the first of the Van Vliets/Van Fleets, and as a third generation American.

Gerrit Van Vliet (whose name is later spelled Van Fleet) had a son named Gerrit Van Fleet (fourth generation American), whom this commentary designates as "Junior."

He was born 5 July 1741 and married Cataleyna Hagerman. By early 1773 in addition to other children, a son named Joseph Van Fleet (fifth generation) was born in Hunterdon County, New Jersey. This child was baptized there in October of the same year. Joseph lived his life as a farmer, after marrying Charity Verbome.

Joseph and Charity Van Fleet had a son in the sixth generation line from Adrian Gerritsen Van Vliet, who was named John and who was born 19 October 1809 in New Jersey. As a young adult of twenty-five in 1834, he married an eighteen year old named Laura Emmons, daughter of Philanous and Susan Wilkes Emmons.

Along with their growing family, John and Laura continued the Van Fleet tradition of moving west for better opportunities, in this case to Michigan.

Their seven children were:

01. Charity Van Fleet, born 21 February 1837 in New York, married John O. Snider and died 26 June 1918 in Marine City, Michigan;

137

02. Jane Van Fleet, born December 1838, married Richard Hollis and died 16 May 1909 in Williamston, Ingham County, Michigan;

03. Albert Van Fleet, born about 1841 in Michigan, married Huldah Van Orden and died on a date unknown, with children William (born 1877) and Anna (born 1876);

04. William Van Fleet, born 4 September 1843 in Dexter, Michigan, married Mary Jane Stewart and died 12 December 1921;

05. Susan Van Fleet, born August 1845 in Michigan, married John B. Dixon and died in 1917 in Williamston, Michigan;

06. Laura Adelpha Van Fleet, born about 1849, married Lorain Rodman and died on an unknown date; and

07. John Henry Van Fleet, born 17 February 1855 in Dexter, Michigan, married Emma Elizabeth Tufts and died 15 February 1936 in Jackson, Michigan.

In the male line, the children of oldest son William and his wife Mary Jane Stewart, all Michiganders, were as follows:

01. Frank Van Fleet, born about 1868;

02. Lester Van Fleet, born 1870 in Dexter, Michigan, married first Georgia A. Walker of Naprine, Ontario, and second Nellie Ann Jones, and died on a date unknown;

03. Laura Van Fleet, born 1872 in Dexter, married Willis Burton Warner, and died on an unknown date;

04. Harry Van Fleet, born Scio Township 12 June 1874 and died 21 June 1874; and

05. Lulu E. Van Fleet, born 14 November 1877 in Scio Township, married James B. Moore and died 8 February 1899 in Webster, Michigan.

John and Laura Van Fleet's youngest child was John Henry. He had three children who were:

01. Richard J.R. Van Fleet, born 20 March 1876 in Dexter, married Maggie May Montona on 8 August 1908, and died 3 February 1936 in Jackson;
02. Walter Henry Van Fleet, born 15 August 1879 in Dexter Township, and died 28 September 1959; and
03. Mary Elizabeth Van Fleet, born 18 February 1881, married Edward Stanford Tubbs and died 11 July 1934 in Denver, Colorado.

Lastly, Walter Henry Van Fleet, grandson of John and Laura Van Fleet who established the Van Fleet family in Michigan, married four times and died at age eighty. These wives were Berdie ____; Helen M. Wetzler, born 19 August 1883 and divorced before 1939; Nettie Drumm, born 1 May 1864, married 27 August 1939 and died 10 May 1947; and Helen Wetzler (again), died 18 August 1965.

Walter Henry Van Fleet's children were as follow:

01. Marie I. Van Fleet, born 20 February 1903, married William Robinette and died 11 October 1925;
02. Lula May Van Fleet, born 26 May 1904, married Louis Andrew Scheaffer and died 11 October 1997;
03. William Henry Van Fleet, married Dorothy Marshick and had a son named William Henry Van Fleet Junior;
04. Walter Edward Van Fleet, born 16 October 1909 and died 17 October 1958;
05. Laura Elizabeth Van Fleet, born 28 December 1911 and died June 1995 in Flint, Michigan; and
06. Vernon Anthony Van Fleet, born 22 January 1913, married Sylvia ____ and died 8 January 1996 in Marshall, Michigan.

DIRCK JANS VAN DER VLIEDT (1630 – c.1690)

Dirck Jans Van der Vliedt was a Dutch soldier who arrived in America in 1660 aboard the ship De Trouw. On 16 April 1663 his wife and two young sons, ages four and nine, sailed from the Netherlands aboard the ship Spotted Cow. The Trouw was the same transport ship on which Adrian Gerritsen Van Vliet arrived with his wife and children in 1662, and one which was used extensively in the trans-Atlantic trade.

Dirck Jans Van der Vliedt settled with his wife and two Dutch-born sons initially in Flatbush, Long Island. Later the family relocated to Hunterdon County, New Jersey.

Dirck Jans apparently was not of the immediate family of the Van Vliets, but rather a distant relationship was most likely, tracing their mutual origins back to the House of Vliet. He was from Rylevelt in the Province of Holland. Over time, however, this family changed the spelling of their surname to "Van der Vliet," to "Van Vliet" and eventually to "Van Fleet," although some descendants are still known by the surname "Vliet."

Those descendants who changed their surname spelling lived in close proximity to descendants of Frederick Van Fleet and Gerrit Van Vliet, grandsons of Adrian Gerritsen Van Vliet. This Van Vliet family, being more numerous, probably precipitated the name changes that occurred in Dirck Jans' family line, possibly to avoid confusion.

Dirck Jans married twice, the first wife being Lyntje Aertsen, and the second being Grietje Van Kirken. The dates of these marriages are unknown, as is the maternity of the five children sired by Dirck Jans Van der Vliedt.

These children were:

01. Hendrick Van der Vliedt, born before 1654 in Holland, probably to Lyntje;
02. Jan Dirckse Van der Vliedt, born before 1659 in Holland, probably to Lyntje;
03. Maria Van Vliet, born in America;
04. Gaertje Van Vliet, born in America; and
05. Garret Van Vliet, born in America.

Nothing is known of Hendrick, and it is possible that he died as a young man. Jan Dirckse Van der Vliedt, however, married and had children named as follows:

01. Grietje Van Vliet, who married Simon Wycoff;
02. John Van Vliet who married Simon's sister Grietje Wycoff;
03. Judith Van Fleet (note the spelling), baptized 20 May 1759, married Richard Hoagland and removed to Mercer County, Pennsylvania;
04. Hannah Van Fleet, baptized 3 March 1781, married John L. Burwell and removed to Mercer County, Pennsylvania (their children including William, John and Lydia Burwell);
05. William Van Fleet, baptized 26 September 1763;
06. Peter Van Fleet, baptized 26 September 1763;
07. Catherine Van Fleet, baptized 6 January 1767;
08. Richard Van Fleet, baptized 21 October 1769 in Somerset, New Jersey, and died in New Bedford, Pennsylvania on 19 February 1850;
09. Sarah Van Fleet, baptized 8 September 1771, married John Newell; and
10. Abraham Van Fleet, baptized 4 November 1773, married Amelia Stephens and lived in Somerset County, New Jersey.

Richard Van Fleet established a family that relocated to Pennsylvania and to Ohio, after he married Sally Hogue in August 1801.

They had the following children over a twenty-three year period:

01. Phoebe Van Fleet, probably born 1801;
02. William Van Fleet, born 1803 and died 1885;
03. Eleana Van Fleet, born 1805 and died 1886;
04. John Van Fleet, born 1807 and was a resident of Youngstown, Ohio and of Brookfield, Ohio;
05. Hannah Van Fleet, born 1810 and married Frederick Price, living in Youngstown, Ohio;
06. Richard H. Van Fleet, born 1811 and died 1846, having lived in Youngstown, Ohio;
07. Sarah Van Fleet, born 1813 married Jonathan Riggs and lived in Shenango, Pennsylvania;
08. Alexander M. Van Fleet, born 1815 and died 1850, lived in Shenango, Pennsylvania;
09. Jesse Van Fleet, born 1817 and died 1851, lived in Shenango;
10. Rebecca Van Fleet, born 1820, married Harry Kile and lived in Pulaski, Pennsylvania;
11. David Van Fleet, born 1823 and resided in Mercer County, Pennsylvania; and
12. Eliza Van Fleet, born 1824, married Adam Sherrif.

Richard's brother Abraham Van Fleet remained in Somerset County, New Jersey, following his marriage to Amelia Stephens. They too had a sizable family over some nineteen years, but just two short of the number of Richard's.

Their children were:

01. Lea Huff Van Fleet, born 1805;
02. Abraham F. Van Fleet, born Neshantre (?), New Jersey in 1807;
03. Rebecca Van Fleet, born 3 June 1808, married John Tunnison;
04. Joseph S. Van Fleet, born 25 August 1811, married Anna B. Hill;
05. Frederick Van Fleet, born 1 August 1813;

06. Brogan H. Van Fleet, born 29 October 1816;
07. Catherine A. Van Fleet, born 14 November 1817;
08. Mary Hoagland Van Fleet, born 9 April 1820;
09. Margaret Van Fleet, born 24 February 1822; and
10. Eliza Stephens Van Fleet, born 23 March 1824.

As noted elsewhere in this commentary, the presence of this Van Fleet family in Pennsylvania and in Ohio tends to confuse researchers vis-à-vis the two lines cited in this work; namely descendants of Adrian Gerritsen Van Vliet and Dirck Jans Van der Vliedt.

In the latter category, there are many descendants in Ohio as early settlers, including Cornelius, John, Jared and Matthias Van Fleet in the general Toledo region, while in the former case, there are many in the Counties of Hardin, Delaware, Seneca and Marion (among others).

Nonetheless, this tracing of Van Fleets well into the Nineteenth Century – their second in America – provides insight into the movement of families in general (and Van Fleets in particular) in a westerly direction.

As a final note, it is curious that among the two branches in question, there is a remarkable overlap in naming patterns, leading one to ask: was this coincidence or were there contacts maintained between these families?

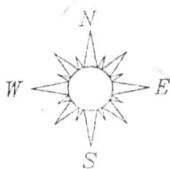

A PORTRAIT OF PENNSYLVANIA

The first Europeans to arrive in the area comprising the present-day Commonwealth of Pennsylvania were Swedish colonists in 1643. They settled on Tinicum Island in the Delaware River. Perceiving that colony as an incursion into its claims, the Dutch West Indies Company sent a military contingent and seized the colony in 1655.

In fact, the Netherlands laid claim to present-day Pennsylvania from at least 1615 onward, and its origins are more correctly described in history as Dutch (and only arguably Swedish) rather than English. However, in 1664 the Dutch surrendered sovereignty over this land to the English, and later in 1681 Charles II conveyed a charter to William Penn for colonization under his proprietorship.

Philadelphia, his capital named for that ancient "city of brotherly love" grew rapidly, in time becoming the second largest city in the English-speaking world. During the American Revolution, it served as the capital of the new nation until captured by the British in 1777, but not before one of this country's greatest founding documents, the (Seven United Provinces-inspired) Declaration of Independence was penned in July 1776. Following full independence from the British, the (again, Dutch-inspired) United States Constitution and then the Bill of Rights were all drafted and ratified in this great city and early capital of the United States of America.

Settlement of the province displaced somewhat sparse Indian tribes, mainly of the Delaware Nation, and took place along the length of the southern third of its territory. Today the state is still uneven in the distribution of cities and towns, the greatest concentration being in the south.

The northern two-third of Pennsylvania remained primitive undeveloped rolling land and woods, well into the Nineteenth Century, particularly in the northwest and mountainous northeastern regions. When extensive settlement came late in the 1800s, it was largely with recent immigrant peoples brought or invited to America to exploit the coal found in abundance in the latter case.

Pennsylvania was one of the original thirteen states, and the third to ratify the Constitution. It has a land mass of 46,059 square miles, making it the thirty-third largest in the American Union. During the early years of the country until the American Civil War in 1861 – along with New York and Virginia – it was one of the three most populous states.

What Brought Van Fleets to Pennsylvania?

The descendants of Adrian Gerritsen Van Vliet began entering Pennsylvania from New Jersey by the mid-1700s, and from New York by the late 1700s. Descendants of Dirck Jans Van der Vliedt came just shortly later, and then from New Jersey.

These Van Fleets – and in several cases, Van Vliets – established themselves in the eastern areas of the Commonwealth by the Federal Census of 1790. They could be found in a number of present-day counties, including Berks, Bucks, Lackawanna, Luzerne, Lycoming and Monroe.

Some of these families included descendants of Dirck Jans Van der Vliedt through Dirck Van Vliet Junior, and Joshua and Abraham Van Fleet (from the line of Adrian Gerritsen via Jan). By the end of the Eighteenth Century, there were numerous Van Fleets and Van Vliets in Pennsylvania.

The Van Fleets were mainly in the Wyoming Valley while the Van Vliets were in the vicinity of Stroudsburg. The Stroud Township descendants have kept the Van Vliet spelling to this day, whereas most others in the state utilized the Van Fleet name.

In any event, what is important to understand is that just as the Minisink Valley was the staging area for many family members to settle New Jersey and Pennsylvania, that state became a point of departure for many other locales in this country further to the west.

Joshua Van Fleet, who resettled to upstate New York from Pennsylvania, remained there only a generation, and similarly upstate resident Daniel Van Fleet Junior's children moved on to Ohio (in many cases, by way of the Erie Canal). Ohio, and then the rest of the American Midwest, beckoned to family members eager to start a new life on their own with better provisions for their growing families.

One is struck by the continuity of family and friendships as these migration events unfold. Much as the move from Kingston/ex-Wiltwyck involved such considerations within the Esopus River Valley; from there to the Minisink Valley; so it was for these connections to play out a role in the settlement of both the Delaware and the Wyoming Valleys. Decisions were obviously well thought out and made by multiple parties, with the purpose of bettering the lives of all concerned in new settlements, always further to the new lands of the west.

Mutual reliance was obviously a key to success in the areas opened up by these pioneers. Exploring the phenomena of friendships and family ties in these new areas, our story continues....

Northeastern Pennsylvania Settlement

The Dutch claimed ownership of Pennsylvania from at least 1615 onward, but the English Crown ignored its claims and proceeded to issue grants as if the New Netherland colony did not exist. As a result of this practice, Connecticut was given all lands extending to the "great body of water," interpreted later as being the Mississippi River.

When William Penn's grants seemingly conflicted with Connecticut's earlier charter, what was set in motion was the basis for conflict that may be described as the first major "civil" war in the new American Nation.

Under a charter from the province of Connecticut, five settlements were planned for the Wyoming Valley (in present-day Pennsylvania) under the Susquehanna Land Company. Given the proximity to the Delaware River and the need for new fertile lands for settlement west of existing colonies, these communities began to attract sizable numbers who "...arrived from New York and Connecticut."

Pittston was one of the original five communities created in 1768, and at that time had "no white man" to count among its inhabitants. Nearby, however, there were large numbers of Iroquois and Delaware Indians at the time of the community's founding.

Named for William Pitt the Elder, Earl of Chatham and friend of the American colonists, Pittston shared a distinction of honoring British parliamentarians who favored the Americans. Wilkes-Barre, another of the original communities, honored "distinguished advocates of liberty" John Wilkes and Colonel Isaac Barre, when it was established by Major John Durkee in July 1769, although its first settlers had arrived earlier in May.

These communities were forced by events to accommodate themselves to a multitude of changing circumstances. Pittston, for example, suffered through high waters on the Susquehanna in 1784, and thereafter was redesigned to encompass a total of thirty-six square miles, constituting an entire township. Zebulon Marcy was the first white settler to build there, and by 1780 the first sawmill was established by Solomon Finn for the benefit of incoming settlers (he later resettled in up-county Luzerne County near Benton Township).

Similarly, Wilkes-Barre saw the construction of Fort Durkee at what was to become Ross Street in the city that ultimately developed at that site. Its boundaries were established by Major Durkee in 1772 but were revised extensively in 1802, to accommodate growth and the placement of streets that were laid out by Thomas Sanbourne for the expanding community.

This development of a thriving settlement around the Susquehanna River and nearby Lackawanna River proceeded with few serious obstacles until the advent of hostilities in 1775 between the American settlers and the British when the colonists took up arms against the Crown.

As a result, all of the major communities in the Wyoming Valley were attacked on 3 July 1778 by the British and their Indian allies under Sir John Butler. The settlements were decimated by the raid, known in history as the Wyoming Massacre. This event was nothing less than the conduct of war by terror, for although of no special strategic value, the Valley was to be an object lesson by the British; that is, to show that support for a rebellious would-be government would meet with death and destruction.

Killing every man, woman and child, and burning every homestead, was the order of the day for the British and Indians vis-à-vis the Wyoming settlers, and coincidentally, later for those in the Minisink Valley regions as well. For the Indians, it was also a welcomed signal that further European occupation would not be tolerated by a victorious English government.

At the time of the Wyoming Valley Massacre, Marya (or Mary) Van Fleet and her husband John Kennedy were living in the region, and were like so many others victimized by the horrors inflicted by the enemy. Quite likely they were located in Wilkes-Barre, which according to Bradsby's HISTORY OF LUZERNE COUNTY, had twenty-six buildings, some twenty-three of which were burned. In their flight for safety in New York, it is possible that a child was lost in their trek.

Their presence is noted here because of developments that would follow in the course of this narrative, once they returned to the Valley after the war's end.

Although Marya and John Kennedy fled eastward to the supposed safety of Orange County, in fact both regions were severely damaged by the British-led raids.

Sir John Guy Johnson headed the attacks in the Minisink region, but his ally was the same Indian chief who earlier had attacked the Wyoming; that is, Joseph Brandt (or Brant). Known by his Indian name as Thayendanegea, a Mohawk chief, racially he was reputed to be part European (German), educated at Dartmouth College, and urbane. Nonetheless, he was dedicated in his ruthlessness in both sweeps to break the back of any European expansion into lands occupied by Indian tribes and nations.

Indians under the so-called Queen Esther engaged in every type of barbaric behavior killing scores of settlers and destroying every standing vestage of their presence. Readers with an interest in this sad chapter in American history that established attitudes toward retribution would do well to look into the Wyoming Massacre in the many histories that detail that event.

In late July 1779, the sweep of Joseph Brandt and his British allies brought terror to the Minisink in a frenzy of destruction, "...burning...twenty houses." Orange County historical accounts of the slaughter clearly state that the Swartwout, Cuddeback, Decker and Van Fleet families (James in particular) were victims of this terror by the British and Indian rampage.

Although the Revolutionary War came to an effective end in 1781 with the fall of Yorktown and the capture of Lord Cornwallis, any peace in the land was not to be forthcoming for the Wyoming Valley. In fact, the Connecticut-sponsored settlements were beset by counterclaims to the region by Pennsylvania titles held by the Penn family, who used armed men to enforce their claims.

In effect, these often violent disputes began in August 1771, and were only temporarily set aside for obvious reasons during the American Revolutionary War.

Civic strife returned quickly but somewhat intermittently to the Wyoming Valley after that event, pitting the Pennamites, or Penn family claimants and their agents, against the "Yankees," or the claimants under Connecticut's laws.

On December 30, 1782, a five man court appointed in August by Congress held unanimously that the disputed title should be awarded to Pennsylvania, whose territory was contiguous. Without awaiting settlement of individual claims, the Pennsylvania Assembly approved a plan to oust the Connecticut settlers in 1783. Militia actions against settlers were denounced by the Pennsylvania Council of Censors, which forced the Assembly to enact measures on September 15, 1782, restoring settlers in their lands under protection of a new Commission on September 9th. After further violence in 1787, a Pennsylvania act of that year brought an equitable and conclusive settlement.

The problems between Pennamites and the so-called Yankees, however, were deep-rooted. On 24 July 1784 in one of the worst outbreaks between these factions, the Pennamites struck at Wilkes-Barre where historical records state that "many dwelling houses in Wilkes Barre are burnt to the ground by Pennamites." Virtually everything was destroyed, save the fortified structure in the center of the settlement. Expulsion of the Yankee settlers followed under Pennsylvanian Alexander Patterson, who had the assistance of Pennsylvania's state militia.

151

Through continued negotiations that lasted for a period of years, peace eventually returned to the Wyoming Valley and its settlers of all backgrounds were gradually incorporated into the fabric of Pennsylvania society. The effort to incorporate the Valley into non-contiguous Connecticut, or even to form a new state as was advocated by many, was averted.

The region as it was known in Pennsylvania was part of Northumberland County, but in 1786 a large area was carved out from this jurisdiction to form Luzerne County, in honor of the nobleman who represented the French Crown before the American Congress during the Revolutionary War. It was later further subdivided, as this commentary relates.

The year 1790, however, is something of a watershed in that the national enumeration reported a total of a mere 4,908 people in this huge territory, making Luzerne the least populated pf the Commonwealth's twenty-one counties. With some eight hundred sixty-seven heads of families, spread over the northeastern state of present-day Luzerne, Lackawanna, Susquehanna, Wyoming and Bradford Counties, as well as parts of others covering some twenty percent of Pennsylvania, densities were virtually non-measurable.

Such a vast area with a miniscule population reflects the frontier nature of the region in question. Further contrasts magnify this point. In 1790, Pennsylvania had 434,373 persons and New York some 340,120, compared with Virginia's 747,810 inhabitants (or 810,000 if the population of the "County of Kentucky," then part of that Commonwealth, is included). America's largest cities were New York, with 33,131 residents, and Philadelphia with 28,522.

152

The Wyoming Valley

The environment into which Orange County migrants came in the 1770s and 1780s was one of great potential, juxtaposed against danger on many fronts. As a newly opened area for settlement, every physical obstacle imaginable had to be overcome, from the clearing of the land to the taming of streams and rivers; and from the development of transport networks to the making of peace with the Indians. As stated, a yet more critical issue for them was coming to terms with the conflicting land claims of many belligerent people from two provinces, over a nearly twenty-five year period.

One might wonder why Van Fleets, among others, would have bothered with this frontier, but in fact the reasons have already been stated. Unlikely heirs to existing farms and agricultural lands in New York in Orange County (which, incidentally, had a hefty 18,478 inhabitants in 1790, while Ulster County had 29,397), the vast lands of Pennsylvania offered the magical "free land for the settling" necessary for essentially disinherited farmers.

But additionally and importantly, the two Van Fleets who settled in the Wyoming Valley were young (Joshua being twenty-two and Abraham being twenty-six years of age); they were veterans of the hardships of the Revolutionary War; they were adventuresome and risk-takers; they were logically eager to make a new and prosperous life for their own families; and finally, they were obviously willing to avail themselves of the extended family infrastructure that already existed in the Wyoming Valley community.

153

The Wyoming Valley of Pennsylvania

The fertility of its soil and its beautiful location in the midst of a smiling valley, invited hundreds from different parts of Orange and Ulster counties to take up residence within its limits. No where else had they found so desirable a spot for a home as on the banks of the noble Susquehanna in that quiet valley. No settlement had been so prosperous, and in 1778 it numbered a population of eleven hundred families.

Stickney's HISTORY OF THE MINISINK REGION

Among the many peoples from western Orange County swept into the westward movement to the Wyoming Valley after the Revolutionary War, one found numerous friends, relatives and "shoestring" relatives of the Van Fleets. Importantly and perhaps critically, Mary Van Fleet and her husband John Kennedy were already in the Valley, as were members of the Decker family, when Joshua Van Fleet arrived in 1784. He was joined by Abraham Van Fleet in 1786, and between those dates and the last years of the decade, there are various references to them in the records of the Susquehanna Land Company. In the following narratives, other names of relatives by marriage, as well as fellow Orange Countymen, are cited.

Importantly too, it is possible that Daniel Van Fleet Senior came to the Wyoming Valley, at least on a short-term or "trial" basis. There are numerous references to a "Daniel" unidentified by a surname in the appropriate time frame, and as will be stated a crucial reference by Joshua to "his father's house" in Wilkes-Barre. But this issue should be addressed in greater detail.

The Deckers were from a family closely allied with the Van Fleets. Because of the common bonds among neighbors as well as kinship ties, their relationship with Joshua and Abraham is important to note. Together with their sister Mary and her husband John Kennedy, there is a well-constructed network of family and friends seen in the patterns of resettlement in the Wyoming Valley. But what about Daniel Van Fleet Senior?

In the Revolutionary War pension claim filed in Ontario County in 1832, Joshua Van Fleet affirmed his birth in the Minisink, and claimed that he was living in Luzerne County "in (his) father's house until it burned in 1784...during the troubles."

155

His "father's house" was cited as being in Wilkes-Barre. Since he was not yet married – an event that occurred in 1785 – he could not have been referring to a father-in-law. Is it not possible that the individual in question was Daniel Van Fleet Senior's home? Alas, the records are not clear on such a point.

Abraham and Joshua Van Fleet are tied together in innumerable ways in the Luzerne County experience, from the signing of the same documents but on different occasions, to being noted as living together or in close proximity in 1790 and (unfortunately) having their surname recorded erroneously in the Federal Census for posterity to read as "Vanflect."

Although Abraham who came to Luzerne County as a young married man with his wife and first born son James, remained in the Pittston region for the remainder of his life (with death coming in 1837), Joshua – perhaps distressed with the turmoil of the Yankee-Pennamite conflict or disappointed in future prospects for the area – removed further north along the Susquehanna watershed to the Tioga area of Athens Township, Pennsylvania, until about early 1800, and thereafter relocated to upstate New York's Ontario County.

The Tioga area was formerly the stronghold of the Iroquois under Queen Esther, surrendered by the Indians following their defeat and expulsion during the Revolutionary War.

Joshua Van Fleet was present in New York for the summertime 1800 Federal census. He settled in Manchester, Ontario County, a small hamlet located in the Finger Lakes region on lands that are very fertile in the sweep of farms that extend along the breadth of New York from Buffalo to the capital at Albany.

156

ABRAHAM VAN FLEET (1760 - 1837)

Abraham Van Fleet was probably the third child born to Daniel and Sarah Cuddeback Van Fleet, and was a fifth generation American. At the time of his birth on 15 January 1760, his family was living in the Minisink Valley of Orange County, the area settled by his grandparents and great grandparents, the Swartwouts, Cuddebacks and Van Vliets.

Abraham was born and reared in tumultuous times. In 1760 the French and Indian War was raging, and at age fifteen the conflict with Britain had begun in earnest. His grandfather Jan Van Vliet Junior played a role in Orange County activities agitating for the American Cause in defense of liberty.

War broke out when he was fifteen and when he was sixteen the Declaration of Independence was promulgated. At age eighteen on 18 November 1778, he enlisted as a private in Captain Daniel Wood's Company of Colonel Mahahn's Regiment, Continental Troops, New York.

In April 1779, Abraham transferred to Captain James Bunnell's Company, Colonel Oliver's Regiment, Continental Troops, New Jersey, and served as a corporal. He transferred again in December 1780, to serve in Captain James Gregg's Company, Colonel Van Schaick's Regiment, which was the First New York Regiment, Continental Troops.

He continued his military service in that unit, otherwise known as the First Ulster, until his discharge as a corporal at age twenty-one with some three years of service to the Revolutionary Cause, on 18 November 1781. His actual discharge came while he was in Maryland.

157

During his service, Abraham Van Fleet fought in three battles, numerous skirmishes and performed the many other tasks expected of enlisted men and non-commissioned officers during the conflict. His pension papers document his role in the Battle of Connecticut Farms, New Jersey; the Battle of Springfield, New Jersey; and most importantly, the Siege of Yorktown. Although the pension papers do not provide detail in any of these events, it is a source of pride to see his name engraved in Yorktown today, and to have pointed out the locales occupied by the First Ulster during the siege that broke the back of British power in America.

Indeed, his service in the military during the American Revolution warranted a pension when such were provided for by Congress. He began receiving a small sum in 1820, and continued to do so until his death at age seventy-seven in 1837.

Perhaps as importantly, he qualified for a Land Bounty Rights award, according to the Daughters of the American Revolution, but there is no evidence he ever claimed one. Certainly his presence in the Wyoming Valley was a function of other factors, those being the availability of land under the settlement programs of the Susquehanna Land Company and the presence of family, friends and former Orange County neighbors.

Following his discharge from the army, Abraham made his way back to the Minisink Valley region where he married Sarah Brown, daughter of Jonathan Brown, another Orange County man. That marriage took place some time in 1785, when he was twenty-five.

It is interesting to note that the pattern of multiple family member weddings continued, with his older brother Daniel Van Fleet Junior marrying Sarah's sister, Martha.

158

Abraham's brother Joshua had already left the Minisink region to settle in Pennsylvania's Wyoming Valley in 1784. The area in question was then still a district of Northumberland County, according to Pennamite claims, but an integral part of Connecticut, under the claims of that state and its chartered Susquehanna Land Company.

In 1786 Pennsylvania established the County of Luzerne encompassing all of the Wyoming Valley itself. Named for the French marquis who represented Louis XVI and assisted the American Cause, it was the heartland of the area devastated during the Wyoming Massacre that left just 3,100 settlers in the Valley after that most tragic event.

Family history and various local history books indicate that Abraham and Sarah Van Fleet arrived in the Wyoming Valley sometime during the summer 1786. They carried with them their only child as of that time, young James, who was described as nearly "eaten to death" by the swarms of mosquitoes that plagued the way between the Minisink and the Wyoming Valley.

It is uncertain precisely where Abraham and Sarah settled, but the Wilkes-Barre community is the most likely spot. That supposition is based on the presence of relatives and friends being there, including his brother Joshua; Joshua's in-laws, the Roberts family; members of the Decker family; Gumaers, Browns, Bidlacks, others and possibly even his father. However, it is also evident that both he and Joshua lived in a nearby settlement called Jacob's Plains (later Plains), with essentially is an extension of Wilkes-Barre. Susquehanna Land Company records locate them both there in Plains. This region was once named for Indian Chief Jacob, and was reported to have fine soils for farming, due to flooding deposits.

When the Federal Census of 1790 was taken, both Abraham and Joshua were living next to or close to each other, since that enumeration recorded their surname as "Vanflect." That clearly demonstrates that their names were recorded at the same time, by the same person and in the same general place for such an egregious error to have occurred.

By the time of the 1800 census, Abraham was living in the Pittston area, another of the original settlements under the Land Company, but Joshua had since left for Tioga, near the New York state border. From there he relocated to upstate New York, settling in Manchester, Ontario County.

Census reporting is important in tracking the Abraham and Sarah Van Fleet family, because church records are absent. Family records and the census data state that they had seven children, born between 1786 and 1804.

These were:

01. James Van Fleet, born 9 February 1786 in the Minisink region;
02. George Van Fleet, born 1796, died in Galena, Delaware County, Ohio;
03. Hannah Van Fleet, born 7 August 1800, and died 1830;
04. Fanny Van Fleet, born in 1804;
05. Mary Van Fleet;
06. Elizabeth Van Fleet; and
07. Rebecca Van Fleet.
08. While the last three children have no known dates of birth, they were undoubtedly born before 1804 and probably before 1796.

George Van Fleet, the second of just two sons, married Christiana Bidlack after he relocated to Ohio in 1818 (her family following the trails to Ohio sometime after 1820), and established a large family there.

Hannah married William Tompkins, and later they followed her brother James to the upper portions of Luzerne (present-day Lackawanna) County, while Mary married Alvah Phelps and then Benjamin Jenkins, and too relocated to the upper reaches of the county.

Elizabeth married William Mullinson, and Rebecca married a Nafus, of the same family that played a prominent role along with the Van Fleets in upper Luzerne County.

Fanny, the youngest child, may or may not have married. She was mentioned by her father at the time he filed pension papers, with a curious statement how he came to live with her, leading one to conclude that she may not have been entirely mentally competent or physically able. Apparently, too, he was near poverty according to those papers.

The eldest child James married Christiana Gardner, as is related later. She was also from an Orange County family, and the surname was most likely an anglicized form of Gardinier. That French Huguenot family played a major role in the history of the Ulster County to Minisink movement of families in the Seventeenth and Eighteenth Centuries.

Abraham Van Fleet was a widower for many years, inasmuch as his pension papers filed in 1820 indicated his wife was dead. Those same papers reflect the fact that he farmed throughout his life in this region, largely in the Pittston area, during the nearly half century of residence there.

A witness to many events in the early settlement of the Wyoming Valley, Abraham was present to see the area grow dramatically. Luzerne County went from 4,900 persons in 1790 to 20,027 in the year he filed his pension papers, and increased by another 15,000 by the time of his death.

This growth was just the beginning, for he was – unknown to him – also a witness to the advent of the coal industry in America, and with it the development of iron and other industry in northeastern Pennsylvania.

In Wilkes-Barre, a local politico, magistrate and inn owner Jesse Fell found a way to utilize the hard black coal that was so troublesome to farmers tilling their fields. Unlike anything known in England, in 1808 he devised a grate that permitted air to flow and the coal to burn efficiently.

As an aside, the Fell House (later called the Old Fell House) that was built in 1787 or 1788 was very much a focal point for community activities in and around Wilkes-Barre. Undoubtedly, it was well known to Abraham Van Fleet and probably to Joshua as well.

Pennsylvania's Counties Before Divisions

In addition to its social functions, the Fell House was often used as a courthouse. A century later in the late 1800s, this venerable establishment was owned and operated by this commentator's maternal great-grandparents, when it served as a hotel and was noted as a historic landmark in that city.

In the following years, the Wyoming Valley became an attractive region for immigration from Europe, with available work in the mines that all too soon covered the very ground once farmed by Abraham Van Fleet and his fellow pioneers. A scant thirty years after his death, Luzerne County had some 161,000 residents, most living in precisely the same geographic locales once home to the Susquehanna Land Company settlers.

Family records do not record an exact date for Abraham Van Fleet's death, but it was sometime at the end of 1837. Pension records make note of that fact as well as the clear indication that he died in the same Pittston area in which he lived so long. He was buried there in a gravesite that has now been lost in time and to the coal industry development of the region.

A Sketch of Fleetville, Pennsylvania

The site of Fleetville was an unbroken wilderness until 1821 when the Philadelphia-Great Bend Turnpike was surveyed by James Van Fleet through the rolling lands of northern Luzerne County. A map of that year showed only a briar patch where the village now stands.

Philadelphians Thomas Meredith and George Clymer had acquired title to much of the land, which they had surveyed to sell acreage for up to five dollars per acre. William Finn, William Hartley and James Halstead were among the first purchasers.

About the same time, the "Factory Road" was laid out from Factoryville to Blakely, creating an intersection and the rationale for founding a village. As late as 1830 there were few settlers, but a village did begin being named "Fleetville" for James Van Fleet, as it was designated officially in 1838.

By 1840 however, Fleetville was growing. It had a shoemaker, physician, hotel (initially built as a temperance house) stores and a post office. By 1851, master carpenter Israel Colvin had designed and built a number of fine structures including the Fleetville Universalist Church in that year, described as "one of the finest meetings houses in this section of the country." Two years later, the FleetvilleBaptist Church ws erected.

By the mid-1850s the community had taken shape but continued to grow for several more decades. In 1880 there were 1,148 inhabitants in Benton Township, about a fifth of whom lived in the Village of Fleetville itself. By then two cemeteries were in place, the Universalist (and Baptist) Cemetery (1827) and the Chase Cemetery (1837).

The Village of Fleetville preserves many of the classic Nineteenth Century buildings erected by Colvin and his workmen, and the rolling hills, streams and ponds that attracted farmers a hundred and fifty years ago now are inviting to suburban-oriented people. Although a shadow of its former self, Fleetville is still something like a Currier and Ives print of a farming community of a by-gone age.

ABINGTON TOWNSHIP est. 1806

407 - Philadelphia Great Bend Turnpike 1819
A·W - Abington·Waterford Turnpike - 1823
---- D.L.+W. R.R.-1850
ooo - D.L.+W. R.R -1915 modernization
...... Northern Electric Street R.R.- 1907

JAMES ALVA VAN FLEET (1786 – 1877)

James A. Van Fleet was born 9 February 1786 in the Minisink region of Orange County, New York, as a sixth generation American of the Adrian Gerritsen Van Vliet line. An early chronicler stated that in that year when his parents Abraham and Sarah Van Fleet relocated to the Wyoming Valley in the summertime, he was carried along in a basket. These reports state that he nearly died from mosquito bites received along the way on the arduous trip by horseback.

The attraction to Abraham in settling his new family in the Wyoming Valley was obvious. He was preceeded there by close relatives and family friends. The availability of land at little cost, moreover, was important for someone not destined to inherit a farm back in Orange County. Moreover, although both the Minisink Valley and the Wyoming Valley had been decimated by the British and Indian raids during the Revolutionary War, prospects for the future in a rich but sparsely populated area seemed infinitely brighter.

The years following his arrival saw growth in the Wyoming Valley. The War had ensured there would be no impediment to westward expansion by government, and indeed that s the direction of continuous movement. Facilitating such, one saw the improvement of communication and transportation under the aegis of both the public and private sectors.

In 1798, a mail route was established between Wilkes-Barre and Great Bend, not far from the New York state border with Pennsylvania (HISTORY OF **LUZERNE COUNTY**). Then in 1819, turnpike construction fever arrived in that corner of the Commonwealth.

166

The Philadelphia-Great Bend Turnpike was chartered in that year from Philadelphia through Easton to Mount Pocono. This toll road then continued past present-day Tobyhanna, Moscow, Dunmore, Providence, Chincilla, Clarks Green, Waverly, Fleetville, Lennox, Glenwood, and Harford, to Great Bend.

Completed in 1826, the Philadelphia-Great Bend Turnpike was a major regional thoroughfare, linking farmers to markets to the south and the east, and making these former hinterlands attractive to development and accessible to new settlers. The dirt was paved over in the 1921 to 1922 period, and the road continues to serve the region well even to the present day.

James Van Fleet had been living and farming in the Pittston area where his parents had settled, until the early 1820s and likely somewhat before. It was in this period – specifically, 1821 – that he contracted employment as a land surveyor for Thomas Meredith and George Clymer, owners of the land speculation and construction company that had set out to build the turnpike from at least Easton through the northeastern part of the state to somewhat past present-day Benton Township.

How James came by the skills to be so engaged is unknown, but like his brother George who was a distiller in Ohio, he had skills as a mechanic and both boys were trained as carpenters.

The book LACKAWANNA HISTORY and family recollections recount that during this employment he saw the fertility and potential of the land in what was then part of Nicholson Township, Luzerne County, and thereafter sold his holdings in the Pittston area. He moved permanently to the region now called Fleetville, Benton Township, sometime around 1826 if not somewhat earlier.

In a note of irony, the lands he allegedly held in Pittston were later found to bear high grade anthracite coal, so the subsequent owners became immensely wealthy by exploiting the very product that made for difficult farming in the early years of the Nineteenth Century. But this was not foolishness on James' part. This coal was uneconomical to transport, and it was not until decades later with the advent of railroads that it gained value as a marketable commodity.

Although the upper reaches of Luzerne County had been well explored in the 1700s, the region's first recorded settler did not arrive until 1810 or 1811. His name was Ezra Bassett, for whom a small lake in Benton Township is named.

The earliest frame houses were built in the 1820s by Thomas Chambers (no relation to the Esopus Valley personage, who had no children) and by John Finn (whose family had also moved from the lower Wyoming Valley).

Another small lake in the area was named Finn's Pond, until changed to Baylor's Lake (this commentator being a descendant of the Baylor family). Then as the area's population grew, the name "Fleetville" was informally adopted in honor of James Van Fleet, sometime by the mid-1830s and officially by the Pennsylvania government in 1838.

The heirs of Meredith and Clymer sold land in the region along their turnpike's right of way for some two dollars and fifty cents to five dollars per acre. The price differential depended on the proximity to the road, among other prevailing conditions.

With fertile lands as highly suitable for farming as these, the area attracted farmers and began to grow sufficiently quickly to warrant separation from Nicholson Township and status as its own jurisdiction.

Although still part of Nicholson Township in 1830, the area was reestablished as Benton Township shortly afterwards, with some twenty-eight square miles. In 1838, the new township was named for Missouri Senator Thomas Hart Benton, a well-known abolutionist.

Like Benton Township, the Village of Fleetville expanded steadily over the years, having a population of two hundred in 1880, out of some 1,148 for the township itself. Its two hotels, two churches (Baptist and Universalist), two stores, school house, wagon shop, shoe shop, saloon and blacksmith shop have for the most part disappeared, but the village continues to this day to be a pleasant community in an area generally known as the Abingtons, some twenty miles northwest of the City of Scranton.

James A. Van Fleet married Christiana Gardner sometime in 1803 in the Pittston area when he was about seventeen. She was born 29 August 1788 in the Wyoming Valley as the daughter of Jesse Gardner, and was fifteen at the time of the union. Jesse Gardner was yet another of the many Orange County settlers who came to Pennsylvania under the aegis of the Susquehanna Land Company, in a similar fashion to Abraham from the same New York state region.

James and Christiana Gardner Van Fleet had thirteen children born between 1804 and 1830.

These were:

01. Eliza Van Fleet, born 21 September 1804, married John Brazie who was of a refugee background, his family having fled the French Revolution;

02. Daniel Van Fleet, born 9 February 1806, married Mary Parker and later Mary Hall;

169

03. Sarah Van Fleet, born 10 February 1808, married Josiah Kennedy (of the John Kennedy family from the Wyoming Valley);

04. Alvah Alanson Van Fleet, born 1 February 1810, and named for a son of James' brother George before moving to Ohio, married Esther Baker;

05. Mary Van Fleet, born 31 March 1812, married Edward Clark;

06. Martha Van Fleet, born 17 April 1814, married a Smith;

07. Caroline Van Fleet, born 20 September 1816, married Sidney Finn;

08. Jesse Gardner Van Fleet, born 22 December 1818, named for his grandfather, married Eliza Finn, sister of Sidney, and later died in Louisville, Kentucky;

09. George Van Fleet, born 25 March 1821, named for James' brother, married Lexa Penina Thacher;

10. Abraham Van Fleet, born 15 June 1823, named for his grandfather, remained unmarried;

11. James Van Fleet, born 12 August 1825, moved west "and was not heard from again" according to family records;

12. Rebecca Van Fleet, born 16 March 1828 and died 30 July 1829; and

13. Hannah Van Fleet, born 19 July 1830, named for an aunt, married Lord Byron Green.

Beyond their thirteen children, James and Christiana had fifty-five grandchildren, eleven with the Van Fleet surname. Some of the descendants of those eleven remained in northeastern Pennsylvania, and descendants can be found there today.

However, as this commentary reflects, others went on to form branches throughout the country, including in as distant locales as California and Washington.

James Van Fleet's farm was situated not far from the center of the Village of Fleetville. It occupied a beautiful site, with a vista of rolling pastures and distant woods spreading over the gentile Pennsylvania landscape. Initially the farm had a log cabin "near the well on the lower side of the old road" to Fleetville, but a frame house was later constructed, where a tenant farmer resided (and the building supposedly remains to this day).

Later in 1861 James' son Alvah built a splendid eighteen room mansard-roofed house on the crest of the hill above the road. Perfectly situated on that hill at the apex of a curved drive, the view downward to the southeast are of magnificent undulating farm lands, and downward to the northwest toward their privately owned Deer Lake, beautifully set like a gem surrounded by green woods.

The farm, that ultimately came to be called Manor Farm and for a few generations home to the Van Fleets, enjoyed a degree of fame as "Grayce Farms" under a subsequent owner, who created a spectacular model dairy operation there. It was sold by the Van Fleet family in the early 1930s.

James A. Van Fleet was known to be a good and successful farmer, but additionally and importantly, he was a farm implements developer and manufacturer. A HISTORY OF LACKAWANNA COUNTY, the book THIS IS WAVERLY and the Lackawanna County website, among other sources, cite the fact that his shop "made nearly all the plows used in the first agriculture of the valley," among other items.

Initially Van Fleet used the gnarled and knotted hard woods of the region to fashion this product, and later after 1840 this was done with iron tips from the foundries of the Scranton family in the nearby community soon named for them. These histories cite that he was a "manufacturer of grain cradles" as well, all skills requiring mechanical ingenuity and an ability to engage in carpentry, reflective of someone with a background in surveying in early America.

Throughout a very long life in Benton Township, James Van Fleet was described as a prominent individual who was highly regarded in the community. He was one of the earliest members of the Fleetville Universalist Church, which had the affiliation of most members of the Van Fleet family until its closure in the early 1920s. Politically, he was a Democrat, even after the Fleetville area became Republican in orientation.

The Fleetville Universalist Church before 1920

Christiana Gardner Van Fleet died 21 July 1833, just short of her forty-fifth birthday. James never remarried, so he lived almost half of his life as a widower until his own death at age ninety-one on 6 September 1877. In his later years, he lived with his daughter Hannah, and her husband Lord Byron Green.

James and his wife Christiana are buried in the Old Fleetville (Universalist) Cemetery, along with many of the other early Benton Township family members and pioneers of this northeastern Pennsylvania region.

James A. Van Fleet left a major imprint on the Village of Fleetville, Benton and the history of settlement, development and agricultural pursuits in Lackawanna County in its earliest years, during and before the area became famous for its mineral and manufacturing activities.

The Founding Father: James Van Fleet of Fleetville, Pennsylvania

James Van Fleet, one of two sons of Abraham Van Fleet, remained in northeastern Pennsylvania for the duration of his life. About the time his brother George relocated to Ohio, establishing a vibrant branch of the family there, James' descendants were reared in what came to be known as Fleetville, Pennsylvania, a prosperous farming community in present-day northern Lackawanna County.

His family consisted of thirteen children, only one of whom – Rebecca – died in her youth. The remaining twelve with their children, most of whom gave rise to the Van Fleets of northeastern Pennsylvania, are noted below, with their children.

James Van Fleet's Children:

Abraham	George	Jesse Gardner
None (Unmarried)	Benjamin Franklin Emmett Luther G. Minerva	Hobart E. Rudolph A. Adda L. Augusta

Alva Alanson	Daniel	James
Galusha A. Merritt B. Sarah Charles G. George Nelson Elizabeth Rebecca Lamitha	Edgar Melissa Marietta Stephen James	None Known (Moved West)

174

Eliza (married Brazie)	**Sarah** (married Kennedy)	**Mary** (married Clark)
Martha J. Thurston Louisa	Sarah Adelia William Murray Abram J. Samuel Orpha James Nelson	Jasper Marion Carolina Ruth Esther Florence Napoleon Chester Emma Mary

Martha (married Smith)	**Caroline** (married Finn)	**Hannah** (married Green)
Nelson Douglas Christiana Fred	Oscar Mary J. James Hannah Mary T. Stark Ida Daniel Hattie	Ida Eva Clara I. William

Note: The Finn and Kennedy families had initially located in the Wyoming Valley earlier as settlers in the Susquehanna Land Company program along with the Van Fleets, later removing to the upper areas of Luzerne County.

ALVA ALANSON VAN FLEET (1810 – 1870)

Alva (or Alvah) Alanson Van Fleet was the fourth child born to James and Christiana Gardner Van Fleet, and a seventh generation American. He was born 1 February 1810 in Pittston, Pennsylvania, before his father relocated the family to the northern part of Luzerne County.

Alva removed as a young man to present-day Benton Township. As a young man, he married Esther Baker, the daughter of Isaac and Louisa Barnes Baker of Clifford, Pennsylvania. Esther had been born while her parents were temporarily located in Trois Rives, Quebec, Canada, but always protested loudly when this fact was jokingly pointed out of her American roots and citizenship.

Alva Alanson Van Fleet

Alva grew to maturity on the farm that his father had established and developed, and which was called Manor Farm in later years. He was described in several history books as a prominent and well-to-do farmer, who in his middle years built a large new home crowing the crest of a hill on the family property.

This eighteen room Victorian style mansard roofed house was designed and built by Julius Youngs in 1861. It stands today as a distinct testament to the wealth that farming once generated in Lackawanna County. Unfortunately for Alva, he was to live there only some nine years before he died of a sudden heart attack at the early age (for Van Fleets) of sixty, on 19 July 1870.

The Manor Farm home of the Van Fleets

In addition to the farm, Alva Van Fleet built and ran a general store in Fleetville, located in a structure that still stands at the main intersection in the village.

However, it was not at this store but rather at another he owned in nearby Wallsville that became somewhat infamous, that a gathering regularly took place among would-be philosophers and political commentators, called "the Crackerbarrel Congress."

In her book THIS IS WAVERLY, Mumford (a Van Fleet family member) wrote about this contingent that included Theron Finn, president; Squire Thomas Smith, vice-president; Uriah Gritman and Alvah Van Fleet, secretaries. In point of fact, these individuals were described elsewhere as "copperheads," or northerners who sympathized with the South during the American Civil War.

Highly opinionated and open to admit their contempt for the Lincoln Administration, they wrote letters to the press in New York and in Pennsylvania. A July 1863 missive to the New York Daily News captures the venom in their strikes against Mr. Lincoln.

We protest the further prosecution of this war against the Southern States...for the subjugation of states, or for any other purpose than the settlement of an honorable peace between the North and the South. We ask ourselves now, as heretofore, for what is all this sacrifice of human life and useless waste of National Treasure? Casting our eyes over the bloody history of this war...unwisely provoked and wretchedly conducted by this corrupt administration, we find the only answer that can be made is that Abraham Lincoln, like Caesar, might be great.... In Washington today sits the President in the chair of state once occupied by the Father of his Country, with his infamous retinue of advisors around him.

Legions of contractors, army sneaks, and myrmidons throng about the White House, bowing and bending the pliant hinges of their knees that thrift may follow fawning; Gobbling up the nation's wealth as jackals and vultures gobble up the life blood of our boys upon the battlefield.

Alva Van Fleet was, needless to say, a rabid Democrat in what was by the time of the Civil War – and forever more has remained – a Republican stronghold in Pennsylvania. Whether he was truly a so-called copperhead is a matter of conjecture, but they were present in sufficient numbers in the area to cause general alarm. Numerous barn burnings of strong Union (and strongly anti-South) farmers occurred in Benton Township and adjacent areas during that unhappy period.

Nonetheless, without doubt, the American Civil War was traumatic for Alva and his family as it was for untold others. In addition to friends and neighbors dying in battle and of disease, Alva's niece (his brother Jesse Gardner's daughter) lived in occupied Louisville, Kentucky; his sister Eliza's grandchildren, John, Ella, Martha, Clarence and Joyce Decker, were all living in North Carolina; and yet other family members had relocated earlier to Albemarle County, Virginia. His daughter Lamitha lost her brother-in-law Henry Davidson, he being a friend of Alva's brother-in-law, Lord Byron Green. Even his eldest son George Nelson, who sought to join the Union Army but without success, was a problem for Alva.

For whatever reasons, Alva Alanson Van Fleet took an unpopular stand on the American Civil War and the Lincoln Administration in particular. Nonetheless, he might be credited for courage in expressing opinions so openly in a day when the vast majority supported saving the Republic in tact.

Alva and Esther Van Fleet were staunch members of the Fleetville Universalist Church for much of their lives, but it was not yet formed when they were married. Esther was described as "a fine, very well-known woman" who was called "Aunt Esther" by many in the community. She lived to be eighty-seven years of age, having been born on 14 July 1813. She died 10 May 1901.

Alva and Esther Van Fleet had eight children, born between 1835 and 1852. They were:

01. Lamitha Van Fleet, born 1835, married Alvah B. Davidson;
02. Rebecca Van Fleet, date of birth unknown, married Mortimer Barker and later Francis E. Loomis, a prominent Scranton attorney and principal of the Universalist Church;
03. Elizabeth Van Fleet, born 1840, married Benjamin M. Green, brother of Lord Byron;
04. George Nelson Van Fleet, born 7 January 1843, married Lavinia Newton;
05. Charles Graham Van Fleet, born 3 June 1847, married Belle Wilson, then Ella Oliver and a third time, died in California in 1908;
06. Sarah Van Fleet, date of birth unknown, married Silas Hartley;
07. Merrit Baker Van Fleet, born 14 October 1850, married Ella Browning (it being noted that his uncle George Van Fleet in Ohio had a son with the same name); and
08. Galusha Alva Van Fleet, born 1852, married Addie Browning (a sister of Ella) then Flora Ann LeSeur on 2 January 1888 in Floyd County, Virginia.

Although the fourth child, eldest son George Nelson inherited Manor Farm, several other children remained in the general vicinity save Charles and Galusha, as detailed in later chapters.

Alva Van Fleet's general store in Fleetville, which he built around 1865, was left to his daughter Elizabeth. She and her husband Menjamin M. Green, brother of Lord Byron Green, ran the store for a number of years before they relocated to neighboring Waverly. Benjamin and Elizabeth established and conducted a general merchandizing emporium in that community, where they lived with their family for many years.

Nonetheless, the Fleetville store building that was built by Alva continued to function as a general store for years, and still stands today. A large and renovated structure, at present it serves as one of many botique-like shops specializing in antiques.

Alva and Esther Van Fleet both died at their beautiful hilltop family home in Fleetvbille, as stated she many years after her husband's untimely death in 1870. They are both buried in the Clark Cemetery in Fleetville.

GEORGE NELSON VAN FLEET (1843 – 1914)

George Nelson Van Fleet was the eldest son of Alvah and Esther Van Fleet. He was born 7 January 1843 in Fleetville, Pennsylvania. At age twenty-two he married Lavinia Lucinda Newton (Newton Lake being named for her family), daughter of Loren and Emily Wilcox Newton of Springville, Dimock Township, Susquehanna County, on 22 March 1865.

Lavinia was born 10 May 1846, and was still in her teens at the time of the wedding. They had met while attending a "select school" (private academy) in Nicholson, Pennsylvania.

From 1867 through 1875, George Nelson and Lavinia Van Fleet had five children. These were:

01. Charles Ray Van Fleet, born 22 August 1867, a twin, his brother dying at birth, married first Nellie G. Clarkson and second Nellie G. Stoddard Baylor, a widow;

02. Elizabeth Emily Van Fleet, born 5 January 1869, married Judge Solomon N. Robinson;

03. Catherine Van Fleet, born 5 December 1870, remained unmarried;

04. Bruce Newton Van Fleet, born 18 November 1873, married Vera Hawker; and

05. Paul Halton Van Fleet, born 7 November 1875, married Ruth Patterson.

Both daughters Elizabeth ("Aunt Lizzie") and Catherine ("Aunt Kate") were school teachers, who argued in a friendly way as to which of them had the longer service (both taught about thirty years, but not consecutively). Elizabeth married Solomon N. Robinson, son of Daniel and Sarah Robinson of Lennoxville, Lennox Township, Susquehanna County, in 1892.

"Sol" was a prosperous farmer and long-time justice of the peace, who served forty-five years as a local justice and judge with that title. They had one child, William Van Fleet Robinson, who married Maude DeVall. In 1958, Elizabeth Van Fleet Robinson died at age eight-one.

Catherine, born in December 1870, died 26 September 1931, never having married. She was an elementary school teacher and like her siblings, a graduate of the Keystone Academy in LaPlume, Pennsylvania (and like Elizabeth, of a Pennsylvania state teacher training institute).

Catherine lived at Manor Farm, and in fact inherited this property when her father George Nelson Van Fleet died. Although she never married, she was rumored to have had a long term relationship with her farm overseer. When she passed away in 1931, it fell to her brother Bruce Van Fleet, a wealthy Massachusetts banker and executor of the estate, to sell the property, ending just one hundred years' Van Fleet residence in the mansion and somewhat twenty-five years more of ownership of this land.

Paul Halton Van Fleet lived in nearby Dalton, Pennsylvania. A salesman by occupation, he was active in public education affairs throughout his life. Married to Ruth Patterson, daughter of David and Carrie Smith Patterson, they had one child, a daughter named Margaret. Born in 1912, she was killed in an automobile accident at age eight.

Bruce Newton Van Fleet was married to Vera Hawker of Scranton, Pennsylvania. They lived in Melrose, Massachusetts. For many years, Paul served as the president of a bank in Melrose. They had three children, Gerald, an Episcopal priest; Bruce Junior, now living in Jacksonville, Florida; and Robert.

George Nelson Van Fleet lived his life as a gentleman farmer, residing in the large home built by his father Alva. He was described as having been "very well known and a prominent local (member) of the Fleetville Universalist Church" by several commentators.

Interestingly, George Nelson had a reputation as a meticulous dresser. He was called "Gentleman George," a reflection of his demeanos and correct dress in frock coat, tie and stiffened white collar, regardless of whether he was walking through rows of corn at Manor Farm or past rows of pews in the Universalist church. This commentator's father had little recollection of the grandfather for whom he was named, but remembered vividly the stacks of celluloid white collars that remained in the family attic long after George Nelson Van Fleet's demise.

It is of interest too to note that during the American Civil War, George Nelson attempted to join the Union Army, but was deemed ineligible for service due to an injury from a horse sustained while early in his teens. That cut in his heel left him with a distinct limp throughout his life.

George Nelson Van Fleet, like his father, was another ardent Democrat in a rock-hard Republican area. He ran for the United States Congress twice, allegedly spending a considerable amount of his personal fortune, only to be resoundingly defeated both times, despite his personal popularity. He simply adhered to the wronf party at the wrong time.

Lavinia Newton Van Fleet died in 1897. George Nelson Van Fleet lived on at Manor Farm until 29 December 1914, expiring at age eighty-one. They are buried in the Chase Cemetery in Fleetville, Pennsylvania.

CHARLES RAY VAN FLEET (1867 – 1951)

Charles Ray Van Fleet, the eldest child of George Nelson and Lavinia Newton Van Fleet, was born 22 August 1867 in Fleetville. He was a twin, but his brother died at birth. No records exist giving his name, nor are there other references to him.

As a child, Charles Ray suffered from polio which left his right arm somewhat crippled. However, he overcame this disability in time, and was able to perform all normal tasks as well as anyone, decreasing attention to what otherwise would have been a noticeable characteristic.

A second physical characteristic was a partial harelip, that was surgically altered and after puberty kept covered with an ample mustache for the remainder of his life, leaving the scar undiscernable.

Charles Ray attended the Keystone Academy, and lived at Manor Farm until his first marriage to Nellie G. Clarkson in 1891 at age twenty-four. Nellie was a member of the family of long-time United States Congressman Galusha Grow of Susquehanna County, Pennsylvania, who was the author of the 1862 Homestead Act. This Act was one of the greatest landmarks in America's history of the opening and settlement of the west.

Interestingly, Nellie's father was an American Civil War veteran who had been a prisoner in the infamous Confederate Andersonville Prison in South Carolina.

Following their marriage, Charles Ray and Nellie G. Clarkson Van Fleet moved to a farm of their own, no doubt acquired with some $5,000.00 accepted from his father, possibly as a loan or in lieu of an inheritance, the basis for considerable family tension in later years.

185

They later relocated to one of Benton Township's finest farms, formerly owned by Welcome Browning and family, and noted as their property on old maps. This farm is referred to as "the Old Homestead" by many Van Fleet family members. Charles Ray built on to the house creating a large twelve room gabled structure in the Dutch colonial style, overlooking the main road and former turnpike laid out by his great grandfather James, leading to the heart of the Village of Fleetville.

The Charles Ray Van Fleet "Old Homestead"

Charles Ray and Nellie Grow Van Fleet had five children between 1892 and 1906. These were:
- 01. John George Van Fleet, born 4 July 1892 and died in 1894 at barely two and a half years of age;
- 02. Rose Esther Van Fleet, born 15 February 1894 and named partly for her grandmother, married first Glenn Hoss and second George Watkins;

03. Charles Ray Van Fleet Junior, born 25 November 1896, married Mildred Travis;
04. Ralph Bruce Van Fleet, born 22 September 1898, married Flossie Stirret; and
05. Howard Clarkson Van Fleet, born 14 April 1906, married Esther Stanton.

Very shortly after the death of his first wife on 20 January 1907, Charles Ray married a young widow, Nellie G. Stoddard Baylor (Baylor Lake having been named for her first husband's family). Her father too had served in the American Civil War from the Benton Township area, and lost an arm in the Battle of Lookout Mountain in Tennessee. She was also a Mayflower descendant.

Charles Ray and Nellie G. Stoddard Van Fleet had three children between 1908 and 1913. These were:

01. George Nelson Van Fleet, born 11 April 1908, married first Loretta Rose Bachman of Wilkes-Barre and second Bernice Ruth Dearborn, died 5 July 1997;
02. Alva Alanson Van Fleet, born 3 December 1910, married Jessie Mae Jones of Georgia and died November 2001; and
03. Helen Elizabeth Van Fleet, born 22 August 1913, married Eli Talvitie, and died 1958.

Among the children of the first marriage, none survives. Rose Esther died in 1984 in Lackawanna County, followed by Ralph Bruce in Tampa, Florida in 1965, Charles Ray in 1976 in Scranton, and Howard Clarkson in northeastern Pennsylvania in 1998.

Among the children born to Charles Ray and his second wife Nellie G. Stoddard Baylor Van Fleet, Helen Elizabeth died in California in 1958 followed by George Nelson in Clarks-Summit, Pennsylvania in 1997 and Alva A. in Tampa, Florida in 2001.

Charles Ray had been a member of the Fleetville Universalist Church and served for some time as its superintendent of Sunday schools. However, a disagreement – the details of which have long been forgotten – arose which caused him to sever his relationship with that congregation, despite the fact that its ministers had often lived with the Van Fleet family.

Despite a stubborn streak and temper that sometimes alienated him from others, Charles Ray was active in many community social activities, including those of most concern to local farmers, the Dairymen's League and the National Grange Federation. He was a member of the Willow Leaf Lodge of Odd Fellows in the 1920s and 1930s, along with several cousins in the Benton Township area. Politically, he was part of the Democrat Party minority in a Republican quarter of the county like his father and grandfather before him.

Nellie Van Fleet was a strong supporter and long-standing member of the Fleetville Universalist Church. She served as a trustee for it until her death in 1920. Due to her generous nature, as stated the church's ministers frequently stayed at the Van Fleet home as long term guests.

Nellie G. Stoddard Van Fleet

Those serving it in its last years residing with the family were not welcome after her death, and with a decreasing membership and the loss of in-kind support, the church became insolvent and closed its doors permanently less than one year after her death, in 1921.

Charles Ray Van Fleet as a young man c. 1888

Charles Ray, who was a widower for some thirty years, farmed in Fleetville his entire life. In old age he retired to the homes first of his daughter Helen Elizabeth in New Jersey, and second to that of his son Charles Ray Van Fleet Junior, in Scranton. He died in that city on 10 August 1951 and is buried between his two wives in the Clark Cemetry, Fleetville, Nellie G. Clarkson (1869 to 1907) and Nellie G.. Stoddard (1872 to 1920).

189

Charles Ray's sons sold their father's farm, largely ending a chapter of over one hundred thirty years of Van Fleet history in the village that was named for their ancestor in Benton Township. There are scattered family members remaining in the general area who carry on the family name. Those Van Fleets whose family history is traced through Fleetville – persons whose ancestry encompasses at least thirteen generations spanning nearly four centuries in America – now make their homes in scores of cities in dozens of states across America.

The children and grandchildren of Charles Ray Van Fleet were/are:

01. John George Van Fleet, born 4 July 1892 and died 1894;

02. Rose Esther Van Fleet, born 15 February 1894, married first Glenn Ross and second George Watkins and died in 1984. Her children were: Ralph Ross, died as an infant; Ralph Ross, killed in 1945 in World War II; Paymond Ross; and Robert Ross.

03. Charles Ray Van Fleet Junior, born 1896, married Mildred Travis, died 1976. Their children were: Roberta, a nurse, married Glen Williams; and Marilyn, a nurse, married Alfred Hafler.

04. Ralph Bruce Van Fleet, born 22 September 1898, married Flossie Stirrett, died 1968. The children were: Ralph Bruce Van Fleet Junior, an insurance broker, and Donald Stirrett Van Fleet, a senior state official in education in Florida and Kentucky.

05. Howard Clarkson Van Fleet, born 14 April 1906, died 1998, married first _____ and second Esther Stanton, with no children being born of either marriage;

06. George Nelson Van Fleet, born 11 April 1908, an Air Force colonel and attorney, married first Loretta Bachman and second Bernice Dearborn, died 5 July 1997. The children were: Mary Joan, born 12 May 1935, a nursing professor, married John J. Burns; George Nelson Van Fleet Junior, born 10 May 1936, an attorney and businessman, married first Patricia Thomas and second as a widower Frances Smith Wilson; and James A. Van Fleet, born 16 January 1940, a former government official and later university dean and professor, married Holly A. Hufsachmidt.

07. Alva Alanson Van Fleet, born 3 December 1910 and died November 2001, married Jessie Mae Jones. The children were: Lee Frances; Martha Jeanne; and Alanson Alva Van Fleet, a former professor and current businessman.

08. Helen Elizabeth Van Fleet, born 1913, married Eli Talvitie, and died 1958. The only child was Gail.

RELIGION AND ITS ROLE IN AMERICAN LIFE

For Americans today who disdainfully witness extremes of religious zealotry around the world, it is difficult to imagine that there was a time when an individual in this country was largely defined by religious preference. Most of the thirteen colonies were founded with an established church, and well into the 1830s long after our Constitution and Bill of Rights had been adopted, there were states with official churches.

But there have always been dissenters. Preaching the gospel of universal salvation in the 1700s there were at least three distinct geographical areas in the south, northeast and central states that saw the rise of a faith known as Universalism. In Philadelphia Benjamin Rush, a signer of the Declaration of Independence and a famed physician, was a father of this religion along with Elhanan Winchester who founded a congregation there in 1781.

Universalism was in part a rejection of the strict Calvinist doctrine on eternal punishment. From its beginnings, Universalism challenged its members to reach out and embrace people whom society often marginalized, a liberalism reflected in its acceptance of freed slaves and (by the 1860s) female ministers.

Universalism has been described as more evangical than Unitarianism, and from its organization in 1793 as a distinct church, Universalism spread its message across the American Union and Canada, fed by such individuals as Hosea Ballou and Nathanial Stacy, and following the advice of Universalist publisher Horace Greeley, on into the west.

What did Universalists believe? Thomas Starr King is credited with stating the difference between Unitarians (with whom Universalists merged in the 1960s) and Universalists: "Universalists believe that God is too good to damn people, and Unitarians believe that people are too good to be damned by God." Specifically, Universalists believed in a God who embraced everyone. This eventually became central to their belief that lasting trust is found in all religions, and that dignity and worth are innate to all people regardless of sex, race, color or class.

Universalism was adopted by Van Fleets in New York and Pennsylvania, notably with brothers Joshua and Abraham accepting it (and certainly in the former case, his line for generations to come). This was a departure from the Calvinist Dutch Reformed Church into which each was born and baptized, and which other lines of the family adhered for many decades before greater diversity entered into the picture.

In the case of the social liberalism of the Universalist Church, there is a clear tie-in with Joshua Van Fleet's New York state constitutional provision to ban slavery, and the tendency of his and other Van Fleets to endorse liberal causes, which historically went hand-in-hand with this (and the Unitarian) religion.

By the late Nineteenth and into the Twentieth Century, Van Fleets were found in many religious faiths, including Mormon, Roman Catholic, Methodist, Episcopal, Presbyterian and Baptist churches, reflecting in many cases perhaps more their location in the country (and availability of choices) than devotion to a particular doctrine, as religion came to play a decreasingly important defining role in identity in America.

GEORGE NELSON VAN FLEET II (1908 – 1997)

George Nelson Van Fleet II was a tenth generation American, born the son of Charles Ray, grandson of his namesake George Nelson, and great great grandson of James Van Fleet, the Northeastern Pennsylvania pioneer, turnpike surveyor, farming implements manufacturer and agriculturalist noted elsewhere in this family history.

George Nelson Van Fleet attended the local one room elementary school in Fleetville, the town named for his ancestor in the mid-1830s, in classes taught by his maiden aunt Catherine. Later, he attended secondary school in Waverly, Pennsylvania, as a schoolmate of Henry Luce of TIME magazine.

George was the fifth child of Charles Ray Van Fleet, and the first born of Charles' second marriage to Nellie G. Stoddard Baylor, a widow whom he married the previous year shortly after the death of his first wife. Two other children followed, Alva Alanson and Helen Van Fleet, before their mother in turn died in 1920, leaving a large and very young family behind from two wives.

Neither George, his siblings, nor his father fully recovered from this loss. His father, embittered by her early death and in faltering financial circumstances, became an increasingly difficult person to deal with, alienating many in the larger family and in the community, including his own children.

Accordingly, George Nelson left Fleetville at the earliest possible moment to pursue his own destiny. Ultimately that led him to a colorful career that included the Army Air Corps (later the United States Air Force), the Secret Service and a lengthy career in the practice of law.

Beginning employment with the Federal Government as a Prohibition Officer in the 1930s just before that era ended, George Nelson transitioned into the United States Secret Service as a special agent, and later Agent-in-Charge, in several offices in the Northeast. Concurrently, he served as an officer (pilot and later in military intelligence) with the Army Air Corps (later the United States Air Force Reserve).

As stated he was a pilot, having learned to fly (before learning to drive a car) at age fifteen during the 1920s, but in World War II he was considered too old for combat missions, those being reserved for men a decade his junior. Nonetheless and most notably, he became a glider pilot and trained for the exceedingly dangerous tasks of landing troops at Normandy during the invasion, and would have seen service in that capacity had not the glider program been abandoned.

However, it was as a senior pilot that he was one of the Allied team that flew to Norway in the waning days of the War, to either accept the surrender of – or to be ambushed and possibly massacred by – Nazi troops who had settled in for the last stand in a Nordic "fortress." Fortunately for all concerned, the Germans opted to surrender rather than to fight.

His career in intelligence, in the Judge Advocate General's Corps in the Air Force, as well as in Federal law enforcement were highly meaningful for George Nelson Van Fleet, a man who had a deep love for the law.

Following his retirement as a senior officer from the Secret Service and concurrently after thirty years from the Air Force Reserve as a full colonel, he took the bar exam for the first time at age fifty-three, and initiated a general practice that would last for some thirty-five years.

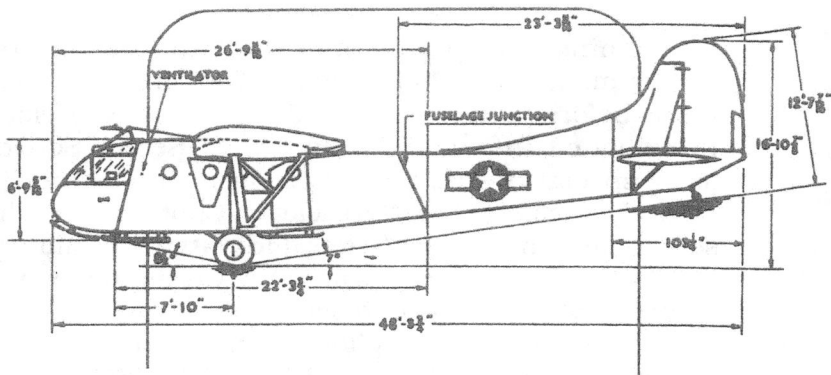

Gliders Were Once Destined for D-Day Invasion

George Nelson Van Fleet married first Loretta Rose Bachman in Wilkes-Barre, Pennsylvania, in June 1934, and second Bernice Dearborn, in Waverly, Pennsylvania in May 1946. By his first marriage, he and Loretta Bachman Van Fleet had three children:

(01) Mary Joan Van Fleet, born 12 May 1935, married John J. Burns, and is a retired college professor of nursing in northeastern Pennsylvania, residing in Scranton;

(02) George Nelson Van Fleet Junior, born 10 May 1936, married Patricia Ann Thomas, and as a widower Mary Frances Wilson, is a business executive and attorney in Wichita, Kansas; and

(03) James Alward Van Fleet, born 16 January 1940, married Holly Ann Hufschmidt, and is a retired international economist and university administrator, presently residing in Naples, Florida.

196

*George N. Van Fleet as a United States Army Air
Corps Captain in 1941*

A lifelong advocate of voluntary and charitable
organizations, George Nelson Van Fleet received
countless awards in his later years from veterans'
groups, the Lions and other civic clubs, as well as
community organizations and the Republican Party.

He was an amateur genealogist as noted in the
introductory comments to this book, who also
served as a regional vice president of the Holland
Society of New York.

In failing health. George and Bernice Van Fleet removed to Clarks Summit, Pennsylvania, in 1996, to be close to daughter Mary Joan Van Fleet Burns. They both died there within two months of each other, she in May 1997 and he on 5 July 1997.

They are interred in the Clark Cemetery of Fleetville, Pennsylvania among many Van Fleet family members of earlier generations from the northeastern Pennsylvania branch.

G. Nelson Van Fleet, James A. Van Fleet and Mary Joan Burns, children of George N. Van Fleet

DIRCK DIRCKSE VAN VLIET (1701 – c. 1780)

Another Van Vliet family branch was established in Pennsylvania deep in the Delaware Valley but not many miles from the Wyoming Valley home of the Van Fleets. This branch was founded in the Stroud Township area, in a time frame contemporaneous with relatives in the Minisink Valley of New York.

Specifically, Dirck Adriansen Van Vliet, brother of Jan Van Vliet Senior, was born in Holland and brought to New Netherland as a child by his returning father and immigrating mother, Adrian Gerritsen Van Vliet and Agatha Jans Spruit. Thus, like his brothers and sisters, he grew to maturity in the general area around Kingston, Rochester and Marbletown, New York, in close proximity to the Hudson River.

Marrying Anna Andriesz (or Andriessen or Andrise or Andries) in the 1680s, this couple had eight children, at least the first of whom was baptized with witnesses Jan Van Vliet, his brother, and Agatha Spruit, Dirck's mother. These baptisms are recorded at the Old Dutch Church of Kingston.

The children of Dirck and Anna Van Vliet were:
01. Ary (Adrian) Van Vliet, baptized 11 September 1686;
02. Ellentje Van Vliet, baptized 1 January 1688;
03. Adries (Andrew) Van Vliet, baptized 5 November 1691;
04. Cornelia Van Vliet, baptized 7 June 1695;
05. Gerrit Van Vliet, baptized 4 September 1697;
06. Rachel Van Vliet, baptized 7 May 1699;
07. Dirck Van Vliet (Dirrick, or Richard), baptized 1 January 1701; and
08. Catherina Van Vliet, baptized 22 November 1702.

199

The publication entitled the Pennsylvania COMMEMORATIVE BIOGRAPHICAL RECORD states that Dirck Van Vliet married a second time, and had three children:

01. Joseph Van Vliet;
02. Derick (sic) Van Vliet; and
03. Charrick Van Vliet.

Their places and dates of birth are not noted. However, the information contained in the BIOGRAPHICAL RECORD for Pennsylvania that described the family history in the last years of the Nineteenth Century is confusing and somewhat inaccurate. It is asserted that Van Vliet lands were acquired from William Penn and that (Dirck) "passed his remaining years in that localitym and died 1744, his remains being interred in Stroudsburg." He would have been in his late nineties, an age not inconsistent with other family members, but in fact the reference is to his son Dirck Junior, not Dirck Senior of the second generation in America.

BIOGRAPHICAL RECORD entries state that both Charrick Van Vliet and Joseph Van Vliet were Dirck Senior's sons, as well as Revolutionary War soldiers. It is more than unlikely that they were the original Dirck's children, inasmuch as to have been so, they would have to have been very old men by the time of the American Revolution.

Presumably, a generation is skipped here, and much more than likely they were really the grandchildren of the Dirck Van Vliet who came to America as a child from Holland in 1662.

The Minisink Dutch Reformed Church records support this thesis. Dirck Van Vliet Senior's son, Dirck Junior, is the one who was married twice (contrary to the Pennsylvania BIOGRAPHICAL RECORD assertion).

200

The first marriage was to Marytjen Chrispel of Hurley, widow of Jacob Hermans, on 24 January 1730. Three children – interestingly but un remarkably, all daughters – were born to this marriage.

Undoubtedly widowed, he was married a second time to Rachel Van Keuren on 27 December 1741. They resided in New York, according to church records, and had at least seven children, including "Tjerk Van Keuren Van Vliet," a creative variation and phonetic spelling of the Dutch name Dirck, whose involvement in the Revolution is unquestioned, given Daughters of the American Revolution members who claim him as an ancestor.

Children born of the second marriage include:

01. Marytjen Van Vliet, baptized 8 August 1742 and named for his first wife, a common practice for widowers to do;

02. Tjerk Van Vliet, 24 April 1744, died in infancy;

03. Judica Van Vliet, 5 May 1745 (witnesses being Gerrit Van Vliet and his wife Jidica Van Neste);

04. Anna Catherina Van Vliet, 1 February 1746 (witnesses being Teunis Swartwout and his wife Rachel Van Vliet);

05. Tjerk Van Keuren Van Vliet (again), 30 October 1748, married Barbara LaBar;

06. Jenneke Van Vliet, 29 September 1750; and

07. Elizabeth Van Vliet, 23 December 1753.

08. In these cases, Dirck Junior would have been about twenty-eight or twenty-nine years of age at the time of the first marriage, and about thirty-nine or so at the time of the second, meaning that children of the second union would have been of the right age for service in the American Revolution.

Note that he was in his fifties when the last of his children was born, a pattern repeated in generation after generation of Van Vliets and Van Fleets. Charrick Van Vliet was described as the great grandfather of the subject of the Pennsylvania biography, that related his son was called Derick. This Derick married Rachel Staples, and they had eight children, one of whom was another Charrick Van Vliet, father of the John W. Van Vliet profiled in the biographical sketch.

The family is further discussed as having engaged in various pursuits, including farming, greenhouse industries, and the building of railroads in northeastern Pennsylvania.

Curiously, in this latter capacity John Van Vliet worked and lived in the greater Scranton region, where other descendants of the earliest Van Vliet settlers lived, all with the anglicized surname of Van Fleet and descended from Jan Van Vliet Junior.

Although this branch of the family's history is not pursued further in this commentary, it provides the basis for other genealogical research for descendants of Dirck Van Vliet, that might be productive vis-à-vis what other information is given on persons with the same family line.

It should be noted, however, that the Van Vliet surname can be confusing for researchers, given the fact that in the mid-1900s a number of Van Vliet families immigrated from the Netherlands, coming to Michigan and several other Midwestern states to establish new lives in America. Nonetheless, those Van Vliets from the New York, New Jersey and eastern Pennsylvania regions are most likely of the old "Knickerbocker" family that arrived in the Hudson Valley during the Dutch colonial era.

202

PART III.

NEW LANDS TO CONQUER:

FROM OHIO THROUGHOUT THE

MIDWEST

A PORTRAIT OF OHIO

The first European to visit Ohio was Pierre LaSalle in 1669. American fur traders arrived sometime around 1685, and during the French and Indian War there was an effort to expel these "English" from the territory.

A part of the American territorial claim at the time of the Revolutionary War, the Americans as represented by Virginians defeated the Indians in 1774, but hostilities were renewed in 1777 and continued for some time. Following a decisive victory by General "Mad" Anthony Wayne at Fallen Timbers near present-day Toledo in 1794, conflict with the Indians ceased, and they were pacified or displaced.

Firmly established as United States territory, the claims of several states – Virginia and Connecticut among them – were abandoned, and Ohio was classified as part of the Western Preserve.

Ohio Territory's first organized settlement was at Marietta, on the Ohio River, in 1788. Settlement initially proceeded along the Ohio River and then inland, but after the completion of the Erie Canal in 1825, the Great Lakes were opened to rapid development and settlers flowed into the interior of the new state from northern parts of the area, via New England and New York.

The dangers to settlement and to life itself in Ohio were alleviated with the 1794 defeat of the Indians, the War of 1812 that saw Oliver Hazard Perry's victory on Lake Erie and William Henry Harrison's invasion of Canada end the threat of British conquest of the Ohio Valley, and the draining of unhealthy so-called black swamps, particularly in the northern third of the state.

Ohio had no substantial American population base in 1790, the year of the first Federal Census. In 1800, there were 45,000 persons, but by 1810, seven years after statehood, there were 231,000 inhabitants. In 1820, some two years after George Van Fleet arrived, and in 1830, during the time when Joshua Van Fleet's children Moses, Miles, Joshua Junior and John Kennedy Van Fleet were arriving, the population figures were 581,434 and 937,903, respectively.

Ohio became a state on 1 March 1803, the seventeenth in the American Union. With 44,828 square miles of territory, it ranks thirty-fourth in the country today. In the context of history, James Monroe was President of the United States when George Van Fleet removed to Ohio, and Andrew Jackson was President when the sons of Joshua Van Fleet began arriving about a decade later.

What brought the Van Fleets to Ohio?

There is a simple answer to this question: Economic opportunity mixed with at least a sense of adventurism attracted Van Fleets to Ohio.

It must be remembered that Ohio was the west, the direction that for thousands of years represented in one fashion or another the direction of the future. More so than Kentucky or Tennessee, lands that preceded Ohio into statehood, it was Ohio that was the bridge between the original colonies and the westward promise of America.

Some lands in Ohio were granted for service in the American Revolution, but it is believed that Van Fleets from several branches found their way to Ohio to purchase – albeit at minimal cost – the lands they acquired.

The flatness and sparseness of rocky land in the state, the fertility of its soil once cleared or drained, and the length of the growing season made farming much more attractive and profitable than elsewhere in the northeast. Thus, Ohio became the better choice for farmers from the east, as arch-typical Americans in so many ways, fulfilling a Jeffersonian dream of a country in expanses of farming communities.

The BUILDING of OHIO

18 Land Grants

Ohio and Its Counties

Van Fleet Heads of Families in Ohio: 1840 Census

(Compiled by Cleo Goff Wilkens 929.4771/W681)

01. Page 184, George noted in Delaware County, Ber. Township (Abraham's son);
02. Page 109, A. noted in Franklin County, Ham. Township (unknown relationship);
03. Page 095, D. noted in Franklin County, Madison Township (unknown relationship);
04. Page 306, Daniel noted in Erie County, Por. Township (Daniel Van Fleet Junior's son);
05. Page 075, Miles Wilkensen noted, Hardin County, Dudley Township (Joshua Van Fleet Senior's son);
06. Page 305, Stephen noted, Erie County, Por. Township (Daniel Van Fleet Junior's line);
07. Page 262, Cornelius noted, Lucas County, Watertown (Matthias Van Fleet's son of the Van der Vliedt line);
08. Page 444, Jacob noted, Miami County, Spr. Township (unknown relationship);
09. Page 277, Jefferson noted, Lucas County, Yor. Township (Levi Van Fleet's son of the Daniel Van Fleet Junior line);
10. Page 133, Joshua Senior, Marion County, Big Island Township (Daniel Van Fleet Senior's son);
11. Page 213, John Kennedy noted, Marion County, Big Island Township (Joshua Van Fleet Senior's son who later went to Indiana);
12. Page 213, William noted, Seneca County, Scioto Township (Daniel Van Fleet Junior's son);

13. Page 214, Levi Senior noted, Seneca County, Scioto Township (Daniel Van Fleet Junior's son);
14. Page 244, John noted, Trumbell County, Youngstown (Richard Van Fleet's son of the Van der Vliedt line);
15. Page 155, Moses noted, Marion County, Mon. Township (Joshua Van Fleet Senior's son);
16. Page 260, Matthias noted, Lucas County, Watertown (Van der Vliedt line);
17. Page 260, John noted, Lucas County, Watertown, (Van der Vliedt line);
18. Page 302, Levi Junior noted, Shelby County, Jackson Township (Levi Van Fleet Senior's son); and
19. Page 153, Jerimah noted, Morgan County, Olive Township (Van der Vliedt line).

CORNELIUS VAN FLEET (1758 - 1841)

Cornelius Van Fleet, a descendant of Dirck Jans Van der Vliedt (Van Vliet, and finally Van Fleet), was born in Readington, New Jersey and baptized 6 March 1759. He relocated to Washington in Lycoming County, Pennsylvania, probably with a young famiy. He died 7 December 1841 in Lycoming County, and it is unclear whether he like several of his children relocated for any time period to Ohio.

Nonetheless, as a progenitor of many Ohioans, he is included here for the sake of continuity. Cornelius Van Fleet married Sarah Shipman sometime in 1781 or 1782, and had nine children between 1782 and 1803. These were:

01. Margaret Van Fleet, born 19 December 1782;
02. William Van Fleet, baptized 2 October 1784;
03. Mary Van Fleet, baptized 12 November 1786;
04. Sarah Van Fleet, baptized 19 August 1787;
05. John Van Fleet, baptized 6 December 1791;
06. Jared Van Fleet, baptized 4 May 1800, married Lucy Dupuis, removed to Olympia, Washington, by 1868;
07. Matthias S. Van Fleet, born or baptized August 1793;
08. Hannah Van Fleet, baptized 18 April 1796; and
09. Elizabeth Van Fleet, baptized 9 January 1803.

John, Jared and Matthias Van Fleet all relocated to northwest Ohio in the vicinity of Watertown, Toledo and adjacent Wood County. Initially, it is believed that they resided in the Dayton area for a while. In any event, they are recorded in the northwest portion of the state by the early 1830s, where their names are reported in local county histories.

208

In 1835, Matthias S. Van Fleet was a colonel in the Ohio Militia, residing in the Wood County area adjacent to the disputed lands abutting the Territory of Michigan. Leading a troop of militiamen under the orders of Governor Lucas of Ohio, an unsuccessful raid was staged during the period known as the Black Hawk War.

Although frustrated in the plan to seize by force the area in dispute, there was a successful settlement later by Federal courts in favor of Ohio, giving that state the land now known as Lucas County, and as compensation the Michigan Territory an area from the Wisconsin Territory, that region known today as the Upper Peninsula.

At the time, the Lucas County region was very sparsely settled. In 1834 there were just forty-three voters in the immediate Wood County area where the Van Fleets settled. Nonetheless, John and Matthias were active in politics, both being listed as "viewers" for Lucas County roads in the 1830s, and as active Democrats representing that party in the state convention in 1841.

John Van Fleet served as county commissioner from 1838 to 1841, having been elected as justice of the peace as early as 1832 in that area. Matthias meanwhile was a trustee for Waterville in the 1833 to 1834 period. Later in 1874 his son was a county coroner.

A son of Matthias, Cornelius Van Fleet II, married Julia Anna Runyon, who like her husband had been born in Pennsylvania before relocating to Ohio with her family. Among their children was a son who ultimately became a California Supreme Court justice, William Carey Van Fleet, and another named Mabry, who joined his brother William's family in California, in association with the Wells Fargo Bank ultimately as a senior officer.

MATTHIAS S. VAN FLEET (1793 – c. 1865)

A descendant of the Dirck Van der Vliedt line through Cornelius (born 1758 and died 1841), Matthias Van Fleet was an interesting figure in the history of northwest Ohio. Born in Pennsylvania after his family relocated there from New Jersey, likely in proximity to the Delaware River around Berks or Bucks County, he settled initially in Montgomery County, Ohio, in or near Dayton. This relocation occurred sometime in the 1820s, inasmuch as he is noted as a head of household there in the 1830 Federal Census, but not in any earlier enumeration.

However, sometime before 1835, Matthias Van Fleet and his young family relocated again to present-day Lucas County. At the time, the area in question was claimed by the state of Ohio as well as by the Territory of Michigan, precipitating an armed struggle for control of this relatively small but strategic strip of land (with excellent ports) along a principal feeder of Lake Erie, the Maumee River.

On 23 February 1835, Matthias Van Fleet, who was then a colonel in the Ohio Militia, led a group of Governor Lucas' Ohioans into the disputed area north of the Maumee River. Although routed by the Michiganders, the event proved crucial to the ultimate settlement of the border issue, with Michigan gaining the Upper Peninsula (from the Wisconsin Territory) and Ohio what became known as Lucas County.

Matthias, who was baptized in August 1793 and presumed to have been born earlier that year, was a farmer by occupation in the Waterville area. Most likely he was accompanied to this region by his brother John. Both he and John appear in many 1830s records.

Specifically, Matthias and John Van Fleet are cited in THE HISTORY OF TOLEDO AND LUCAS COUNTY as frequent office holders. Both were selected as "viewers" for Lucas County roads in December 1835, and were participants in the state Democratic Convention on 30 November 1841, when that party opposed the Whigs at the polls.

John Van Fleet was born in 1791, and was a county commissioner for Lucas in the 1838 to 1841 time frame. John also served as a justice of the peace in Waterville, being elected to that post on 21 June 1831. In 1832 Matthias was elected a county trustee and supervisor, a role filled again in 1835. John virtually alternated, similarly serving in these capacities in 1833 and again in 1835. Then, Matthias later served as a Democratic supporter for Franklin Pierce in the national election of 1852.

John Van Fleet owned property which he acquired from William J. Ketcham in 1836. Additionally, Lucas County records state that he sold property in 1840 to John O. Ensign. Matthias was recorded as selling property to his son Charles, sometime in 1843, among the tax and property records of the county.

A third younger brother journeyed with Matthias and John Van Fleet to northwest Ohio; namely, Jared. Taxpayer lists for Waterville in 1838 include his name, as well as his brothers, and he was noted for service as a grand juror as early as 1836 in Lucas County records. He is recorded as well in the 1840 Federal Census, as noted.

Jared Van Fleet was baptized 4 May 1800 in Pennsylvania, and may have been born the prior year. It is certain that the Jared and Lucy Dupuis Van Fleet obituary reported in the OLYMPIA TRANSCRIPT in Washington state later in the century is theirs, reflecting a later move.

Matthias Van Fleet and his wife had several children, among whom were Charles and Cornelius Van Fleet II.

Charles was born on 19 March 1822 in Dayton, Ohio, and later married Sarah Webb. He and Sarah had a daughter, named Helen I. Van Fleet who was born on 10 November 1847. A second child was Henry F. Van Fleet who was born 13 December 1839, and who like his father and grandfather, was a farmer in Waterville.

The last two known children were Cora Van Fleet and Fred W. Van Fleet, who was born 2 March 1857. Two other children in this marriage died young. Charles Van Fleet himself died 10 November 1884.

Charles and Cornelius Van Fleet were both members of local Ohio militia units as noted in 1844. Like his father Colonel Matthias Van Fleet, Cornelius was an elected officer serving in various capacities. Civically, he also served the community, including in an unspecified role in 1850 as a township official. In 1874, he was listed as the county coroner.

Matthias was the grandfather and Charles the father of Frederick Van Fleet. He was born in 1857 and later in life was reported in local histories as a substantial northwest Ohio citizen. In 1889 he established the Sugar Ridge Stone and Lime Company. In the Perrysburg community, he was listed as a faithful member of the Presbyterian Church in 1895 in that town.

Cornelius Van Fleet II's son was a most distinguished jurist in California. This commentary includes a chapter on Judge William Carey Van Fleet and his remarkable career in Democrat Party politics, in San Francisco and on the bench in "the Golden State."

JEREMIAH VAN FLEET (1793 – 1854)

Jeremiah Van Fleet, son of Garret and Phoebe Welton and a descendant of Dirck Jans Van der Vliet (of the New Jersey family), was born in Hardy County, (present day West) Virginia. Jeremiah's siblings included Peter, Phoebe (married Nimrod Simon), William, Rebecca (married John Coler) and Hannah (married George Gadd) Van Fleet, some of whom resettled in Ohio with the extended family.

As an adult Jeremiah relocated to Olive Township, Morgan County, in southeastern Ohio, directly opposite his not-too-distant relatives Matthias and John Van Fleet in northwestern Ohio. He wed to Margaret Armstrong and thereafter they had at least two sons, and likely many more children, including George (who married Sarah Ann Ward 6 May 1851) and John Van Fleet, a Civil War veteran.

George and Sarah in turn had eight children:

01. William Van Fleet, born 7 August 1853;
02. John W. Van Fleet;
03. Margaret Ann Van Fleet;
04. Francis Van Fleet, born 27 January 1872, married Stella _____, served as a distinguished Colorado educator and died at Colorado Springs 9 April 1937;
05. James Buchanan Van Fleet;
06. Theresa A. Van Fleet;
07. Joseph E. Van Fleet (whose son Donald, of Harrodsburg, Kentucky, was killed in a Japanese attack on 30 November 1942 when his ship was struck); and
08. Benjamin Van Fleet.

Jeremiah died in Olive township in 1854 at the relatively young age of fifty-seven. His father Garret was noted living there in the Ohio 1850 Federal Census at age ninety.

HENRY FRANK VAN FLEET (1849 – 19__)

In the line of Dirck Jans Van der Vliet, the Matthias Van Fleet line resided in Dayton by the early 1800s before relocating to northwest Ohio.

Specifically, Charles Van Fleet, a pioneer of this general Toledo region, was born in Dayton on 19 March 1822 and married Sarah Webb who was born in Syracuse, New York, on 13 March 1828, after her parents relocated west via the Erie Canal.

Charles had removed to northwest Ohio with his parents in 1831, after his father purchased a farm near what is now Waterville, Lucas County. At the time it was described as "little but wilderness to be seen in many miles," by MEMOIRS OF LUCAS COUNTY.

Clearing the land was a long and arduous task, but the financial rewards of farming the resulting rich lands were evident in that Charles and his wife had ample time to devote to the Presbyterian church and to politics.

Charles, an avid Democrat and promoter of his party in state elections, served as a township trustee, member of the school board, and held various other unspecified offices. He died 10 November 1884, followed by his wife Sarah 28 August 1889.

Six children were born to them, two who died in infancy. Those surviving were:

01. Helen I. Van Fleet, married Jacob W. Urschel of Toledo;
02. Henry Frank Van Fleet;
03. Cora V. Van Fleet, who married Wilson W. Spencer of Bowling Green, Ohio; and
04. Frederick W. Van Fleet, a well known manufacturer of tiles in Finley, Ohio.

Henry Frank was born on the family farm two miles northwest of Waterville, on 13 November 1849. He received his early education at local schools near the farmstead and later pursued studies at Maumee Seminary while helping his father in farming activities. He himself became a farmer as soon as his age and finances permitted.

Additionally, Henry Frank Van Fleet entered business. He was instrumental in founding the Waterville State Savings Bank, later serving as president. He was treasurer and director of the Citizens' Telephone Company and a substantial stockholder in the Waterville Butter Company as well.

Like his father, he was a staunch Democrat who served for years as a Lucas County commissioner, elected property appraiser and school board member.

He married 19 June 1872 to Sarah M. Bradley, who was originally from Summit County but whose family relocated to Lucas County some years earlier. She was born 29 October 1850. The couple had three children:

01. Nellie B. Van Fleet, born 5 September 1876, married Arthur Longbrake, a lawyer, of Summit County, Ohio;

02. Laura Lenore Van Fleet, born 12 December 1878, married D.J. Farnsworth, manager and superintendent of the Citizens' Telephone Company of Waterville; and

03. George M. Van Fleet, born 7 April 1881, married Anna Taylor and engaged in farming.

Henry Frank and Sarah Van Fleet were members of the Presbyterian church. In addition to his Democrat Party political activities, he was an active Mason.

GEORGE VAN FLEET (1796 - 1852)

George Van Fleet was born 1 February 1796 in Pittston, Pennsylvania, the younger of two boys born to Abraham Van Fleet and his wife Sarah Brown. Abraham was born in Orange County, a son of Daniel Van Fleet Senior and a fifth generation American descended from Adrian Gerritsen Van Vliet. He and his wife removed with their infant son James to the Wyoming Valley of Pennsylvania in the summer of 1786, the year of his elder son's birth.

Abraham and his brother Joshua Van Fleet, who was some four years younger, were pioneers in the Connecticut-sponsored settlements along the Susquehanna River, along with other relatives and Orange County, New York, neighbors. By the time George was born, however, Joshua had relocated to the upper reaches of the river to the vicinity of Tioga. Within a few years Joshua and his growing family moved again to Manchester, New York, to the Finger Lakes region of the central portions of the state.

George and his older brother James *by twelve years) grew up in the Pittston area, but no records exist on their early life. By about 1821, James was long married. Earlier he had begun working as a surveyor for the Philadelphia-Great Bend Turnpike in northeast Pennsylvania. How and where he acquired those skills remains something of a puzzle, as does the origin of his skill as a tool and implement maker. James relocated to the upper part of Luzerne County by the early to mid-1820s, a more fertile region conducive to the farming activities in which he engaged for much of the remainder of his life following completion of the turnpike, and as related elsewhere in this narrative.

It is not known how their father Abraham disposed of his farm later in life, but in fact he died in 1837, by which time both sons had moved on to other locales and pursuits. In any event, George did not remain on the family farm after his brother left, and had departed on foot for Ohio in 1818 at age twenty-two. It is generally believed that James inherited the farm, because family lore states that he sold or "traded" the land there for new and more promising holdings in present-day Benton Township. However, George having some capital in Ohio to acquire land and businesses in the 1820s soon after arriving there, and James purchasing land at about the same time, leads one to conclude that there was some financial settlement between them of an inheritance or other family funds or assets.

George proceeded to Ohio in the company of G.A. Nash. Two years after his departure, his father Abraham filed for a Revolutionary War pension, and stated that he was living at that time with just one daughter. Consequently, the male line of Van Fleets in lower Luzerne County ended, since James was gone. The several daughters save one where long married as well.

George Van Fleet arrived in Galena, Ohio – then called Zoar – sometime in 1818. This community had but a handful of settlers at that time, and the plat of the village itself was only just completed (two years earlier) by William Carpenter of nearby Sunbury.

The name Zoar, from the place where Lot sought refuge after the destruction of Sodom and Gamorah, lasted but a brief time until a post office was established. It was discovered that another village had that "address," so in 1834 Galena came into existence.

217

George Van Fleet first established himself in Delaware County as a carpenter, although this activity appears to have been somewhat short-lived as a principal activity. From the beginning of the community, the need for a grist mill was evident, the first being built about 1810. One such mill built by Benjamin Carpenter was acquired by George in the 1820s, and run by him as a successful venture for many years.

George Van Fleet was also noted to be a distiller in history books on Delaware County. Quoting from a HISTORY OF DELAWARE COUNTY, it was noted that there were during his lifetime three "stills" operating in Berkshire Township. One was just north of the village, and was built in 1820 by Joseph and Steven Larkin. "This they soon after sold to George Vanfleet (sic), an early settler in Galena, and built another just below the town...."

Although the HISTORY OF DELAWARE COUNTY is somewhat difficult to follow at times, it appears that another local and highly profitable industry was tanning. George Van Fleet was described as the owner of such an operation as well, which continued long after his death and ended only in 1873.

There is no indication how or where George learned any of the skills related to carpentry, distilling, milling or tanning, if indeed he personally engaged in these to any extent. What is more interesting is to note that in addition to land, he held numerous business interests requiring (and earning) considerable amounts of capital.

Four years after arriving in Galena, George married Christiana Bidlack, a daughter of Hileman (a tombstone for his daughter noted Philemon) Bidlack, who – like George's father – was an early Wyoming Valley settler.

Her background, however, was New England, and there is a logical connection here to the ill-fated settlement of the Wyoming under the aegis of Connecticut.

The Bidlack family arrived in Ohio from Pennsylvania by team sometime in 1820. The 1880 HISTORY OF DELAWARE COUNTY noted that she was "a descendant of the Puritans," and probably that meant that the family had gone to the Wyoming Valley from Connecticut under the Susquehanna Land Company auspices. She had been born in Pennsylvania in 1804, and thus was still in her teens when she married in 1822 (or possibly 1821) young George, who was about twenty-four.

George Van Fleet died relatively young on 28 October 1852, somewhat more than three years short of his sixtieth birthday. His wife Christiana followed many years later in 1873. In their years in Delaware County, there is no question that they were aware of the nearby presence of Joshua Van Fleet after 1835 or 1836, and of their various cousins, since all of those family members were in the adjacent County of Marion not even thirty miles distant. Moreover, naming patterns reflect some sustained communication. However, there is no ability to demonstrate continued contact with them, since no journals or other records related to such exist.

George and his wife Christiana Bidlack Van Fleet had a total of eight children, all of whom survived. These children were:

01. Thomas Van Fleet, born 10 October 1823 in Galena, Ohio, married first Elizabeth Perfect and second Lucy Carpenter;

219

02. Alva Van Fleet, born 1830, married Caroline Vandermark, and died 5 October 1902 in Galena (note that his brother James had a son named Alva born in 1810);

03. John Van Fleet, birth unknown, married Rebecca McCabe on 4 October 1857;

04. Hiram Van Fleet, birth unknown, married 3 March 1857 to Thirza Bancroft;

05. James Van Fleet, born 1828 and died 1907 (named for George's brother);

06. Merritt Van Fleet, birth unknown and died in 1908 (a Civil War veteran with a name shared by a cousin in Fleetville, Pennsylvania);

07. Lydia Van Fleet, birth unknown, married John Huff on 1 January 1845; and

08. Eliza Van Fleet, birth unknown, married Harry Slack.

Much of the information on the children of this union, all of whom save one remained in the Galena area, is taken from Galena Cemetery records where George and Christiana Bidlack Van Fleet are buried.

The presence of several males in the saixth generation George Van Fleet line, who remained in central Ohio, is important in describing how that state came to have so many Van Fleets. This narrative, however, concentrates only on his son Thomas Van Fleet, who was born 10 October 1823 in Galena, the first child of this Van Fleet marriage.

Thomas attended school in Galena and helped in farm to age seventeen, when he began working at the joiner's trade with Warren Allen, John Cullison and a Sterns, for some four years. Being an adventuresome lad, in 1847 at age twenty-four he traveled to (perhaps southern) Illinois making fan mills for Thomas Phillips of Cincinnati.

In 1848, he went to Smith's Mills, Hopkinsville, Kentucky, where he engaged in the same activity and in passing made the acquaintance of then-Governor Powell. In 1849 he bought a team and went to Springfield, Missouri, where he stayed until 1852, engaged in the manufacture of fanning mills with Thaddeus Sharpenstine. But in that year, he returned to his home in Galena.

On 12 May 1852, Thomas Van Fleet married Elizabeth Perfect, who was born in 1825 the daughter of William Perfect. They traveled extensively in the 1850s, to Iowa, Missouri and Wisconsin, returning to Ohio to engage in the mercantile business as well as in milling in a partnership. Two years later after trading his shar eof the store, Thomas took full ownership of the mill, which was to be his major activity for the remainder of his life.

Thomas and Elizabeth had four children, including Lucy and Jay, both of whom died young, and Kate and Charlie, who survived to adulthood. Elizabeth died in a mill accident when her clothes became entangled in the machinery, and later in 1863 Thomas remarried.

Thomas' second wife was Lucy E. Carpenter, born 1832, a descendant of the same pioneer family – large in size – that had platted the community of Galena, and had opened a number of businesses. Thereafter, Thomas and Lucy had four children, all of whom survived, including: Nellie, who married Russell Bigelow; Frankie; James, who married Mary Leary; and Carpe (for Carpenter),who married Esther Smith.

In concluding comments on this branch of the Van Fleet family that take the reader into the Twentieth Century, it is difficult to speculate on the maintenance of family ties.

221

George Van Fleet left Pennsylvania presumably never to return. Yet, he named his children Alva(h) and James, the latter his brother's name and the former one of that brother's children. Other recurring names are themes in the family line, including Hiram, Thomas, Eliza and James, even in the context of the Joshua Van Fleet family.

What relationships were preserved over the years and few miles that separated these individuals, or letters perhaps, can only be thought about, since unfortunately no hard evidence exists on the durable linkages among these and other Van Fleets of the Nineteenth Century.

LEVI VAN FLEET (1793 – 1850)

Levi Van Fleet, a sixth generation American, was the son of Daniel Van Fleet Junior and his wife Martha Brown. He was born near Goshen, New York, in the general Minisink region, and at age seventeen relocated to upstate New York with his parents and siblings. They settled in the Cayuga County area of the Finger Lakes.

Levi served as a soldier in the War of 1812, not unlike so many others in upstate New York, living in close proximity to Canada. However, like others in the Daniel Van Fleet Junior family, son Levi was not to remain in this locale for long. Shortly after he married Mary Ann Smith somewhere near Syracuse, they relocated to Ohio.

A farmer by occupation, Levi was noted in the Seneca County Federal census of 1840, along with another of Daniel Van Fleet Junior's children, William (born 29 February 1779). He resided there for most of the decade of the 1830s, and perhaps arrived in Ohio somewhat earlier in the late 1820s before removing to present-day Fulton County, Ohio. He was there in Fulton in 1850, the year of his death, and is buried in the Raker Cemetery there.

Levi and Mary Ann Van Fleet hadseveral children, but all of their names may not be recorded for a lack of information.

Those children known to have been born to them include:

01. Rebecca Van Fleet, born 4 December 1822 at Syracuse, New York;
02. Henry Harrison Van Fleet, born 11 February 1825 in Cayuga County, New York; and
03. Garrett B. Van Fleet, probably born between 1827 and 1830.

Two other children may have been born to them; namely, Jefferson Van Fleet and Otis Van Fleet, based on the fact that they are recorded as living in Fulton County in Federal Census records as contemporaries of other Levi Van Fleet family members.

Henry Harrison Van Fleet, second of their known children, was born in Cayuga County, New York on 11 February 1825. On 13 June 1850, he married Ruth Strong, a daughter of Jesse and Sarah Myers Strong, who were from the Tiffin area in Seneca County, Ohio.

A daughter named Clara Virginia Van Fleet was born to them (date unknown), as well as a son Jesse LeGrande Van Fleet, who died young. Other children included:

04. Herbert Virgil Van Fleet, who relocated to Kansas by 1889;

05. Celia Irene Van Fleet, born 2 January 1855 and died 1 March 1889, having married George W. Tressler; and

06. Florence Van Fleet, born 1858, married Joel Smith and died at the young age twenty-six in 1884.

Like her husband Reverend Joel Smith, Florence was a missionary in China. She died very young, possibly of illness contracted there or possibly in childbirth, and was buried in Kinkiang Province near the Yangtze River. For reasons that are unknown, as a child she was reared by her aunt Rebecca Van Fleet Fowler rather than by her stepmother.

As implied by the above paragraph, Henry H. Van Fleet was left a young widower, and later remarried a second time. However, no children were born to this union, and those children by the first marriage were for the most part reared by his second wife.

JOSHUA VAN FLEET (1764 – 1848)

This chapter could well place the subject Joshua Van Fleet in New York or in Pennsylvania, but Ohio is selected because of his death there and the more important role that his children played vis-à-vis that state.

Joshua Van Fleet was an accomplished – yet for some family researchers, a problematical – member of the Van Fleet family. Born on 22 July 1764 in the Minisink region of Orange County, he was the son of Daniel Van Fleet Senior and his wife Sarah Cuddeback. He was a fifth generation American, descended from Adrian Gerritsen Van Vliet.

Joshua's arrived in the world in troubled times. He was born in the year following the end of the French and Indian War, a conflict that had dire consequences for the people of the Minisink Valley and portends of even worse times for disenfranchised Indians ahead. The Minisink had been raided by French allied Indians who ravaged the frontier lands of New York. The horrors of the times might best be understood by viewing Hollywood's film "The Last of the Mohicans."

By the time Joshua reached his teenage years, by 1775 America was already engaged in conflict with Great Britain. His older brother Daniel and his elderly grandfather Jan Van Vliet Junior had signed declarations against the English. Within just a few years his father and brothers Daniel and Abraham would be in arms against the Crown.

In July 1779 some four years after the outbreak of hostilities, the Minisink region was again aflame, this time torched by the British and their Indian allies. It was at this time that Joshua enlisted in the service of the American Revolution, at age fifteen.

Joshua's service lasted over some three years' time in the New York Troops. He enlisted in 1779 as a private for one month under Lieutenant Tryon, and was drafted on 1 June 1780, serving eighteen days in Captain Shepard's Company in Colonel Wisner's Regiment. He enlisted on 10 June 1781 for six months in Colonel Wessenfel's Regiment, and then was discharged at Albany.

Following the War, he returned to the Minisink region and in 1784, he relocated to the Wyoming Valley of Pennsylvania. The connection here with his sister Marya and her husband John Kennedy is noteworthy. For Marya and John were pre-Revolutionary War settlers in the Wyoming Valley. In the Wyoming Massacre, their daughter is mentioned (as Mrs. Cornelius [Catherine] Courtwright) as fleeing Wilkes-Barre, and her mother as helping people along the way to the relative safety of the Minisink.

Indeed, when Joshua filed his pension papers in Ontario County, New York, in 1832, he stated that although born in the Minisink, he had lived in "his father's house" in Wilkes-Barre, "until the troubles" which referred to the burning of "Yankee" homes in July 1784. He was not married at that time, so his reference was not to a father-in-law, but likely to Daniel Van Fleet Senior, his natural father, who is believed to have relocated (if ever so) briefly in the Wyoming Valley with his daughter, her husband and family, as well as other relatives. These ultimately would have included – in addition to the above – two sons, Abraham as well as Joshua.

John Kennedy lost his wife Marya in the mid-1780s, and then married Margaret Armstrong Van Vliet, widow of Joseph Van Vliet of that family that settled in the Delaware Valley.

226

They returned to the Wilkes-Barre area not later than 1787, since he was listed on a jury roster on 4 September 1787 for Nescopeck Township. It is possible that the Kennedy home in Wilkes-Barre that was known to have been spared destruction during the Wyoming Massacre, was burned by the Pennamites in 1784 marking the time John Kennedy reclaimed his stake in the area, and causing him to relocate to Nescopeck.

The Susquehanna Land Company records make various references to both Joshua and Abraham Van Fleet from 1784 through the late 1780s. These state that on 18 October 1784, Joshua and three others were fired upon at Jacob's Plains by thirteen men of "Armstrong's Party," a group of Pennamites, and the four escaped by fording the river. Then, Joshua signed a 20 February 1785 petition for protection from the Pennamites by the Pennsylvania state legislature, and on 24 May 1786, he entered into the 24 December 1785 "recognizance" along with various others, including Benjamin Bidlack and Elisha Decker (it being noted here that later nephew George Van Fleet would marry a Bidlack).

On 1 February 1787, Joshua Van Fleet, "husbandman," signed an oath of allegiance to Pennsylvania at Wilkes-Barre, and on 21 April 1787, Abraham signed the oath to support the laws of Pennsylvania, both doing so at Jacob's Plains (then an extension of Wilkes-Barre and today known simply as Plains). Joshua and Abraham both signed an 18 September 1787 complaint against a Pennamite agent by the name of William Montgomery. Other complaint signers included Benjamin Bidlack and Moses Roberts, Joshua's father-in-law in the latter case and later the father-in-law of Abraham's son George in the former.

227

The Luzerne County Grantor Index to Deeds (Number 1) states that Joshua Van Fleet sold land in Athens Township, present-day Bradford County, on the Susquehanna River near the New York state border. That occurred on 2 January 1790, the sale being to Putnam Catlin (the deed was recorded 19 April 1796).

In 1785, Joshua married Sabra Roberts, whose family had also come from Orange County to the Wyoming Valley a short time earlier. Her father was Moses Roberts, who – along with various other family members – fought in the Revolutionary War, and as luck would have it, also against the Pennamites as a matterof survival in that region.

The 1910 HISTORY OF HARDIN COUNTY (Ohio) stated that Joshua and Sabra Van Fleet had fourteen children, nine sons and five daughters. It also noted that Sabra died 21 November 1813, but this is incorrect. The ONTARIO REPOSITORY, a newspaper in Canandaigua, New York, that served the region where she and Joshua were living at the time, stated correctly in an obituary that she died on 29 August 1817.

The Hardin County history did, however, note correctly that he later married Elizabeth Brady Odell, who was a widow, and that said union took place 26 January 1819. It further noted, again correctly, that she was one "by whom he had no children."

A small book entitled THE READY RECKONER that Joshua Van Fleet kept contained a flyleaf on which he listed the names (and provided several notations) regarding his children. These were:

01.   Mofe (Moses) Van Fleet, born Tuesday, 28 March 1787, named for his father-in-law, married a Truelove, died 23 August 1855 at Big Island, Ohio;

228

02.   Mary Van Fleet, born Saturday, 16 August 1788, married Paul White, died 16 October 1850 at Big Island;

03.   Joshua Van Fleet Junior, born Monday, 6 February 1790, married Susan Nichols first, _____ Fay second, and Susan Frost third, and died in Moultrie County, Illinois, 13 December 1860;

04.   Ruth Van Fleet, born 31 Septembeer 1791, married David Reed, died childless 3 February 1849;

05.   John Van Fleet, born 3 October 1793, died 23 September 1796, likely named for his grandfather;

06.   We-enthroegh (sic) Van Fleet, born 15 December 1795 and died 7 October 1796;

07.   John Kennedy Van Fleet, born Saturday 20 February 1798 and died 26 October 1844, being named for his Joshua's brother-in-law, married Nancy Brady (died 20 October 1827) and then Sarah Avery 14 January 1829, and he then died 8 January 1849 (and when his father's estate was settled his family of seven children was largely in Steuben County, Indiana);

08.   Miles Wilkinson Van Fleet, born 30 April 1805, married Elvira Caroline Knapp (died 19 April 1837) and then Nancy Wright on 9 September 1838 and then Elizabeth Lester, and died 11 April 1892;

09.   Samantha Van Fleet, born Tuesday 4 November 1807;

10.   Sabra Van Fleet, born 11 June 1809 and died 9 September 1817;

11.   Thomas Van Fleet, born Sunday 19 August 1810 and died 28 August 1817;

12.   Cynthia Van Fleet, born 3 September 1812;

13.   Henry   Van   Fleet,   born   Thursday,   23
February 1813 and died 29 August 1817.

Sabra Roberts Van Fleet died at age forty-eight on 29 August 1817, according to local newspaper notices. Her death was within days of one, and hours of two of her youngest children; that is, Sabra (age eight), Thomas (age seven) and Henry (age four). Undoubtedly, they all died of the same disease, possibly cholera, given the time of the year noted.

The listed children do not total fourteen, and one name is known to be missing; that is, James (who married Elizabeth King). References are made to this son in the settlement of Joshua's estate, as is related later, as the child who brought suit for his share in same.

James Van Fleet resided in Hart County, Kentucky, and was recorded there in the 1820s and in the 1830 census. He is noted as Joshua's son in Commonwealth records, with specific reference to Hart County historical accounts.

The second marriage of Joshua to Elizabeth Brady Odell in 1819 lasted for the remainder of her life. She died on 1 March 1842 at age sixty-nine, some six years or so after she and her husband relocated to Marion County, Ohio. As is noted, he followed her in death somewhat less than six years later.

The first six or seven of Joshua and Sabra Van Fleet's children were born in Pennsylvania in the greater Luzerne County area, including the seventh in that state's northernmost reaches, around Tioga. Joshua left the lower Wyoming Valley to resettle in the upper reaches of the Susquehanna River near the New York state border, around 1790. The family then abandoned the Athens Township area by early 1800, at least in time to be counted in the Federal Census in central New York that summer.

These facts are entirely consistent with Joshua's pension papers that aver that he lived in the Wilkes-Barre area for five years (1784 to 1789), then Tioga, and then in Manchester for thirty-five years (meaning until 1836, according to the pension and court records).

Joshua settled for the longest single period of his life in Manchester, Ontario County, and came to be one of the region's most notable citizens. Prior to the tragic loss of his first wife and several children, he served as a member of the New York state legislature for several years, being elected in 1812 and again in 1814. He was also elected to the constitutional convention in 1821, and served on the committee that drafted the provisions to permanently abolish slavery in the state (having been eliminated by statute in 1817).

Joshua Van Fleet

231

Additionally, he served as a county court judge for some years, although the exact length of this service is undetermined. His election to office and to the bench were reflections of his dedicated involvement in the Democrat Party during most of his life, as clearly indicated by the constant reporting on him in the local newspapers.

There is another dimension to Joshua Van Fleet's military service to his country, that being a reported three month stint in the New York Militia during the War of 1812. Reputedly, he held the rank of colonel, and later in life was addressed with that honorific.

Joshua, like his relatives in Pennsylvania, was a member of the Universalist church. This fact is of some special interest, because that was the religious faith of the Joseph Smith family before their (short-lived) adherence to Methodism and then to what became known as the Mormon church.

They attended the same (and only) Universalist church in Ontario County. That now brings this narration to a point where the Van Fleet family connection to the Latter Day Saints religion should be related. It is more than a colorful anecdote, and has come down through Joshua's grandson Alford White.

Being a prominent and relatively prosperous citizen of the Manchester area in Ontario County, Joshua was approached by Joseph Smith, his colleague Sidney Rigdon (he being a defrocked Baptist minister), and one other unidentified person (likely Oliver Chowdry or more remotely Martin Harris), shortly after the claimed visit to Joseph by the Angel Moroni, when he was shown the burial site of the Golden Tablets on the Hill Cumorah.

Joseph Smith, Sidney Rigdon and their associate visited Joshua to seek his help in financing the publication of the translation of the Golden Tablets. Joshua was quite familiar with the Smith family that lived less than seven miles away, and even more so with the Hill Cumorah where the tablets were said to be found, since it was equidistant between his home and theirs.

However, this familiarity with the Smiths and some of their questionable dealings led Joshua to only consider paying for the publication, on condition that he see these tablets for himself. As his grandson wrote, "They came to Joshua's home with a box about thirty inches long and twelve inches square, covered with a black cloth. When Joshua asked these men to see the Golden Tablets, Smith said, 'Oh, no! No man must look upon these plates but me.'"

Joshua then slapped his hand down on the top of the box. The three men jumped on him, whereupon grandson Alford and Joshua began struggling with the three, who retreated with their treasure. Joshua was thereafter to note with frequency that when he slapped his hand down on the box, it felt like it was full of sawdust, ashes or sand.

It was sometime early in 1836 in all likelihood that Joshua left New York state for Ohio. His pension papers make Ontario County notations for the fall of 1832, the year he filed a claim under a June 1832 Congressional Pension Act, and continue with the last date being at the end of 1835, within a short time of his quitting the state. The pension issue is resumed and documented further in Marion County, Ohio, with a date of 1836 when he appeared in court, requesting the transfer of his claim to that jurisdiction, fixing his arrival in Ohio.

Joshua cited his reasons for being in Ohio in those court records, an advanced age being evident, as a desire to be near his children. Indeed, at the time that he appeared in Marion County court, his sons Miles, Joshua Junior, John Kennedy and Moses Van Fleet were all well established there, having arrived somewhat earlier and over a period of years from 1828 through at least 1831. Son James had gone to Kentucky quite some time before, probably as early as 1817 or 1819. Several daughters were also in Ohio, all within a few miles of other family members.

Marion County is located north of present-day Columbus. The county is contiguous to Delaware County, where George Van Fleet, son of Abraham and nephew of Joshua, had settled in 1818, and within a few miles of Seneca County where the sons of Daniel Van Fleet Junior, Levi and William, were living (both in Tiffin, then called Scioto Township).

In the 1840 census, there were twelve others listed as heads of households under the surname Van Fleet, and there is a close family relationship among at least seven. Others are distant relatives from the New Jersey Frederick Van Fleet and from the Dirck Van der Vliedt lines in that state as well.

In beginning this commentary, it was mentioned that Joshua Van Fleet was enigmatic for some researchers. This is partly because his origins are not church-recorded, possibly given the problems within the Dutch Reformed community at the time of his birth. Additionally, he is reported in some sources as being of a "Holland Dutch" (as opposed to German "Dutch") background, which is correct but misinterpreted to mean he came from Holland. In fact ,some centenary publications aver he arrived in America with a brother (Jan or James) at age twelve. The truth is much more mundane.

234

Joshua was born in the Minisink, according to government records and his sworn court testimony in pension papers. He did not immigrate to America at age twelve. To assume he would lie about that, given his past military service, occupancy of the bench and years in the state legislature, is to do him grave injustice. Indeed, local Minisink area Dutch Reformed Church records exist which *may* show he was the son of Daniel Van Fleet Senior, grandson of Jan (or John) Van Vliet Junior, and great-grandson of Jan Van Vliet Senior, who coincidentally arrived in America from Holland at age twelve. And too, he was the great-great grandson of Adrian Gerritsen Van Vliet, an adventurous, pioneering early "Knickerbocker" colonist who established a great line in America.

He likely never spoke Dutch fluently, in contrast to all of his ancestors and many in the community in which he was reared, but he would have had some familiarity with that language through church connections as well as the community, using common expressions of the Minisink in his idiom. Such linguistic traits lingered long in the isolation of the Minisink, as indeed they did even in the more sophisticated reaches of the Hudson Valley, where Theodore Roosevelt's mother continued to speak Dutch until the 1840s.

It should not escape researchers either, that Joshua never used the name Van Vliet (in enlistment papers, for example, and later in life), which is Dutch, but rather always the anglicized "Van Fleet" form then being employed by some (like Daniel Van Fleet Senior) other young and contemporary – but far from all – of that Van Vliet family in the area. As a recent immigrant, he would never have instantly "changed" this honored and noble name.

Lastly, there simply was no Dutch immigration to English controlled America at the time Joshua allegedly arrived, as any scholar will assert. If any did occur, it would never have been to so backwater an area as the distant and dangerous Minisink Valley, let alone even to the colonies which were already at war when Joshua was twelve years old.

Joshua is thought by some to have been the father of two children by his second wife, but clearly this is not the case. Both her age when one (by the name of William) would have been born 00 some sixty years – pushes even the plausible into something for the Nineteenth Century medical record books. Moreover, there is no evidence to support this assertion, but there is historical documentation to refute that claim. Again, the middle of stories not transcribed nearer the time of the events reported, yields errors and skips generations in the retelling.

How do we substantiate the flow of statements relating to events in the life of Joshua Van Fleet? In addition to the contemporary newspaper reports from Ontario County; published county histories in Ontario (New York), Hardin and Marion Counties (Ohio); pension papers and court proceedings in New York; and official state histories of Pennsylvania, Ohio and New York, there is also the matter of Joshua's estate, settled in court in Marion, Ohio, in 1849.

Apparently, Joshua's death in January 1848 touched off a conflict between his son James, who lived in Kentucky, and James brother Moses, over the distribution of shares from the inheritance. Marion County court action settled the matter and in court reports named all heirs to Joshua Van Fleet's estate.

These persons included five surviving children, with daughter Ruth having been noted as deceased with heirs of her body in 1849 before probate, and John Kennedy Van Fleet as long deceased, with seven heirs of his body (Joshua's grandchildren) inheriting their father's share. No son by the name of William is mentioned, but Joshua Van Fleet Junior was cited as living in Coles County, Illinois, and was listed as an heir to Joshua's estate.

There is great importance to unraveling whatever mystery there is to Joshua's life and times in this document, because the Van Fleet descent of many depends on it. Indeed, often that which is left unsaid or unwritten speaks as much as that which is stated or recorded. This probate document clearly identifies who was a child of Joshua Van Fleet Senior and who was not, in addition to providing information on yet another of his line; that is, John K. Van Fleet's seven children.

The truth of Joshua Van Fleet is a simple one. He grew up in the Dutch and English provincial and sheltered family-oriented world of the Minisink. He served honorably as a very young man in the American Revolution. He pioneered in the Wyoming Valley with other family members and then in Tioga with his own young family. He removed to Manchester and lived a highly productive life in farming, community affairs, the law and state government.

Joshua then retired to spend his declining years in Ohio, near several of his surviving children, a man of some substance in worldly possessions. He died in 1848, was buried in Pleasant Hills' Cemetery near the City of Marion, and is remembered appropriately as a distinguished American in the histories of Pennsylvania, New York and Ohio.

MILES WILKINSON VAN FLEET (1805 – 1892)

Miles Van Fleet was one of the younger children born to Joshua and Sabra Roberts Van Fleet, after their relocation to upstate New York. He lived in the Manchester, Ontario County area until removing to Ohio with several of his siblings in the 1828 to 1831 period, as a young man.

Unlike his brothers John Kennedy, James and Joshua Van Fleet Junior, he was sufficiently content to stay in Ohio for the duration of his life. Consequently, there are members of the Van Fleet family today in that state that trace their descent to him.

Miles Van Fleet farmed in Marion County and in Hardin County as well, and married three times. His first wife was Evelyn Caroline Knapp, daughter of John and Melinda Knapp. She was from Warsaw, New York.

This marriage took place in 1831 when he was twenty-six, and is the year that he removed to Ohio, where he acquired land.

He and Evelyn Caroline Knapp Van Fleet had two children.

These were:

01. Lucy Ann Van Fleet, married J.W. Bartram of Hardin County on 20 October 1835; and

02. Henry Theodore Van Fleet, born 9 March 1837 in Big Island.

His daughter Lucy married into a well-known and wealthy family, and his son Henry T. became a prominent local attorney.

Miles was widowed early in life, and married a second time to Nancy White in 1842. Apparently, she too died not long afterwards, and he married a third time sometime in 1851 to Elizabeth Lester. He died in Ohio in 1892 and is buried there.

HENRY THEODORE VAN FLEET (1837 – 1891)

Henry T. Van Fleet was the son of Miles Wilkinson and his wife Caroline Knapp Van Fleet. He was born in Ohio at Big Island on 9 March 1837, not far from his grandfather Joshua Van Fleet Senior's home, and as such was a seventh generation American.

Henry was reared in Hardin County on the family farm, attending schools in Bellefontaine and in Marion County as well. After teaching for several years, he took a commercial course in Marion, and then read law with Judge John Bartram, of the family of his sister's in-laws. On 16 June 1860, he was admitted to the state bar of Ohio.

Henry T. Van Fleet practiced law until 1862 when he joined the Ohio Volunteers as a second lieutenant. He served until 10 January 1863 when he resigned due to ill health. He returned to Ohio and practiced law. He engaged in criminal law for some years before moving into civil law as a principal activity, engaging in litigation in state and federal courts.

An active member of the Democrat Party, Henry T. Van Fleet was known as a "stump speaker" for their candidates, and was nominated for a state senate seat in addition to serving as a delegate to state and national conventions. However, in Republican dominated Ohio, he was an unsuccessful office seeker.

On 29 September 1861, Henry T. married Eleanor S. Shields, daughter of M.P. Shields of Marion County. They had only one child, a son named George Henry Van Fleet. George graduated from nearby Ohio Wesleyan, and then became a prominent attorney as well.

Additionally, George wrote for and then edited the Marion (Weekly) Star in the City of Marion, beginning in 1885. This newspaper was owned by his close friend Warren G. Harding, and this relationship was noted years later in a conversation with General James A. Van Fleet. Obviously though, there was a change of political loyalty in this part of the Van Fleet family.

Henry T. Van Fleet, like his father, was also a farmer. His main activity was in stock raising. However, his pursuits were numerous and in addition to farming, the law and editing, he raised funds for railroad construction. A man of some wealth and of great social standing, he is remembered in Marion County history, where he died 26 November 1891 and is buried.

Henry T. Van Fleet

They Were Not All Generals: A Private's Story

This commentator has been fascinated by Ohio's history, inasmuch as that state seemed to be the "American melting pot" for Van Fleets from various New York, New Jersey and Pennsylvania branches, who established deep roots there in some cases, or who again relocated to found others across the country.

The notation of a "General Henry C. Van Fleet" house, one of the beautiful Federal period "variation on the Greek temple plan" Nineteenth Century homes in historic Maumee on the Maumee River, Lucas County, was particularly interesting. In tracing Henry C., several things were discovered. He was a descendant of the Dirck Jans Van der Vliedt line, like others in the Maumee and Watertown areas; and he was also a private in the American Civil War.

More importantly, as a young soldier he was captured by Confederate forces, imprisoned for a while in a Richmond tobacco warehouse and then transferred, ultimately being incarcerated in the infamous Andersonville Prison.

When freed, he was a passanger aboard the "Sultana," a paddlewheel steamboat that overloaded as it was with former Union prisoners, was making its way north (and home) when its boiler blew up.

About 1,700 soldiers were killed in this greatest American maritime disaster of all times, but Henry C. Van Fleet – scalded and initially left for dead – survived (but just barely) his injuries.

Henry C. Van Fleet returned home to Maumee and lived a long and fruitful life, being given the honorific for his sacrifices to the American Union of "General."

Sultana - Appalling Steamboat Disaster

A PORTRAIT OF MICHIGAN

Lands constituting Michigan were first visited by European explorers from France in 1616. In 1641, fur trading began with the French, who later established their first settlement in this territory in 1668.

Given its strategic location, following the French and Indian War in 1756 to 1763, all of French Canada was ceded to Britain. Much as the French had utilized the services of the Indian population for fur trading and as allies in war, the British enlisted the aid of the indigenous peoples during the American Revolution and again in the War of 1812. In the interim years, Indians were defeated at the Battle of Fallen Timbers in Ohio by "Mad" Anthony Wayne, in 1794.

In the second confrontation, the British seized Fort Mackinac and Fort Dearborn (Detroit) from the Americans. However, Oliver H. Perry's Lake Erie naval victory and William Henry Harrison's land victories, by 1813, carried the war well into Canada, rendering British interests in Michigan useless.

Michigan became the twenty-sixth state in the American Union on 26 January 1837, during Andrew Jackson's presidency. Some years earlier the struggle with Ohioans over the border was settled in favor of Ohio.

Van Fleets played an important role in this event as Ohio militia agents of that state's Governor Lucas. The struggle for control of a small strip of land along the Maumee River determined the actual configuration of the "Wolverine State" when the Upper Peninsula was added to its territory as compensation for the loss of present-day Lucas County, Ohio.

Although it has 56,809 square miles of land, its total territory including water makes Michigan rank as the eleventh largest state. Its population was just 212,267 in 1840, three years after statehood, but by the outbreak of the American Civil War, it was nearly four times that size, being expanded by large numbers of European immigrants. Today it is the eighth most populous state in the country.

What Brought Van Fleets/Van Vliets/Van Vleets to Michigan?

Once again, the continual search for inexpensive land in suitable farming areas enticed this family, like countless others from eastern states, to migrate to Michigan.

With vast areas in the Lower Peninsula with fertile and well-watered land on reasonably flat plains, this locale was determined to be perfect for farming. Additionally, Michigan is rich in forestry resources and proved to be fruitful for orchard-related production as well as vineyards.

Indeed, those same characteristics enticed many Europeans to immigrate during the Nineteenth Century, including large numbers from Holland in the middle of the 1800s. Among those were Van Vliets, most of whom retained their surname causing some confusion between Van Vliets descended from Adrian Gerritsen and Dirck Jans Van (der) Vliet. These newer immigrants are jokingly described by this commentator as "the latter day Dutch" versus the Hudson Valley Dutch.

The lines of the Van Fleets in Michigan can be traced through several families, one of the Adrian Gerritsen Van Vliet line and the other of the Dirck Van der Vliedt line.

PETER P. VAN VLEET (1765 – 1820)

The Van Vliet name in America has undergone several changes or variations, reflecting spellings and pronunciations current in a given region. As indicated, Jan Van Vliet Senior's son Frederick (nee) Van Vliet relocated to New Jersey and the family name generally became the anglicized "Van Fleet." However, not all members of this family utilized that particular spelling.

A variation on the Van Vliet name was Van Vleet, introduced in New Jersey, New York, Ohio and Michigan, probably before being found elsewhere in the country, through Dirck Adriansen Van Vliet's New Jersey line.

His son by Judith Van Neste was Gerrit Van Vliet, born 17 June 1697, and grandson Willem Van Vliet, born 16 August 1730. In turn, William's son by Adriantje Wykoff was Peter P. Van Vleet – his spelling – who was born 4 October 1765. He lived in New Jersey's general Minisink region, where like New York, the events of the Revolutionary War caused great local disruption.

Following the march of General Sullivan against hostile Seneca Indians of the Iroquois Nation in New York, after their devastating raids in the Minisink in July 1779, soldiers returning to Orange and adjacent counties told stories about the wonderfully fertile lands and rolling forests of the upstate "Lake Country." Many of the settlers of the Minisink region were sufficiently inspired by these tales that a migration further into northwest New York began.

In 1794, Peter P. Van Vleet – as he was spelling his name in simplified fashion from "Vliet" – and his wife Mary Blue, along with their sons Jared and Ezekiel, started out for the fabled Lake Country.

Carrying all of their worldly possessions on a single wagon drawn by two cows, their "draft animals" did double duty, furnishing milk for the family as well as drayage for their goods.

The trip took six weeks over a so-called improved road, that in fact was an Indian trail only slightly widened and leveled in spots. This was then known as the southern route, and followed the waters of the Susquehanna and Tioga Rivers to Newton, now called Elmira. There they left the rivers and turned north following Indian trails to what is present-day Seneca County, New York.

On arrival in these forested lands, the first weeks were spent with the wagon turned upside down to provide shelter and protection while some land was cleared and a cabin built, just north of the village now called Lodi. A deed was recorded on 13 May 1797 for one hundred and twenty acres.

On 8 December 1802 Peter and Mary Van Vleet bought from Joshua Wykoff some two hundred and five acres, located about a mile south of Lodi. The site is marked today by the remnants of some family graves.

It is apparent that the Van Vleet family took an active part in the development of the Lodi community. They were one of the first families to come to this wilderness area, and not unexpectedly Peter ran for local office. He was elected constable of the town in March 1804.

Both Peter and Mary Blue Van Vleet died in Lodi and are buried there in the local cemetery. Their children remained in the region for a while, before scattering to other locales in America.

Peter was born or perhaps baptized 17 December 1765 in Somerset County, New Jersey. Mary Blue was born 1 September 1770 and was baptized in October in the Harlingen Dutch Reformed Church.

246

Following their marriage, Peter and Mary had twelve children, who were:

01. Jared Van Vleet, born 2 March 1791, married first Dolly Swartout (sic) who was born 1791 and died 1835, second Clarissa Clarkson (born 1799 and died 1882), and died 23 November 1876, being buried on the family farm at Kendaia, New York;

02. Ezekiel Blue Van Vleet, born 31 March 1793, married Jemima Townsend (born 19 August 1797 and died 26 January 1863), and died 22 September 1825;

03. George Van Vleet, born 4 September 1795, married Helen Merrill (born 26 October 1789 and died 7 June 1872), and died 27 January 1878, and is buried near Newfane and Olcott, New York;

04. Isaac Van Vleet, born 24 May 1797 and died 24 October 1825, and is buried in Lodi Cemetery;

05. Peter P. Van Vleet, born 23 February 1799, married Lois Swartout, sister of Dolly (born 2 February 1802 and died 2 July 1878), removed to Ridgeway, Michigan, and died 21 January 1879 leaving descendants Harley and Glenn Van Vleet;

06. Hannah Van Vleet, born 1800 and married Abraham Cadmus, lived in Michigan and had four children, dying there in 1878;

07. David Van Vleet, born 1802 and died 1874;

08. James Van Vleet, born 1803, married Elizabeth ____ (who died 26 October 1825 and is buried in Lodi), then Betsy Russell, died 1882 and is buried in Reynoldsville, New York;

09. Patty Van Vleet, born in 1806, died in Ridgeway, Michigan on 31 March 1882;

10. Mary Van Vleet, born 6 June 1807 and died in Dexter, Michigan in 1889;

11. John Van Vleet, born 25 June 1809 and died in 1858, and is buried in Newton Cemetery, Calhoun County, Michigan; and

12. Rubin Van Vleet, born 1812 and died 1892.

Jared Van Vleet married Dolly Swartout first and then Clarissa Clarkson. His children included Peter J. Van Vleet, born 1815 and died 1910. In turn, Peter's children were: Ann Van Vleet, Clara Van Vleet, Emma G. Van Vleet, Anna Van Vleet, Charles Van Vleet, Samuel Van Vleet, and Edward Van Vleet.

Jared's second child was James Van Vleet, who married Mary Ann Cooley and then Sarah Witmore. James' children were: Albert B. Van Vleet, Ann Elizabeth Van Vleet, Jared Van Vleet, and John Van Vleet, all of whom resided in Michigan.

Jared's third child was Barney Van Vleet, who married Caroline P. _____ first, and Jane Gilligan second, and had one child by each; namely and respectively, Edward Y. Van Vleet (died young) and Clark Van Vleet.

Jared's fifth child (his fourth, Coe, has no records) was Montgomery Van Vleet, who married Jane Brooks and removed to Peoria, Illinois.

Jared's sixth child, son Edward Van Vleet, married Helen Dunlap, and lived his life in Ovid and Interlaken, New York.

Jared's seventh child, son Jared Van Vleet Junior, died a year after his birth, but the eighth child, Ethan Watson Van Vleet, married Mary Swartout and lived in Plymouth, Michigan, having children Mary D. Van Vleet (remained in New York state), Edmont Van Vleet, George Van Vleet, Amy Van Vleet, William Robert Van Vleet (went to Denver) and Richard L. Van Vleet (went to New York City).

Jared's ninth child, son Anthony Van Vleet, married Hannah Mitchell, and had children Fred, Grace and Roy Van Vleet. Anthony Van Vleet operated a stage coach in Aurora, Illinois.

Curiously, daughters Mary Jane Van Vleet by Jared's first marriage, and Rachael Van Vleet, Clara Van Vleet and Caroline Van Vleet all by his second, did not produce children.

In moving to the next generation, Edward Van Vleet, the sixth child of Jared and Dolly Van Vleet, and his wife Helen Dunlap Van Vleet, lived their lives in Romulus, New York, and are buried in Union Cemetery in Ovid.

Their children were:

01. Henry Judson Van Vleet, born 29 July 1856, married Mary Helen Stout (born 25 July 1855 and died 2 May 1937), and died 22 October 1940;

02. Fred J. Van Vleet, born 25 May 1855 and died 7 July the same year;

03. Libby Van Vleet, born 20 January 1860 and died 18 September 1865; and

04. Carrie and Cora Van Vleet, twins born in August 1868 and died 9 September 1869.

In the following generation, Henry Judson Van Vleet carried on the family name. As indicated, he was born in 1856 and married Mary Helen Stout on 31 December 1883 at age twenty-seven.

They had the following children:

01. Jay Stout Van Vleet, born 20 January 1887, married Lilian Nicholson on 18 December 1906;

02. Henry Lee Van Vleet, born 11 November 1891, married Edna Cassidy and died 8 April 1941;

249

03. Clarence J. Van Vleet, born 8 December 1893, married Marguerite Miles on 22 August 1922, and then Florence Finn on 12 June 1928;

04. Eva Van Vleet, born 6 July 1895 and died September 1918;

05. Edward Ashley Van Vleet, born 10 October 1899, married Ruth V. Engel on 19 November 1921; and

06. Mary Helen Van Vleet, born 7 June 1901, married Herbert L. Walthart on 7 August 1926, and died 3 February 1961.

Jay S., Henry L. and Edward A. Van Vleet married and had families that continue the Van Vleet name today in Michigan and elsewhere. Their respective families are as follows.

Jay Stout and Lilian Nicholson Van Vleet had the following children:

01. Gladys S. Van Vleet, born 14 March 1909, married first Harry Washburn and had a son Keith, and second married William Farnam (Jim);

02. George Van Vleet, born 13 July 1913, married Mary Marshall 29 June 1935 and had children Martin George (born 1936), Peter Jay (born 26 June 1939 and died in the United States Air Force in Bamburg, Germany on 23 October 1962), Mary Gretchen (born 1944) and Bruce Edward (born 1945) Van Vleet;

03. Clive Van Vleet, born 25 December 1915 and married Jean Hiller;

04. Jessie Van Vleet, born 18 October 1918 and married Jack Guyer in 1941; and

05. Arthur Van Vleet, born 7 December 1924, married Doris Ticknor and had children Alan (born 18 December 1948), Eric (born 11 June 1950) and Karen (born 7 March 1952) Van Vleet.

Henry Lee and Edna Cassidy Van Vleet had the following children:

01. Orpha Priscilla Van Vleet, born 15 November 1916, married Jack Scanlon and had one son, Lea;

02. Vivian Edna Van Vleet, born 31 July 1918, married William Hadden in 1939, and had one son Gary Harrison;

03. Henry Lee Van Vleet Junior, born 24 April 1920, married Ruth Clark and had three sons, James Van Vleet (born 14 December 1950 in Japan), Michael E. Van Vleet (born 20 August 1951), and Gordon B. Van Vleet (born 20 March 1957), and retired from the United States Air Force as a major;

04. Mary Jane Van Vleet, born 25 March 1923 and died 21 February 1928 of diphtheria;

05. Charles Cassidy Van Vleet, born 2 June 1928, married Alice LaVigne and had three sons, Phillip Van Vleet (born 22 March 1953), Charles C. Van Fleet Junior (born 16 February 1958) and William J. Van Vleet (born 5 March 1963); and

06. David Van Vleet, dentist, born 16 December 1931, married Norma Husted on 17 November 1951, and had children Nancy Lynn Van Vleet (born 31 March 1953), David Eric Van Vleet (born 22 February 1961) and Lee Morris Van Vleet (born 25 March 1966).

The youngest brother, Edward A. and his wife Ruth Van Vleet had the following children:

251

01. Edward Ashley Van Vleet, died at six days;
02. Gerald Engel Van Vleet, born 15 October 1923, married Janet Sutton and had children Gersen Lee Van Vleet (born 15 May 1944) and David Sutton Van Vleet (born 7 April 1948); and
03. Dorothy Anne Van Vleet, born 4 June 1935, married Floyd Hicks in 1950 and had two children, Judith Anne Hicks (born 15 September 1957) and Thomas Jay Hicks (born 13 March 1960).

The Van Vleet Cocktail

Jay Preston, a contributor to this commentary, reported that his daughter brought back maple syrup from Indiana. Wondering about the uses to which this product could be put, he was surprised to find two entires on a website for a "Van Vleet Cocktail," one in Dutch and another in English.

1 ounce of lemon juice plus 1 ounce of maple syrup plus 3 ounces of rum. Shake with ice and pour into an old fashion glass.

Enjoy yourself and toast to your Dutch ancestors!

A PORTRAIT OF INDIANA

Although Indiana is home to some of the largest Indian mounds in North America that date from a long-lost thousand year old civilization, for Europeans the first knowledge of the area came through explorations of the French in the Seventeenth Century. However, it was not until 1731 or 1732 that a trading post was built at Vincennes, although Pierre LaSalle had visited the present-day South Bend region as early as 1679 and again in 1681.

As a result of the French and Indian War, France, which had claims in the area, ceded the Indiana territory to the English in 1763. In turn, the English ceded the region to the United States, following the Revolutionary War peace settlement in Paris.

During the War of Independence, the British had been defeated by American forces under General George Rogers Clark at Vincennes in 1778, and elsewhere in the area a year later, effectively ending English control of today's Indiana.

Following the Revolutionary War, hostilities continued with the Miami Indians who defeated American forces twice in 1790. However, at the decisive Battle of Fallen Timbers in 1794, General "Mad" Anthony Wayne was victorious, and later at Tippecanoe in 1811, General William Henry Harrison crushed the threat of the Indian Confederation under the leadership of Tecumseh.

Some five years later on 11 December 1816, Indiana was welcomed as the nineteenth state in the American Union. With a total of 36,420 square miles, it ranks as the country's thirty-eighth largest. In population it had 75,000 inhabitants in 1816.

253

That number however increased dramatically, and in 1840 – the census year closest to the arrival of the first Van Fleets – the population had jumped to 685,866. Indiana was the tenth most populous state in the Union in that year.

What Brought Van Fleets to Indiana?

John Kennedy Van Fleet is the first known member of this family to settle in the state. He relocated with his family to Indiana in the second half of the 1830s, likely during the last years of Andrew Jackson's presidency.

Indiana was still undergoing rapid settlement, and their selection of Steuben County in the state's northeast corner abutting Michigan to the north and Ohio to the east was undoubtedly because of the availability of inexpensive and fertile land for farming, John Kennedy Van Fleet's occupation.

Earlier this man had been well settled in Kentucky and for a period of time in Ohio as well. He left behind a sizable and seemingly close family in central Ohio for the uncertainties of Indiana, scarcely a decade after settling in the Buckeye State where so many of his siblings – and by then his father as well – were located.

Some of the family members remained in Indiana after the early death of John Kennedy, and in all probability there remains a vestige of Van Fleets living there that can trace their line of descent through him.

However, none lives in the Steuben County area today, and those elsewhere and others interested in the Van Fleet genealogy will have to trace their line through other and hopefully more thoroughly detailed sources.

JOHN KENNEDY VAN FLEET (1793 – 1845)

The linkage between Joshua Van Fleet and his Aunt Marya and her husband John Kennedy is clearly demonstrated in the naming of a son for this uncle by marriage. John Kennedy continued to be a close friend and helper for young Joshua in the Wyoming Valley, and for his brother Abraham as well, although his wife Marya in fact died just around the time of their arrival in that region. Consequently, the naming was an act of great respect and appreciation for family closeness and mutual support in a pioneer environment.

John Kennedy Van Fleet was born in northeastern Pennsylvania, where his father Joshua endured considerable hardships during the Yankee-Pennamite Wars which involved him as well as multiple members of the family.

Nonetheless, John was a child of about seven when the family relocated to upstate New York, leaving behind the Tioga, Pennsylvania, area for Manchester, Ontario County. He grew to maturity there before relocating to Kentucky likely in the late second decade of the 1800s, and then to Ohio where he was in the early 1830s.

John Kennedy Van Fleet married Nancy _____. They had some ten children, who were:

01. Christopher B. Van Fleet, the eldest child and probably the same person noted in Marion County history as an American Civil War soldier;

02. Abigail Van Fleet, married James Harraman before 1850 and had ten children, five of whom survived;

03. Ruth Van Fleet, who was named for John's sister;

04. Thomas Van Fleet;

05. Melvina Van Fleet;
06. Nancy Ann Van Fleet, named for her mother;
07. Elizabeth Van Fleet;
08. John (possible middle name Kennedy) Van Fleet (possible Junior);
09. Samuel Van Fleet; and
10. Joshua Van Fleet, named for the paternal grandfather and an uncle, who married Mary Goforth in the 1860s.

For reasons that can only be surmised, John K. Van Fleet and his family relocated to Steuben County, Indiana, sometime before 1840, having resided only about a decade in Ohio and a similar period of time in Kentucky, respectively (where he evidently maintained some property even after quitting the state).

It was in Indiana's Steuben County that he died at the comparatively early age of fifty-two of unknown causes, leaving a sizable and very young family behind.

John Kennedy's death occurred four years before his father Joshua's, and in the settlement of the Joshua Van Fleet estate, John's living children of his body were cited by name, and designated as the heirs of the portion to which he would have been entitled.

Although it remains for other researchers to outline the whereabouts of John Kennedy's descendants, one might speculate that several moved to other states, as partial information would indicate, particularly to Illinois and to Michigan.

In terms of immediate family, although his nephew Dr. Martin Nichols Van Fleet resided in Indiana for some years, he resided at almost the opposite end of the state, before he relocated to Moultrie County, Illinois.

A PORTRAIT OF ILLINOIS

Illinois was explored in the Seventeenth Century by various Frenchmen, largely engaged in the fur trade. In 1673, Louis Jolliet and Father Jacques Marquette arrived in the area, followed by Pierre LaSalle in 1680. LaSalle constructed a fortification and base of operations for the French Crown near present-day Peoria.

The first settlements in the region were at Fort St. Louis on the Illinois River in 1692, and a second in 1700 at Kaskaskia. However, following the French defeat by Britain and her American allies in the French and Indian War, the area was ceded to Britain in 1763.

During the somewhat later struggle for American Independence, the presence of British garrisons at their back posed a threat for Americans. Under General George Rogers Clark, in 1778 the American Revolutionary Army took Kaskaskia from the British without a shot.

Domination of the territory by the Americans followed, although the Indians continued to pose problems for European settlement for decades to come. In 1832 during the Black Hawk War, the Indians were defeated, thereby opening the region for permanent settlement.

In 1818 the country was led by President James Monroe, and Illinois became the American Union's twenty-first state. In the following Federal Census in 1820, the state was reported as having 55,121 inhabitants (compared to 12,000 in 1810). By 1840 when several Van Fleets were present, the population had increased to over 476,000. It reached 1.7 million in 1860 on the eve of the American Civil War, making it the fourth most inhabited American state.

257

Illinois encompasses 57,918 square miles, ranking it twenty-fifth in the Union. Its land is very flat for the upper two-thirds of the state, well suited for agricultural production.

What Brought Van Fleets to Illinois?

Like the situation in Ohio and elsewhere, the availability of low cost land that was fertile and cheap made the settlement of Illinois attractive for farming families.

This fact, in combination with a tightening farm environment further east, land costs and probably limited prospects for inheriting farms (or parts thereof) for many of the male children in large families, produced a tendency to move on – always in a westward direction.

Opportunity was evident in these family moves, so the continuous relocation was a characteristic in and among younger generations throughout the decades of the Nineteenth Century. Thus it was so for the Van Fleets and for many others, for whom census records note birth places further to the east.

JOSHUA VAN FLEET JUNIOR (1790 – 1860)

Joshua Van Fleet Junior was born to Joshua and Sabra Roberts Van Fleet in the area of Wilkes-Barre, Pennsylvania, on 6 February 1790. Later as an infant the family relocated to Tioga, Pennsylvania, and then as a young child, they removed again to the Manchester area, Ontario County, New York, where he remained until as late as 1817 as a young adult, when he settled in Kentucky.

Joshua Junior's brother James (born 1800) and quite likely brother John Kennedy Van Fleet (born 1793) departed upstate New York to establish themselves further south and west in the expanding United States. His siblings Miles Wilkinson and Moses Van Fleet removed to Ohio settling in and around Marion County, where they were later joined by their father Joshua Senior and his second wife Elizabeth Odell Van Fleet in the mid-1830s.

However, James, Joshua Junior and quite likely John Kennedy Van Fleet moved earlier still to Kentucky, for reasons that are of considerable interest to historians.

In 1796, Gideon Granger, who was to serve as a Postmaster General of the United States, acquired 64,184 acres of land in Kentucky. When he retired, he settled in Ontario County in upstate New York, and thereafter promoted the sale of farmsteads in Kentucky from his lands, which were known as "Granger's Great Tract."

Encompassing most of Hardin County, this massive Granger holding lapped over to include lands in neighboring Hart and LaRue Counties as well (the reader should note that county lines were later redrawn), precisely the area that attracted the Van Fleets for settlement.

259

Granger's principal land sales operations occurred between 1812 and 1826. Since this is the precise time frame in which Joshua, James and John K. arrived in Kentucky, unlikely to return again to upstate New York, and given the fact that Granger was a neighbor of the Van Fleets in Ontario County, the rationale for settlement in central Kentucky by descendants of an old Knickerbocker family is quite evident.

But there is an added dimension to this. James was a young seventeen years of age at the time, but Joshua Junior was twenty-seven and John twenty-four. Joshua was married at that time to Mary Ann Nichols, which is commented upon later, and her family was anxious to relocate to Kentucky. Thus, movement there – like historical movements throughout this family's history – was undertaken with a larger and extended family group, that likely (but inconclusively) included brother John Kennedy Van Fleet.

Family information indicates that Joshua Van Fleet Junior relocated from Kentucky to Illinois in December 1828. However, he was recorded in Kentucky in 1819, 1823, and 1826 and even later in 1852, not long before his death. His brother John Kennedy Van Fleet is later found in Steuben County, in northeastern Indiana, indicating clearly that they opted for other locales for longer term settlement and for reasons that are unknown. John was noted only once in the 1819 period in Kentucky.

James Van Fleet remained in Kentucky, being cited there from the 1817 date through the rest of his life. Indeed, the Van Fleet family found in the Commonwealth for the most part traces to him.

Joshua Van Fleet Junior married Mary Ann Nichols on 1 January 1815, in Ontario County, New York. Thereafter, they had seven children.

These children were born between 1815 and 1829, and were:

01. Martin Nichols Van Fleet, born 9 October 1815, married Maria Louisa Smith on 19 April 1846, and died 29 September 1895 in Illinois;

02. Henry H. Van Fleet, born 12 September 1817;

03. Sabra Samantha Van Fleet, born 20 August 1819, married Samuel Holden, and died 1 June 1899 (she being named for her paternal grandmother);

04. Samuel Nichols Van Fleet, born 7 November 1821 and died young in 1850;

05. Sally Nichols Van Fleet, born 17 September 1826 and died 3 August 1851; and

06. Edwin L. Van Fleet, born 11 September 1829 and died 27 September 1851, and is buried in Huron County, Ohio.

On 12 August 1830, Joshua Van Fleet Junior lost his wife Mary Ann Nichols, due to unknown reasons, allegedly on her way to Vermilion, Illinois. Since this event was not likely childbirth, it was probably illness or an accident.

With a need to have a mate to help raise a young family, on 22 November 1831 in Edgar County, Illinois, a marriage license was granted to Joshua Junior and Sarah Fay, about whom nothing is known.

However, what is known is that Joshua and Sarah Van Fleet had a child named William Van Fleet, who was born on 20 January 1833 in or around Little Sandusky, Ohio, in the general Marion County area where his siblings were living at the time, and where his father Joshua Van Fleet Senior would settle within a few years.

It is possible that Joshua Junior, who had traveled extensively in the country for that period of time, could have sought the assistance of his extended family (brothers and unmarried sisters) to assist with rearing his young children, explaining why he and his new wife and family were in Ohio for a period of likely at least one year.

No other children are known to have been born of this marriage. The biographical sketch of William Van Fleet, who left Illinois in the early 1880s for Florida where he established a new family line, is reported under his name in the chapter on Florida Van Fleets.

Joshua married a third time, to the widow Susan Frost, on 9 September 1841 in Coles County. No children are known to have been born to this marriage. She died 21 May 1851, leaving Joshua Van Fleet Junior a widower for the nine-plus remaining years of his life. He died on 13 December 1860 at age seventy in the home of the Underwood family in Moultrie County, Illinois, not far from his son Dr. Martin N. Van Fleet, and where he had farmed for much of his adult life.

Joshua Van Fleet did not use the designation "junior" in his name, causing some confusion for researchers. In another note on his life, his activities in Edgar, Coles and Moultrie Counties possibly brought him into contact with local lawyer and Congressman Abraham Lincoln, giving rise to comments by his son William, who claimed to know Lincoln personally.

MARTIN NICHOLS VAN FLEET (1815 - 1895)

Martin Nichols Van Fleet was the first child born to Joshua Van Fleet Junior and his wife Mary Ann Nichols, both of Ontario County, New York. His birth was recorded on 9 October 1815, and he was a seventh generation American descended from the Jan Van Vliet line through Daniel Senior and Joshua Senior and Junior Van Fleet.

At an early age, Martin Nichols relocated several times with his family, first as a child to Kentucky and then to Illinois. As a young adult, he apprenticed to become a physician, and thereafter practiced medicine in Roseville, Parke County, Indiana, which is close to the Illinois setting of his father.

It was in Parke County that he met and married Hoosier Maria Louisa Smith, who was born 20 January 1827, being some twelve years his junior.

In 1846, Martin Nichols Van Fleet was reported as being in Numa, Indiana, which is when he likely married. In January the following year, the first of Martin's and Maria Louisa's children was born. Over an eighteen year span some nine more were born, all in Illinois. Their children were:

01. Maria Eudocia Van Fleet, born 22 January 1847 in Indiana, married Lyman G. Perry and died 31 March 1913;

02. Thermantia Van Fleet, born 10 August 1848, married James Franklin McKissick and died 6 February 1927;

03. Simpson Bennett Van Fleet, born 23 September 1850, married Eleanor Savage and died 26 February 1913;

04. Morse Van Fleet, born 16 June 1852, married Amanda Margaret Jacoba (possibly Jacobs) 7 July 1875, and died 7 November 1929;

05. Prescott Van Fleet, born 25 March 1854, married Sarah Ann Lytle and died 12 July 1939;

06. Charles Emerson Van Fleet, born 30 June 1856 and died 24 (or 21) August 1857;

07. Cecilia Van Fleet, born 20 May 1858 and died 2 August 1860;

08. Lyman Trumbull Van Fleet, born 29 August 1860, married Harriet Kulp and died 20 March 1910;

09. Augusta Van Fleet, born 7 November 1862, married Jacob Beck and died in 1953; and

10. Emma Lucretia Van Fleet, born 22 April 1865, married Howard Rossean, died 10 September 1944.

The Dr. Martin Nichols Van Fleet family did not remain long in Indiana, and in fact, only their first born child was an Indianan. They relocated (he in effect returning) to Illinois, as had his father Joshua Van Fleet Junior, and established a strong family presence in that state thereafter in Champaign, Coles, Piatt, Moultrie and Marion Counties, largely in the late 1840s to 1860s time frame.

Martin Nichols had Van Fleet wanderlust in his veins, and moved several times as an older man, including to New Mexico and California. But several of his children spread across America, establishing other and more permanent lines including in the state of Washington, from which most of this material was provided by Vernita Van Fleet in the 1980s. Most notably, the family established roots in southeast Iowa, northeast Kansas and southeast Nebraska, in the years following the post-War period.

Returning to the above listing of children, the surviving son Morse Van Fleet and his wife Amanda Margaret Jacoba had seven children. These were:

01.	Perry Prescott Van Fleet, born 20 May 1876, married Mary Elva Starr and died 9 January 1924;
02.	Roscoe William Van Fleet, born 25 March 1878, married Anna Mahalia McQueen (death unknown);
03.	Emma Mary Van Fleet, born 8 September 1879, married Carl Edison Walker (date of death unknown);
04.	Jesse Morton Van Fleet, born 7 February 1881, married Genella Parker (date of death unknown);
05.	Lulu Pearl Van Fleet, born 11 July 1886, married Scott Lloyd Coffey and then James Alexander Jamieson, died 9 August 1962;
06.	Chester Arthur Van Fleet, born 24 June 1883, married Vada McCracken and died 16 February 1915; and
07.	Herschel Carl Van Fleet, born 15 May 1889, married Caroline Virginia Green (date of death unknown).

Of these children, only the offspring of Perry Prescott Van Fleet and his wife Mary Elva Starr are known. They had three children as follow:
01.	Byron Lester Van Fleet, born 26 September 1902, married Mary Elizabeth White (date of death unknown);
02.	Mildred Louise Van Fleet, born 3 May 1904, married Rolland Smith Taylor and died 17 June 1973; and
03.	Vernita Dorothy Van Fleet, born 5 July 1913.

Byron Van Fleet carried on the Van Fleet name into the next generation. He married Mary Elizabeth White 30 June 1926, and they had four children, three of whom survived to adulthood:
01.	Lester White Van Fleet, born 29 March 1928 and died in April of the same year;

265

02. Sarah Katherine Van Fleet, born 14 May 1929, married Thomas B. Brand and had children Ellen Irene and Matthew Lester;
03. David Starr Van Fleet, born 7 June 1931, married Alveris Bonnell; and
04. Douglas Lester Van Fleet, born 8 November 1932, married Ann Fitch and had children Alice Jean, Janet Louise and Laura Ann.

Dr. Martin Nichols Van Fleet

Wanderlust

A recurring theme throughout many Van Fleet lines over generations is one of movement – sometimes seemingly constant. Martin Nichols Van Fleet, trained as a physician, was born in Illinois but lived for a while as a young practioner in Indiana before returning to Illinois, moved frequently in his later adult years. Several letters of his survive attesting to this movement.

In one, "a mile above Fort Dodge" on 24 June 1862, he wrote to his daughter "Docia" (Eudocia) as follows:

We are here and well, we have plenty of work. Grasshopers are taking almost everything here to live on.... I do not know where I will winter but if I can find out where there has been anything raised I will move to that country rather than pay the provisions of this country.

Sam Dubois was out last week for goods and he and (Mr.) Bell says the grasshoppers are not doing much harm on the Sioux (River) but seem to be afraid they will. So am I and have been ever since they laid their eggs last fall and I am more than glad that I did not plant or sow anything for them to destroy.

Some twenty-five years later as an aging man, Martin Nichols Van Fleet wrote again to Docia some "ten miles from Weed, New Mexico" on 2 April 1887, as follows:

I received your very grateful letter day before yesterday and was truly glad to learn that you were all tolerably well, I am as well as I ever was in my life.

267

Last December I weighed 145 lbs. Day before yesterday I weighed 156 lbs., so you see I am on the gain again.... I think you need not worry about my taking care of myself for with the little bad health I have had I have not had to take to my bed nor have I been so that I could not cook and eat my meals....

As for getting wood, that is almost nothing (since) wood is plenty all around close to my house and the very best of dry pine. This is not a prairie country but a mountainous country one mountain and another with a narrow canyon between and the best of springs and plenty of pine timber. I built my house close to one of the springs.

Well, this Creat's birthday, I suppose you remember it well for it snowed ...that morning but cleared off a beautiful day. Well, this has been a beautiful day too so far but a little cool. What do you think, I have been mauling rails this forenoon to repair the fence and clear off the ground for my potatoes and rutabagoes and turnips and beets.

I am living more than a hundred miles from a railroad and that is very inconvenient but this is a healthy country. But I do not know whether I will stay here or not. I started last June 6th for California but my horse died and I could not go on then, maybe I will this summer or fall.

My nearest neighbors are a mile and a half over east and one west. But they are mighty good neighbors. I pulled an awful big tooth for one this morning. I generally get a dollar a piece for pulling a tooth. I got $30 for an obstetrick case this winter 25 miles away from my home and have had two others since nearer house for which I am to have ten dollars each. There is not much sickness in this country, one fellow run away owing me ten dollars but he is in jail which pays me some. This is good game country (and) I often get (paid with) a piece of deer....

A PORTRAIT OF KENTUCKY

Kentucky was the first area west of the Allegehany Mountains settled by American pioneers. Daniel Boone, one of this country's greatest fok heroes, led settlers through the Cumberland Gap on what became known as the Wilderness Trail, a reflection of of perception of what lay ahead and what was left behind for these adventurous people.

The area was in fact the western portion of Virginia, and for a time it was called Kentucky County. The first permanent settlement was at Harrodsburg in 1774. Daniel Boone's establishment of Fort Boonesborough in 1775 ensured a redoubt for settlers in the event of an Indian attack.

These raids were unceasing almost from the beginning, since this period marked the outbreak of the Revolutionary War and the British spurred the Indians on to attacks during America's struggle for independence. Forays did not cease until George Rogers Clark captured British forts in the Indiana and Illinois territories in 1778, definitively ending the British, Tory and Indian menace.

Settlement moved ahead rapidly in the region, and when Virginia dropped its land claims Kentucky became the fifteenth state in the American Union on 1 June 1792. Its star and stripe added to the flag gave a total of fifteen of each and created the "Star Spangled Banner" celebrated in our national anthem (but thereafter the number of stripes reverted to thirteen to honor the original union).

Kentucky is a commonwealth, reflecting its Commonwealth of Virginia heritage. Two years before statehood in the first Federal Census, it reported 74,000 residents, but it had an astonishing 221,000 and 407,000 in 1800 and 1810, respectively.

269

By 1820, the year closest to the first Van Fleets arriving in the commonwealth, there were 564,317 counted in the national enumeration, making it the fifth largest state in population. In size, however, its total land area is just 40,411 square miles, making it thirty-seventh of the fifty states.

When Kentucky became a state, George Washington was President, and when John K. and James Van Fleet arrived there, James Monroe was in the newly rebuilt and refurbished (after the British burning in the War of 1812) White House.

What Brought Van Fleets to Kentucky?

It is understood that Joshua Van Fleet Junior, John Kennedy Van Fleet and James Van Fleet all traveled to Kentucky as early as 1817. At that time, coming from New York as they did, they undoubtedly passed through Ohio. One would wonder why that new underpopulated state (1803) would not have attracted their attention, but in fact an explanation lies in a further chapter of American history that directly ties central Kentucky to Ontario County, New York, home of these Van Fleet boys.

In 1796, Gideon Granger, who was to serve as a Postmaster General of the United States, acquired 64,184 acres of land in Kentucky. When he retired, he settled in Ontario County in upstate New York, and thereafter promoted the sale of farmsteads in Kentucky from his lands, which were known as "Granger's Great Tract." Encompassing most of Hardin County, this holding lapped over to include lands in Hart and LaRue Counties as well, precisely the area that attracted James (and John K. temporarily) Van Fleet for permanent settlement.

270

Granger's principal land sales operations occurred between 1812 and 1826. Since this coincides exactly with the time frame in which James Van Fleet arrived in Kentucky, to the best of his descendants' knowledge never to return to New York or to relocate elsewhere, and given the fact that Gideon Granger was a Van Fleet neighbor in Ontario County, the explanation for his settlement there is too obvious to overlook.

Although Joshua Van Fleet Junior did not remain long (settling instead in Ohio for a while) and John Kennedy Van Fleet came and went over the years, James Van Fleet stayed put. He married in Hart County (then still part of Hardin) and reared children, being counted as a property owner as early as 1823 and again in the 1830 Federal Census.

James Van Fleet was the founder of the Van Fleet line in Kentucky. His permanent relocation there as opposed to his brothers' choices of Ohio, Indiana and Illinois, was endorsed by many of his descendants, since the long line of that family remains well established in the "Bluegrass State" to this day.

JAMES VAN FLEET (1800 – 1861)

James Van Fleet was born to Joshua and Sabra Roberts Van Fleet in Farmington, New York on 7 February 1800. That is the same year that his family relocated further upstate in new York, to what is now the Manchester area in Ontario County.

A sixth generation American descended from Adrian Gerritsen Van Vliet through grandson Jan Junior and great grandson Daniel, James grew up in a farming environment but at a very early age – possibly seventeen in 1817 – he struct out on his own, traveling to the Commonwealth of Kentucky.

It is possible and rather likely that his initial foray was undertaken with brother Joshua Van Fleet Junior and almost certainly with brother John Kennedy Van Fleet, but neither stayed long. Thereafter, James was reported as a resident of Hart County in 1823, where he was recorded as a property owner. He most likely married there in that year but not later than 1824.

James Van Fleet married twice. His first union was with Amanda _____, by whom he had as many as six children, three of each sex. The information of this wife, marriage and date of death is unknown. Moreover, the names of his possible six children are not all rcorded, since the 1830 Federal Census cites him as the head of household with just three children between one and ten (a category). Possibly there was a child by the name of Joshua.

The known children were:

01. Adeline Van Fleet, born 6 September 1824 in Munfordville, Kentucky (date is certain);

02. Caroline Van Fleet date of birth unclear; and

03. Joseph Van Fleet, date of birth unclear.

The second marriage took place in Hart County in 1834. James married Elizabeth King, who had been born in New York state on 23 May 1814. She was the daughter of Arthur and Nancy Tharp King. They had eight (and possibly ten) children between 1835 and 1847. They were:

01. James T. Van Fleet, born 1835 in Hart County;
02. Henry Clay Van Fleet, born 1 April 1836;
03. Mary Ann Van Fleet, born 1837 in Hart County;
04. Sarah E. Van Fleet, born 1838;
05. Elizabeth M. Van Fleet, born in 1840 in Hart County;
06. John Van Fleet, born in 1842;
07. Idrael K. Van Fleet, born 1 January 1845 in Hart County (also spelled Iredell), a Union Army veteran of the American Civil War; and
08. William Moses (Alonzo) Van Fleet, born in 1847 in Hart County and died there 25 January 1881 at age thrity-three. He was also a veteran of the American Civil War.

Other children are tenuously identified as Alonzo (presumably a different child from the one cited above) and Jarel (or Jared). It is also possible that Jarel is a misspelling of Idrael.

On 15 January 1850, James filed a petition against his brother Moses Van Fleet and other siblings for a share in the real estate of their father, Joshua Van Fleet Senior. In accordance with court proceedings, some land was sold by Sheriff David Epler. In 1852 James and Elizabeth sold the remaining Ohio land he received, and returned to continue farming in Hart County until their deaths. James died there in 1861.

James' sons William Moses Van Fleet and Idrael Van Fleet are traced here to illustrate a part of the family lineage in Kentucky.

Idrael (or Iredell) Van Fleet was born in Hart County on 1 January 1845 and died there 14 February 1917 of pneumonia. He distinguished himself in service to the Union Cause during the War Between the States. He married twice, the first union being with Georgia Ann Cosby in 1870 (died around 1890). They had the following children:

01. Jim (James?) Van Fleet, born 1870 or 1871;
02. David C. Van Fleet, born 1871;
03. U.S. Grant Van Fleet, born 1872, died October 1947 in Jefferson County, Kentucky;
04. James T. Van Fleet, born 1877; and
05. Mary E. Van Fleet, born 17 April 1885, married Ossie Fuqua.

Idrael then married Burley Lee Taylor, daughter of Peter and Elizabeth Logsdon Taylor, in Hart County in 1898. She was many years his junior, having been born 14 February 1878. Their children were:

01. Edward Hobson Van Fleet, born 13 September 1901 in Hart County;
02. Frederick Van Fleet, born 27 October 1903 in Bonnieville, Hart County; and
03. Edith May Van Fleet, born 7 March 1908 in Munfordville.

Upon Idrael Van Fleet's death, his widow remarried and had two children unrelated to the Van Fleet line.

Edward Hobson Van Fleet, grandson of James and great grandson of Joshua Van Fleet Senior, was born in 1901 and died of cancer 25 September 1778 in Bowling Green, Kentucky. He had served in the United States Army (1924 to 1926), and on 27 January 1927 he married Lois Violet Tinsley of Cannleton, Indiana. Their children were:

01. Edward Hobson Van Fleet Junior, born 3 March 1928 in Warren County, Kentucky, died the same day;
02. John Wallace Van Fleet, born 15 may 1929 in Ownesboro, Kentucky;
03. Grover Frederick Van Fleet, born 8 August 1931 in Bowling Green;
04. James Edward Van Fleet, born 5 December 1933 in Bowling Green;
05. Frank Craig Van Fleet, born 2 November 1938 in Bowling Green; and
06. Judith Gail Van Fleet, born 10 July 1943 in Bowling Green.

Frederick Van Fleet, grandson of james and great grandson of Joshua Van Fleet Senior, was born in 1903 and died 23 December 1981 in Butler County, Kentucky. He had married twice, first to Catherine Van Cleve to whom one son was born; that is, Bobby Joe Van Fleet in 1932, later killed in an accident, and then to Ruth Sumner.

Frederick and Ruth Van Fleet had the following children:
01. Max Van Fleet;
02. Jay Van Fleet;
03. Scottie Van Fleet;
04. Doug Van Fleet; and
05. Brenda C. Van Fleet, born 1945 and died 17 march 1960 of lukemia.

John Wallace Van Fleet ws born in 1929 and was the grandson of James and great grandson of Joshua Van Fleet Senior. He served in the United States military – first the Navy (1945), then the Army Air Corps and later still the United States Air Force – from 1945 to 1969. He married twice, to Ruth Lohrman in Fairbanks, Arkansas on 26 May 1951. Their children were:

01.   Kathy Jean Van Fleet, born 11 July 1952 in Sioux City, Iowa;

02.   Bruce Wayne Van Fleet, born 28 December 1955 in Shreveport, Louisianna;

03.   Patricia Lynn Van Fleet, born 7 August 1957 in Shreveport; and

04.   Angela Maria Van Fleet, born 17 September 1959 in Barcelona, Spain.

While serving in Thailand during the Vietnam War, John (known as Johnny) Van Fleet married in a traditional Thai ceremony Supatra Viradecha, by whom he had a son named Anurak Viradecha Van Fleet (called Noe), born 3 October 1965. He remains in contact with his American family, although he resides in Italy with his wife Anna, mother and Italian stepfather.

John Wallace Van Fleet worked for the United States Post Office following retirement from the military, later relocating to Silver Springs, Florida where he died in 1989. A sports complex in East marion, Marion County, Florida is named for him in recognition of his work in recreation.

Grover Frederick Van Fleet, great grandson of Joshua Van Fleet Senior, was born in 1931. He married Betty Adams on 20 June 1953, by whom he had three children. They were:

01. Lisa Gayle Van Fleet, born 19 November 1963;

02. Jacqueline Kay Van Fleet, born 9 January 1956 and died about a year later; and

03. Lynnette Van Fleet, born 30 December 1961.

James Edward Van Fleet, great grandson of Joshua Van Fleet Senior, was born in 1933. Small in stature, he trained as a jockey and later became a trainer, eventually moving into management for horse farms in Kentucky. He married Doris Cox on 5 December 1952.

Their children were:

01. Vicki Joean Van Fleet, born 16 June 1954 in Bowling Green; and
02. James Edward Van Fleet Junior, born 24 February 1956 in Bowling Green, Kentucky.

Frank Craig Van Fleet, great grandson of Joshua Van Fleet Senior, was born in 1938. He attended local schools and college at Western Kentucky University, at St. Leo University in Florida and at the State University of New York. In addition to specialized Department of Defense training schools, he is a National War College graduate.

Frank Van Fleet retired from the United States Army as a colonel. In his military career he served both as an enlisted man as well as an officer.

Enlisting in the Guard in 1956, he was mobilized for the Berlin Crisis in 1961, serving at Fort Knox. His active duty ended in 1961 but he remained in the National Guard, returning again to active duty in 1975 where, among other assignments, he served over ten years at the Pentagon.

Colonel Van Fleet retired from the Army in 1993, and at present he operates a consulting business in northern Virginia area serving the American defense industry.

He married Erma Joyce Fleming on 16 December 1961. She was originally from Indiana but her parents were Kentuckians, and as a child she returned with them to that state.

She and Frank Craig Van Fleet had the following children:
01. Mark Allan Van Fleet, born 2 February 1963, married Xi Chang in Huntsville, Kentucky, by whom he had a son Kyle Frank Cheng Van Fleet; and

277

02. Maria Ellen Van Fleet, born 12 June 1965, married Thom Thitijumnong in Alexandria, Virginia in 1985, father of Emily Thitijumnong (born 1987). Maria then married Andrew Sirotta in 1992, who is the father of Elizabeth and of Jacob Sirotta (born 10 March 1993 and 9 January 1997, respectively).

James Van Fleet's son William Moses Van Fleet, undoubtedly named in part for James' brother Moses, married Sarah Eliza Whitman, probably after the American Civil War. Later he died at the young age of thirty-three, leaving a young widow behind with a sizable family. As stated, he was a Civil War veteran as well, having fought for the Union Cause.

The children of William M. and Sarah Van Fleet were:

01. William Henry Van Fleet, born 1869 in Hart County;
02. Anna Elizabeth Van Fleet, born in Hart County, married William Jesse Brown;
03. Samantha Van Fleet, born 1875, married Shoudy Wilson; and
04. Hattie Gertrude Van Fleet, born 1877, married Wallace Warder.

Kentucky's Filson Club in Lousiville is the state repository for historical and genealogical records. So many Van Fleets still reside in Kentucky, that for those tracing their family trees with roots in the commonwealth, this organization is a remarkable resource.

PART IV.

ONWARD TO AMERICA'S

BORDERS

PORTRAIT OF FLORIDA

America's frist and greatest tropical territory, Florida came into possession of the United States through the ceding of parts of a vast backwater holding by Spain. Once having the flags of other countries fly above it, including those of Spain, France and Great Britain, gradually the boundaries of the state were established and it was admitted to the American Union in 1845.

The climate of Florida mitigated against its attractiveness by settlers until well into the 1900s. During the American Civil War as a southern and slave-holding state, it seceded along with the rest of the region to join the Confederate States of America. However, its war contributions were of minor importance in the scope of events, although its punishment for rebelling was of no small consequence.

Florida languished for years following the Civil War, but various developments in American technology came to play a major role in its transformation from 1875 through 1925, and certainly more so since that time.

These included frequent steamer service serving Atlantic and Gulf coast ports; all-weather road connections for cities and towns; the conquest of the state's worst enemy, yellow fever, by Dr. Walter Reed; and ultimately the widespread use of electricity that made possible refrigeration, electric fans and finally air conditioning.

Today, Florida is the fourth most populous American state after California, Texas and New York. Within two decades it will rank third. It owes this growth to the movement of persons from throughout the land who seek new lives in a tropical environment.

279

What Brought Van Fleets to Florida?

Van Fleets played a significant role in the development of Florida. In the 1850s, the first noted to reside within the state died of yellow fever in Jacksonville. Others came to the state in Federal Army uniforms, with Stewart Van Vliet being noted during the Seminole Wars and again at the end of the American Civil War.

But it was really in the early 1880s that the first of the modern adventuring entrepreneurs, William Van Fleet a railroad builder, arrived from Illinois, establishing a family remaining in part in the state to this day.

Lastly, mention is made of another relative who established himself as well in the Florida of the 1920s, during the real beginnings of growth in the state. Ralph Bruce Van Fleet's contributions to education and to organized recreation in Tampa Bay and ultimately throughout the South are noted.

Today, Florida is the home to growing numbers of Van Fleets, more of this family surname than any other state except California. These Van Fleets and Van Vliets owe much to their historical – or perhaps newly rediscovered – peioneering kinsmen who contributed to making Florida an American paradise.

WILLIAM VAN FLEET (1833 - 1919)

William Van Fleet was born 20 January 1833 near Little Sandusky, Ohio, in what was then part of Marion County, not far from the homes of various aunts and uncles, all of whom had relocated to that state from New York within the previous decade.

William's father was Joshua Van Fleet Junior, by his second wife Sarah Fay, whom he had married as a widower somewhat more than a year earlier. Joshua Van Fleet Junior was a sixth generation American, being descended from Adrian Gerritsen Van Vliet through Jan and Jan Van Vliet Junior, Daniel Van Fleet and his father Joshua Van Fleet Senior.

Joshua Van Fleet Junior was born in northern Pennsylvania, but grew to adulthood in upstate New York in the Manchester, Ontario County area. As a young man in his twenties, he relocated to Kentucky with two siblings and the family of his wife, Mary Ann Nichols, daughter of Adam Nichols. There he remained until about 1828 when he initiated a move to Illinois. His wife died in 1830 on way to Vermilion County, Illinois, leaving Joshua Junior with numerous small children, the last born just the year before in 1829.

In Edgar County, Illinois in 1831 Joshua Junior took out a license to marry Sarah Fay. Where they were married is unknown, but somewhat more than a year later their son William was born, likely during a sojourn in Ohio near Joshua's extended family.

William was not to spend much time in Ohio, and grew up on a family farm in eastern Illinois. His father, undoubtedly a widower for the second time, married a third time on 22 September 1841 to Susan Frost, in Coles County. She later died there in 1851.

Nothing of consequence is known of William's childhood, but one might assume he preferred to be on his own at an early age.

According to family lore, William became a purser at age seventeen in 1850 (some say fifteen, or 1848) on a Great Lakes steamer plying the route between Chicago and Buffalo. Living as he did in east central Illinois, it is logical that he began his career on the water from not-distant Chicago, the city that he was to make home for his early adulthood.

In later life, William Van Fleet gave only scanty vignettes about his early years, but it is assumed he was not anxious to spend much time either in farming or possibly in his stepmother's house. The career on the Great Lakes did not likely last too long, and by the outbreak of the American Civil War, William was noted as having become a sutler – a procurer of supplies for the Union Army – in the western theatre of activity. This not-all-together honorable profession might explain another curious statement that as a post-War businessman in Chicago, his net worth was noted at some $20,000.00, a substantial fortune for a young man in those days, and one that could only have been garnered through highly profitable war dealings.

William Van Fleet invested capital in the theatrical business in Chicago. He had made that city his home as early as 1861 (but likely later), but it was in the next decade that he was registered as a substantial stockholder in the old Dearborn Theatre. This establishment was well known in Chicago for its productions, as well as a menagerie that was kept on the premises.

William Van Fleet married for the first time likely in the late 1860s or early 1870s. Although that marriage ultimately failed or more remotely ended in his wife's death, it left him the father of one daughter, Sabra, born in 1873 and undoubtedly named for his grandmother.

282

William Van Fleet married a second time, in 1877. Her name was Medora Roxanne Schofield, reputedly of the family for which Schofield Barracks in Hawaii was named. She was the daughter of Eliphalet (sic) Steele and Martha Ann Hayes Schofield of Utica, New York. Medora Roxanne was born there on 16 August 1848, and was fifteen years her new husband's junior.

William Van Fleet was a businessman and was reported to have had the acquaintance of many prominent persons, including President Abraham Lincoln. It is difficult to say much about this point, other than it is plausible since Van Fleet lived in the Moultrie/Coles/Edgar/Vermilion County areas, in very close proximity to Decatur and even to Springfield, both places where Lincoln practiced law. Moreover, it is possible that Lincoln's constituency encompassed parts or all of these counties, in terms of his election to the United States House of Representatives.

One further note may be made of the fact that as a sutler, William Van Fleet and a business partner named Moore wrote President Lincoln in 1864, offering to sell him horses for the Federal troops.

In the late 1870s, William Van Fleet and a business associate Alfred Parslow became interested in the potential for railroad building in post-War Florida. Anxious to open this state's vast resources to development, its government was making concessions for railroad construction making the state attractive to entrepreneurs.

In 1879, they came to Florida arriving in Tampa from Cedar Key aboard the coastal steamer Lizzie Henderson. They began looking for an appropriate route to connect that region to the populated areas of the northeastern part of Florida, thereafter raising capital and chartering a railroad company in this venture.

283

The railroad in question was named the Jacksonville, Tampa and Key West Railroad. For many reasons, the original routing was changed, but finally when it was built it came to run from Tampa by way of present day Plant City, Peace Creek (now called Bartow), Auburndale, Kissimmee, Orlando, to Sanford, the last call for steamers on the St. Johns River, and on to Jacksonville.

Surveying for the line began in 1881, and by 1885, the road had reached Palatka. However, due to competing railroad construction in the south Florida area, among other factors related to poor business practices, this grand project was never completed under Van Fleet's railroad presidency. The railroad went bankrupt soon after arriving in Stanford from Jacksonville, far short of its planned connections. Ultimately in 1899 what remained of this chartered rail system was sold to the Henry B. Plant interests, which completed the line. That company later still was absorbed into the Atlantic Coast Line.

For a period of years in the late 1880s and early 1890s, William Van Fleet resettled his growing family in New York and for a while, in nearby New Jersey. Several of his children were born in New Jersey, although the intent was to remain in the north only for a short period of time, while a yellow fever epidemic ran its course in Florida.

William Van Fleet and his young family did not return to Florida until the early 1890s – probably in late 1892 – taking up residence in the region where he spent so much time exploring and surveying for the ill-fated railroad. He held land there in his own name, for it is reported in the family that when he first came to the present day Auburndale region, he "fell in love" with the numerous lakes and thick virgin forests of pine.

284

Both William Van Fleet and his partner Alfred Parslow bought and homesteaded tracts on three lakes which William named Lake Alfred, for his friend and business partner; Lake Medora, for his wife; and Lake Van (Fleet), for himself. He also named Lake Mattie for their first child, Martha Melita Van Fleet, who was known throughout her life as "Mattie."

It is of interest to note that many of these lakes were later joined together through a system of canals, designed and dredged by William's son Richard R. Van Fleet.

Following his financial difficulties and ultimate termination of his railroad interests in bankruptcy, William Van Fleet entered the similarly uncertain phosphate mining business with several ventures, located near Kissinger Springs, Florida. These were not large or even sizable mining operations, being described by several sources, including his son James, as "pick and shovel" undertakings. They were not very successful either, and later in life it was necessary for William to revert to various small business activities for a family livelihood, principally in the town of Bartow.

William and Medora Van Fleet had seven children. These were:

01. Martha Melita Van Fleet, born April 1877, married Albert Dickey, and died November 1976;

02. William Robert Van Fleet, born 19 December 1880, died unmarried 11 January 1944;

03. Richard R. Van Fleet, died as an infant;

04. Lois Medora Van Fleet, born 1884, married James S. Dickinson, died 1974;

05. Richard Rensellaer Van Fleet, born 19 September 1887, first married Josephine Mayo and second Susanne Levesque, died August 1976;

06.   Albert Eudelmar Van Fleet, born 1890, married twice, and died 1981; and

07.   James Alward Van Fleet, born 19 March 1892, married first Helen Moore and second Virginia Skinner-Higgins Wells, and died September 1992.

As stated, William had married earlier in Illinois, and had a daughter named Sabra, obviously named for his grandmother Sabra Roberts Van Fleet. There is no information about his first wife's name, marriage, death or divorce.

Nothing is recorded of this first marriage, or the ultimate fate of his daughter, other than some notations of gifts recorded in his account books from the 1880s.

There is another notation from a different source (United States 1880 Federal Census) that would imply that a Nadone (could this be poor handwriting transcribed from Medora?) was in Ashtabula, Ohio with a seven year old daughter Sabra and a two year old named Martha, but no further information is available on this other than a family recollection about a daughter raised by relatives. Another indicates that there may have been two children. Like so many other things relating to William Van Fleet, much is shrouded in mystery, leaving one to conclude he shared little information (and then probably selectively) with his family later in life.

With declining business fortunes, life for the Van Fleets in the early 1900s was much more difficult than anyone of them had ever experienced before. William's last business venture was a newspaper kiosk in Bartow.

It is believed that with the last of his personal connections, William persuaded friends to arrange an appointment for his youngest son James Alward to the United States Military Academy.

As a result of his fatherly intercession, William inadvertently ensured one of this country's most brilliant military careers in the wars of the mid-Twentieth Century, that of General James A. Van Fleet.

After giving up their small bungalow in Bartow, William Van Fleet and his wife lived with their daughter Mattie near Auburndale toward the end of their lives. William died 3 February 1919 leaving less than two hundred dollars in assets, following his wife Medora who passed away just some five months earlier on 7 October 1918.

A Presbyterian and a Democrat in his politics – perhaps reflective of Florida necessity at the time – both William and Medora Roxanne Van Fleet were laid to rest in the old Auburndale Cemetery, through their church affiliation.

William Van Fleet

JAMES ALWARD VAN FLEET (1892 – 1992)

James Alward Van Fleet, one of America's greatest Twentieth Century generals, was a descendant of Adrian Gerritsen Van Vliet through his son Jan, grandson Jan Junior and great grandson Daniel Van Fleet Senior.

Appropriately James Alward's grandfather Joshua Van Fleet Senior and great granduncles Abraham and Daniel Van Fleet Junior, as well as their grandfather Jan Van Vliet Junior and father Daniel Van Fleet Senior, were all American Revolutionary War patriots and veterans.

Joshua Van Fleet Senior's grandson William Van Fleet was born in Ohio shortly before his arrival in that state. However, William's father Joshua Van Fleet Junior was not there long.

Young William moved to Illinois in childhood when his father Joshua Junior took his sizable family there. As a young man William was an entrepreneuring businessman in Chicago before removing to Florida in the 1880s.

Although the Van Fleets took up residence in Florida during the period of William's railroad building years, yellow fever caused the family to flee to New York and later to adjacent New Jersey for several years. It was during that time that William and Medora Roxanne Schofield Van Fleet had at least three of their seven children, including the youngest, James Alward, who was born 19 March 1892 in Coytesville, New Jersey.

Later that same year, the Van Fleet family returned to Florida and took up residence in Bartow, Polk County. It was there that James attended the Summerlin Institute, developing his athletic – not to mention mental – skills that would serve him well in later years.

He graduated from Summerlin in 1911, and with his father's invaluable assistance with some well-connected friends, obtained an appointment to West Point. He graduated from "the Point" in 1915 in "the class on which the stars fell." Some of his classmates included General Dwight D. Eisenhower and General Omar N. Bradley.

Immediately upon graduation, Lieutenant Van Fleet found himself in the United States Army incursions into Mexico, chasing Pancho Villa and his raiders. His "baptism of fire" came during that short-lived action. Then as America entered the First World War, he served in France, ultimately commanding an American Expeditionary Force machine gun battilion, that won him two Silver Stars and a Purple Heart. He finished service in that conflagration as a major.

Thereafter, James Alward Van Fleet's career seemed to stall badly. Between 1918 and the outbreak of the Second World War, he served variously in university Reserve Officers Training Corps assignments and command of infantry units. Both afforded him time for his love of football, allowing him the opportunity to twice coach the University of Florida (among others) and the Army team based at Fort Benning, Georgia.

However, these assignments did nothing for his military advancement. He did not have the opportunity to serve on a senior staff; was not assigned to Washington; and did not have a "sponsor" among the senior military or political leaders of the era.

The only service school that he ever attended was the Advanced Course at Fort Benning. He concentrated on marksmanship, tactics and the training of infantrymen then, as he did later in his military life.

289

When the Second World War erupted, he continued that same essential concentration as commander of the 8th Infantry Regiment, training officers and soldiers who moved on as cadres to other units. In January 1944, he and the 8th shipped to England and intensified their training. On D-Day, this fifty-two year old colonel, who at one time had almost been retired for age, led his regiment ashore as the assault force at Utah Beach.

As the regiment advanced from the beachhead through Ste. Mere-Eglise and beyond, Colonel Van Fleet's leadership was best described by General Omar N. Bradley who stated he was "earning about three Distinguished Service Crosses a day."

By 1 July 1944, James Alward Van Fleet was a brigadier general and assistant division commander of the 2nd Infantry Division, commanding the task force that broke the German resistance within the Brest Peninsula. Shortly thereafter, he was given his second star and command of the 90th Infantry Division, a unit that under a different commander had performed so poorly that consideration had been given to disbandment.

Under General Van Fleet, the 90th drove toward Metz, executed what General George S. Patton described as "one of the epic river crossings of history" and spearheaded the drive from the south through the Ardennes during the German counteroffensive.

In February 1945, seven months after entering combat as an overage regimental commander, General Van Fleet was given command of XXIII Corps and a training mission in the United Kingdom. A month later, he was called forward to command III Corps at Remagen where, as described by General Courtney H. Hodges to Van Fleet, "Things are pretty messed up."

General Van Fleet used his infantry and engineers to clear obstacles in the bridgehead area and then committed the 7th Armored Division to the exploitation in the Ruhr as German rsistance disintegrated.

Throughout his tour in Europe, General Van Fleet was described as knowing where the front was, as evidenced by two more Purple Hearts. His personal bravery and leadership were recognized with three Distinguished Service Crosses and many other decorations awarded by the United States and its allies.

General James A. Van Fleet

In the next chapter in his life, when Greece was almost defeated by Communist infiltration and under attack from within by Marxist sympathizers, Lieutenant General Van Fleet was named point man for the implementation of the Truman Doctrine in February 1948. He was sent with the instructions that the Communists were to be defeated and driven out. The success of this campaign is measured by the facts that no Americans lost their lives in the ensuing struggle; Greeks were trained and fought to save their own land; and the Communists were vanquished from Greece.

When Lieutenant General Van Fleet returned to the United States, he was given command of the Second Army, a post he held for only a few months until sent to the Korean battlefront in command of the United States Eighth Army.

He was Commander of the Eighth Army and attached Korean Army and United Nations Forces in Korea from 14 April 1951 until 12 February 1953. He was promoted to four star rank in July 1951, and retired on 31 March 1953 at sixty-one years of age, with the permanent rank of full General.

In May through July 1954, General Van Fleet conducted a survey of the military, economic and political situation in the Far East, traveling with the rank of Ambassador.

He was a special representative of President (one-time classmate and former General) Dwight D. Eisenhower. It was during that time that he advised the United States Government to avoid involvement in Vietnam, an irony in view of the war that was to come in which many of his family members would see service.

General James A. Van Fleet, photographed for the American Sunday magazines, during the Korean War.

293

In 1961 President John F. Kennedy recalled General Van Fleet to active service to conduct a survey of National Guard and Special Service Forces units. As a result of that service, General Van Fleet is considered one of the most important figures in the development of the United States Army Special Forces, the "Green Berets."

Colonel Bruce F. Williams (whose writings are used in this commentary) once observed in ARMY magazine that however distinguished these post-war assignments were, it was during that one year in Europe that General Van Fleet put into practice the tenets of leadership he had followed in the years from 1915 up to the Second World War, and it was during that time that General George C. Marshall and others became aware that here was a consummate professional who had indeed been prepared for the test of battle.

General Van Fleet stands out as the general who did not fit the established pattern and who among his contemporaries, including West Point classmates, was different to an unmatched degree. Colonel Williams write that *"...soldiers everywhere should look...to the recounting of this record in which lies the story of a soldier never found wanting, the most tested U.S. troop commander and infantryman yet to serve his nation."*

General Van Fleet's battle awards included three Distinguished Service Crosses; four Distinguished Service Medals; three Silver Stars; four Bronze Stars; two Air Medals; three Purple Hearts; the Distinguished Unit Citation; and – his most prized possession – the Combat Infantryman's Badge.

Additionally he was decorated by the governments of Greece, Korea, Iran, Ethiopia, Thailand, the Philippines, the Republic of China, Great Britain, France, Belgium, the Netherlands, and Colombia.

02. Dempsie Catherine Van Fleet, born in 1917, married (eventually Major General) Joseph A. McChristian, who later served as Chief of Intelligence (J-2) in Vietnam. They had three children: Joseph A. McChristian Junior, known his entire life as "Tanker," including during his cadet days at West Point, Sara and Lilian; and

03. James Alward Van Fleet Junior, who was born in 1926, graduated from the United States Military Academy in 1948, and was killed in Korea while serving as an Air Force captain. He married and had one child, James Alward Van Fleet III, born in 1949.

In many respects, General Van Fleet's life was blest as well as cursed. A child whose family knew very hard times, his military career began positively enough, but slowed almost fatally until 1944, as luck would have it because of a misunderstanding.

The absence of promotions in the long period before 1944 was attributable to James being mistaken for another contemporary West Pointer with the surname (astonishingly) of Van Vliet, a man identified with a drinking problem. James Alward – a lifelong teetotaler – was thought to be that unreliable fellow, a tragic error until a well intentioned person by the name of (General) Omar N. Bradley forcefully straightened out the confusion during the war. Thereafter, as noted in the first part of this chapter, his ascent was spectacular but commensurate with his military leadership skills and personal bravery.

The tragic loss of his only son was one from which he never fully recovered. James Junior chose the Air Force following his graduation from West Point and with that, some very dangerous missions over Korea during that War.

295

It was during a bombing run that his plane was struck by enemy ground fire, exploded and disintegrated in mid-air. There were no survivcors or remains to be found.

Air Force Captain James A. Van Fleet killed in Korea in 1952.

Lost In Korea, April 4, 1952

Nonetheless, family lore has it that the General and his wife Helen secretly hoped their son survived, and somehow was being held by the North Koreans, but witnesses – including one known to this commentator – had reported that there was no possibility of such happening.

Meanwhile, other situations in the family proved too difficult for him to overcome in terms of raising his grandson, causing further strain and frustration for a general accustomed to control. This was an added burden for a man whose sole son was lost in combat while he was in a command position in the Korean Theater.

Immensely successful in business, General Van Fleet's military thinking, summed up in his oft-used phrase – and eventually his epitaph – as "The Will To Win," had some unfortunate familial dimensions as well. He was well known to run roughshod over other family members in terms of anything he set his mind to, eventually causing more than minor problems for his kin.

Throughout his life General Van Fleet traveled, an avocation he followed with diligence after retirement from the Army. He was a big game hunter and had impressive trophies from around the world, especially Africa before shooting safaris became less fashionable. He was a frequent guest of the politically (and militarily) powerful, who welcomed his charming sometime practiced countryboy-like company. He counted among his close personal friends the shah and empress of Iran, President Rhee of Korea and Ethiopian Emperor Heilie Selasse.

General Van Fleet was widowed and somewhat more than a year later married a second time to long time associate in Korean-related activities Virginia Skinner-Higgins Wells in November 1984, when he was ninety-two and she was sixty-five. She then died unexpectedly in the spring 1985.

When he died, he was given a military burial with full military honors. He is interred in Arlington Cemetery along with his two wives and a marker that pays tribute to his falled son as well.

Aside from his prowess in battle, General Van Fleet was brilliant on the gridiron. He was a 1976 honoree of the Football Hall of Fame as a West Point starter and as a coach for his work with the University of Florida.

A Speech Worth Noting

The following remarks were delivered by General James A. Van Fleet, United States Army (Retired), in accepting the Distinguished American Award from the National Football Foundation and Hall of Fame at the Waldorf Astoria Hotel, New York City, on 7 December 1976 (at age eighty-four).

Football and the Game of Life

Mr. Chairman, Your Eminence Cardinal Cooke, President Kazmaier, Mr. Speer, Fred Russell, Colonel Leonard Henry, and Gentlemen:

THIS IS A most happy evening – a wonderful, glorious evening. I thank all concerned for the National Football Foundation and Hall of Fame's Distinguished American Award in this Bicentennial Year. I thank, especially, the Tampa Chapter, many other chapters in Florida and across the nation, and many persons like Rex Farrior, Tom McEwen, Charlie Bachman, and Ray Graves. I shall treasure this Award as my highest decoration, and I will do my best to live up to its high ideals.

I AM especially honored tonight to be here in the presence of these scholar-athletes – to see them, to know them and to gain the confidence that the future of our country will be in good hands. To all of you, my whole-hearted congratulations.

FATHER HESBURGH, of Notre Dame University, in accepting this Award last year, responded with a most scholarly address on the virtues of football and scholarship. The year before, Bob Hope produced a houseful of laughter then closed with a stirring salute to football.

298

I HAVE ALWAYS loved football! It is the GREAT American game. It teaches TEAMWORK, the principle on which our nation weas founded. The pioneer who built his home in this new country depended on ALL of his neighbors coming to "raise the roof" in a single day. We are still a nation of pioneers with the love of freedom and independence in the marrow of our bones! But football is rapidly taking over as the best – and perhaps the only – replacement of that pioneer spirit.

I AM A combat soldier. Until tonight, my most prized possession has been the Combat Infantryman's Badge. I served twelve years with civilian components, eight years of which were commanding ROTC units and coaching football at Kansas State, South Dakota State and the University of Florida. I have often said if you can handle an ROTC unit and a football squad, you can command an Army – or a Bowl invitation.

SURELY, FOOTBALL and armed combat have much in common. Both MUST have Team Spirit, High Morale and The Will to Win. Our military units and football teams possess the finest manpower America has ever produced, the best equipment, great skills and the most thorough training or coaching. But when the whistle blows, victory is dependent upon THE WILL TO WIN. Call it school spirit, alumni support, fighting spirit, team unity – morale, momentum, or, to use the ancient Greek motto, "Come back carrying your shield, or upon it."

I WISH TO mention a few military events relating to Morale and THE WILL TO WIN:

(1)   GENERAL OMAR N. BRADLEY – Shortly before D-Day, General Bradley assembled all the officers of the 4ᵗʰ Infantry Division and attached units to give them a serious talk on the D-Day landing at Utah Beach. It was a solemn occasion, and I was reminded of the firey pep talks to fight for dear old Alma Mater when I was a young football player and later used often myself when I was a coach. There were some twenty generals on the platform facing about 1,000 of us, ranging from colonels in front to second lieutenants in the far back. General Bradley started off by saying, "This is going to be the greatest show on earth, and you, gentlemen, are privileged to have grandstand seats." He was interrupted by Brigadier General Theodore Roosevelt Jr., a great and loveable soldier, who in a clear base voice that reached all ranks, whispered, "Hell, Damnit! We're not going in the grandstand! We're right down there on the gridiron!" We laughed, we shouted, with General Bradley joining in, and the anxiety and the tension were relieved. We left that meeting together, relaxed, wanting to go and determined to win – just like trotting out for the kickoff. Yes – all wanted to be a part of "The Greatest Show on Earth." Administrative officers, forced to stay behind, went back to camp weeping.

(2) GENERAL GEORGE S. PATTON – At the close of World War II, I commanded the III Corps of General Patton's Third Army. I invited the General and his Third Army chaplain for the memorial Day services at the Military Cemetery near Nuremburg. After the ceremony, General patton walked among the many graves with their wooden crosses and identification tags, removed his helmet and kneeling at one of the graves prayed for a long minute. Standing, replacing his helmet and saluting that hero, he walked toward the crowd of some 5,000 G.I.'s and addressed them, "The chaplain made a beautiful speech today covering the greatness of our soldiers, their sacrifices and their Will to Win. But he didn't come here to weep, but to honor them, and to THANK God and them (pointing to the graves) that we Americans are still alive to breed men like them."

(3) GENERAL GEORGE C. MARSHALL – After World War II, I was summoned to Washington to report to General George C. Marshall, then Secretary of State. He told me about the serious situation in Greece and that Queen Frederika had requested him to send over a combat general to take over the training and fighting of the Greek Army. Among other questions, he asked me if I could instill in the Greeks the Will to Win. My reply was that

301

Greece was a soverign nation, united by a common language, a common religion, a passion for freedom and that I felt confident we could instill the WILL TO WIN. He told me the job was mine.

GREECE – HOME OF DEMOCRACY – and how those Greeks love it! Two Greeks, and you have three captains! But united and pulling together like complete teamplay in football, victory is certain.

YES SIR, with limited American weapons, which your taxes paid for, tough training and carefully selected aggressive leaders, the Greeks won their own freedom without a single American rifleman.

SINCE OUR STRENGTH is not without limit, we should use it to aid only worthy allies. And is any ally worthy who is not eager to raise infantry to defend his native soil?

MANY OF YOU here tonight have served your country on the battlefields of Korea and Vietnam. You know there are no good second place winners. Quoting General Douglas MacArthur, "There is no substitute for victory." Surely, we experienced – full measure – our country's agonies at a time when the Will to Win, on the home front and elsewhere, disintegrated. Liberty cannot endure without leaders inbued with the spirit and the ability to influence and inspire others with the Will to Win.

YES, we must instill that ideal in our players, in our subordinates and encourage it in our superiors, our people and our government. When our national Will is weak, it impairs our alliances and encourages all forms of aggression. BUT, when our Will is strong and resolute, we improve our alliances and discourage aggressors.

I AM CONFIDENT that our new President, whose ancestors as did mine, fought in the American Revolution, will keep us free if we all unite in helping him.

IN CLOSING, I wish to quote again General MacArthur, who as you know, was our Foundation's first Chairman of the Advisory Committee, and I quote "Upon the fields of friendly strife are sown the seeds that, upon other fields, on other days, will bear the fruits of victory."

THAT, GENTLEMEN, is Football's contribution to THE GAME OF LIFE.

James A. Van Fleet
General, U.S. Army (Ret.)

James A. Van Fleet

RALPH BRUCE VAN FLEET (1898 – 1965)

Ralph Bruce Van Fleet was the son of Charles Ray and Nellie Van Fleet, and a great grandson of James Van Fleet. This ninth generation American was born on 22 September 1898 in Fleetville on the family farm, and attended local elementary schools, like his siblings being taught by his maiden Aunt Catherine.

Ralph Bruce, like other Van Fleets, continued his studies at the Keystone Academy (now College) in nearby LaPlume. Upon graduation he moved to northcentral Pennsylvania and entered Mansfield State Normal School (now Mansfield University).

Ralph Bruce graduated from Mansfield in the class of 1917, and one day later enlisted in the United States Army in which he was to serve for the duration of the First World War, then in progress.

When discharged, he returned to Fleetville where he received an appointment at the nearby one room Marsh Brook School. He replaced a teacher who had had difficulties with parents. Following words and fisticuffs with this individual, a new parental calm descended and thereafter school authorities called upon Ralph whenever problems arose with parents.

After some nine years of service to local schools in Benton Township, Ralph Bruce Van Fleet left for Florida, becoming a school principal in Pinellas County junior and senior high schools. It was at Pinellas Park High School that he met and married another teacher, Flossie Fern Stirrett, who was originally from Illinois.

Ralph Bruce and Flossie Van Fleet had two children. These were:

304

01. Ralph Bruce Van Fleet Junior, born 29 September 1929 in Clearwater, Florida, and married 17 December 1950, had one son Ralph Bruce Van Fleet III; and

02. Donald Stirrett Van Fleet, born 23 May 1931 in Clearwater, married Imelda Dorsey and had daughters Susan and Annette Van Fleet.

After moving south, Ralph Bruce Van Fleet became involved in organized athletics, among other accomplishments, developing a Florida championship softball team. Competing in the national playoffs, his team found that there were different rules being utilized in various parts of the country, so at the Milwaukee playoffs he and his colleagues drafted and codified the rules of the game under the newly formed National Softball Association.

Thereafter he served for many years as a Regional Director of the National Recreation Association (NRA), a district that encompassed South Carolina, Georgia, Florida, Alabama and Mississippi. His recognition for work in recreation was often and impressive, receiving awards from Florida and other states.

Over his career he was instrumental in establishing two hundred and evelen recreation departments in the five southern states in which he worked as a regional director for the National Recreation Association.

Ralph Bruce Van Fleet died suddenly of heart failure on 19 December 1965 at age sixty-seven, and is buried at Sylvan Abbey Memorial Park in Clearwater. He was followed in death by Flossie Fern Stirrett Van Fleet in 1986, who is interred there as well.

Son Ralph Bruce Van Fleet Junior resides in Tampa, where he engages in the insurance business he has owned for most of his life. His son Ralph Bruce III is a senior executive with a national banking corporation, residing in Philadelphia.

His brother Dr. Donald S. Van Fleet has been a major figure in senior educational administration positions at the state levels in Florida and in Kentucky. In both capacities, he has been associated with Democratic administrations.

Additionally, he has served for many years as a much-honored superintendant of school systems, most recently in Jacksonville, Florida. Retired as a nationally known educational consultant, he resides in Bradenton, Florida.

Mansfield graduate
Ralph B. Van Fleet

306

A PORTRAIT OF NEBRASKA

Nebraska was first explored by Europeans under the Spanish and the French, who sought to identify mineral riches or to develop the fur trade. Later as part of the Lewis and Clark Expedition, the territory was transversed in the 1804 to 1806 period.

It was not until 1823, however, that the first permanent settlement was made at Bellevue, near Omaha on the Missouri River, by the Americans who acquired the region as part of the 1803 Louisianna Purchase.

Importantly, the settlement of Nebraska like much of the Great Plains came about as a result of three events: the Union victory in the American Civil War; the construction of railroads; and the passage of the landmark Homestead Act written by Congressman Galusha Grow, a relative of the Pennsylvania Van Fleets.

After a bloody history prior to and during the Civil War as part of the Kansas-Nebraska Territory, Nebraska entered the American Union as a new state on 1 March 1867 during the presidency of Andrew Johnson. Although sixteenth largest in landmass, its population was and remains small, presently ranking about thirty-eighth in the country.

What Brought Van Fleets to Nebraska?

Free or inexpensive land. The availability of land considered adequate for farming in some places and excellent in others, brought thousands to the American Plains in the decades following the 1860s Civil War through the First World War (1910s).

307

Many immigrants were attracted (indeed, recruited) to this region of the United States, particularly by railroad companies, which were anxious to liquidate their land grants along the rights-of-way for their tracks.

There were many from American farming families who made the trek across the country to the Great Plains, and some as in the case of the following family who came from further north – Canada – to make a home in this vast region.

Untold numbers came to America from Europe as well. The ethnic composition of the state, with a sizable Scandinavian, German and Irish population, attests to the draw of farming activities and the lure of other gainful employment during and following the construction of the railroads across the continent.

ROBERT AUSTIN VAN FLEET (1849 – 1922)

In the commentary *Not All Patriots: America's First Civil War*, reference is made to John Van Fleet and family who removed to Canada following the Revolutionary War.

In fact, there were several Van Fleets named John. John Van Fleet II was a son of Isaac Van Fleet, born in Readington, New Jersey, in 1779, who in turn was the son of John Van Fleet, born in Readington on 12 October 1751. He died in 1831 in Canada, where he relocated with his family.

After this third generation in Canada – that is, with John Van Fleet II – a change was in the works for at least part of his family; namely, his son Robert Austin Van Fleet.

Robert Austin Van Fleet, born in 1849 in Bronte, Ontario, married Betsy Boice in 1880. Records indicate that by that decade he was living in the American Plains. Specifically, he married in Sidney, Iowa, to Sarah Ellen Miller, and a daughter was born in Fremont, Iowa, in 1882.

Within five years, however, the family had moved to Nebraska, where they were recorded for the duration of their lives, all other children being born there and their dying there. Their children were:

01. Olive Van Fleet, born 1882 in Fremont, Iowa, married first John Nicholson and second Henry Nelson, and died without issue in Omaha, Nebraska;

02. Emma Van Fleet, born 1887 in Otoe, Nebraska, married Charles Green and died in Omaha;

03. Miles Van Fleet, born 1889 in Nebraska, died in infancy;

04. Harry Van Fleet, born 1890 in Nebraska, married and died in 1910 with no issue;

309

05. James Franklin (Frank) Van Fleet, born 1896 in Plattsmouth, Nebraska, married Hallie Zorn and died in 1921 in Omaha;
06. Melissa Van Fleet, born 1897 in Plattsmouth, married Otto Lushinsky;
07. Asa Van Fleet, a triplet born 1899, married Reva Colvert and died 1979 in Omaha;
08. Amos Van Fleet, a triplet born 1899, died as an infant;
09. Jesse Van Fleet, a triplet born 1899, died as an infant;
10. Madeline Van Fleet, born 1900, married Raymond Roberts; and
11. Edith Van Fleet, date of birth unknown, married Steve Visocsky and lived in Kansas.

Sadly, there were few in this line to continue the Van Fleet name in addition to James Franklin (Frank) Van Fleet. Born in 1896, he married Hallie Zorn, the daughter of Russian and Austrian immigrants, in Ralston, Nebraska in 1921. Thereafter they had two children before his death in 1921 at age twenty-five. These were:

01. Charles Robert Van Fleet, born 7 January 1919 in Ralston, married Alice Toupal; and
02. Guy Frank Van Fleet, born in 1921 and died in Omaha in 1930.

Charles Robert Van Fleet married Alice Marie Toupal, daughter of Bohemian refugees, in Hiawatha, Kansas, on 30 November 1946. They had three children, to wit:

01. Gretchen Elli Van Fleet, born 5 September 1950 in Omaha, married Klaus Linder in 1970;
02. Karl Frank Van Fleet, born 5 May 1952 in Omaha, married Lori Ann Watson 1980; and
03. Erik Toupal Van Fleet, born 21 February 1959 in Omaha.

A PORTRAIT OF COLORADO

Colorado became United States territory in part through the Louisianna Purchase in 1803, and in part through conquest as a result of the Mexican War. It had been settled by the mysterious Mesa Verde Indians two thousand years ago, but not until the 1800s was it explored by European people. In 1806 Lieutenant Zebulon M. Pike discovered the peak that bears his name.

With 104,100 square miles, eighth largest of the states, Colorado's population began from a small core. In 1860 there were 34,000 people and a decade later just 39,000.

As railroads expanded, however, so did the population, growing to 197,327 by 1880. Just four years earlier on 1 August 1876, Colorado became the thirty-eighth state during the Administration of President Ulysses Simpson Grant.

What Brought Van Fleets to Colorado?

Charles Graham Van Fleet, followed by his brother Galusha Alva, were the first known Van Fleets to come to Colorado, the former having come – allegedly – for his health and the latter to serve in his brother's mayoral administration.

Colorado presented many opportunities for highly entrepreneurial individuals, particularly in mineral related activities. For Charles Van Fleet, the practice of law, land development and mining endeavors proved profitable, although other Van Fleets who followed in future generations saw service in justice administration, education and ranching.

CHARLES GRAHAM VAN FLEET (1847 – 1908)

Charles Graham Van Fleet was born 3 June 1847 in Fleetville, as a young son of Alva Alanson Van Fleet. A BIOGRAPHICAL HISTORY OF BOULDER, COLORADO comments that his father "was a farmer and merchant by occupation, and a man of large influence and wealth in Luzerne County, where he resided until his death...."

Charles was sent to public and private institutions for schooling, at age twelve entering the Wyoming Seminary near Wilkes-Barre under the totorship of the Reverend Dr. Rubin Nelson, an eminent member of the Methodist Episcopal church. He graduated from that institution at the age of eighteen, and then attended Clinton Liberal Institute in Clinton, New York, for some two years, after which he began to read law under the Honorable E.L. Merriman of Lamberton and Merriman in Wilkes-Barre, Pennsylvania.

Following his initial training, he relocated to Scranton and completed his law studies in the office of the Honorable E.N. Willard. Some two and a half years later he completed his training for the bar, and following admission formed a partnership with his then-brother-in-law M.J. Wilson, as well as with his sister Rebecca's husband Francis E. Loomis.

He was in this practice for some ten years, during which time he was actively involved in the booming real estate market in Scranton. He is described to have "erected a number of fine buildings, including a ...residence for himself." He was also reputed to have been engaged in some coal mining operations, which were then enjoying great expansion in Pennsylvania, fueling industrial growth in the northeastern United States.

In 1875 just one year before Colorado gained statehood, Charles Graham Van Fleet quit Scranton for the west, leaving for California according to contemporary accounts. While en route, he stopped in Colorado and after visiting various parts of the state, became enamored with the climate and growing business opportunities, specifically in Boulder. This, despite the fact that the total territorial population was barely 40,000, about two-thirds that of the City of Scranton. He resumed his law practice in that locale, and followed up on investments in the mining industry as well.

Van Fleet was an investor in the Smuggler Mine, and was also chief owner and operator of the Balarat Concentrating Mill, located near the Smuggler Mine. In 1888 when his brother Galusha Alva married a second time, he reported his profession as "mine operator," which would reflect his involvement in brother Charles' activities, as noted elsewhere in this commentary. Then as late as 1904, Colorado mining reports stillconnected Charles Graham's name to these mining industry operations.

Meanwhile in Boulder, he continued his earlier practice of dabbling in real estate, and among other activities he erected the Van Fleet Building, an impressive structure that is still standing on the Main Street in a beautifully restored central city district of that college community.

Charles Graham Van Fleet was involved in local politics, and in April 1879 he was elected the first mayor of Boulder (established 1871) for a full term, which was all of one year. Two persons had served very brief periods in office earlier, but his term in 1879 to 1880 marked a new charter for the city. The HISTORY OF CLEAR CREEK AND BOULDER VALLEYS noted all mayors were "excellent citizens."

313

In addition to his travels to Colorado, while living in Boulder he ventured to the New Mexico Territory, the Arizona Territory, back to Pennsylvania and to Mexico, all on matters of business.

In 1873, the Protestant Episcopal church became established in Boulder. A parish was the outcome of actions of interested parties, called St. John's Episcopal Church. This church stands today at Pine and Fourteenth Streets. Charles was a vestryman for this parish, and a staunch supporter.

Some of his travels obviously related to personal agendas. He was married three times, his first marriage to Isabella C. Wilson, daughter of Dr. John Wilson of Factoryville, dissolved for unknown but undoubtedly scandalous (for the times) reasons, while living in Boulder. He had two children by this union, a son Edwin Van Fleet and a daughter Nora Belle Van Fleet.

A Boulder census in June 1885 reported his former wife and two children as being in that city, but presumably he had divorced and left for the eastern United States by that date. What condition he left his family in is questionable, since his former wife remained in the family home and operated it as a boarding house.

His return to Pennsylvania saw a second marriage on 29 September 1887 to Ella Oliver, of Troy, New York, but it too ended in divorce. He adopted a child in conjunction with this second marriage, and had no children of his body by her.

Charles Graham Van Fleet remained in the Troy area for several years, practicing law there following this second marriage. However, later in his life he did finally go to California where he was reported to have married a third time, to a person who was employed in his household.

Charles Graham was involved in land transactions in California, as is reported in records for that state. Additionally, family lore indicates that he was a mayor again, most likely in San Jacinto, the area where he lived. Although his children ultimately relocated to California with their mother, who remarried, there is scant evidence that contact was maintained.

Charles Graham Van Fleet was reported in San Francisco papers to have died a suicide in 1908.

Charles Graham Van Fleet

GALUSHA ALVA VAN FLEET (1852 - 19__)

The last child born to Alva and Esther Baker Van Fleet was Galusha Alva, in 1852. His siblings included George nelson, who inherited Manor Farm in Fleetville, and Charles Graham Van Fleet, a Colorado lawyer and businessman. He was named for Galusha Frow, a relative and long time United States Congressman from Susquehanna County, Pennsylvania, whose fame stems from penning the Homestead Act of 1862.

Galusha Alva Van Fleet married Addie Browning in 1873 at age twenty-one. She was the daughter of Orin and Minerva Capwell Browning of Fleetville, a particularly prosperous farmer. At about that time he received properties in Benton Township as an outright gift from his parents. Although he settled in this area of upper Luzerne County for a while, he was not destined to remain.

"Galush" or "Duke" as he was most often called, like his closest brother Charles Graham, was also trained as a lawyer. But like him, he left Pennsylvania to try his luck in the west. It is known that he lived in Colorado at least briefly, and later he settled in Salem, Missouri, by the end of the 1880s. He was still reported there in the Federal Census of 1900.

He was in Boulder, Colorado in the 1879 to 1889 period when his brother Charles was serving as mayor, and during that period he himself served as a constable.

Family lore relates that Galusha was handsome but light on morals. He was described as a ladies' man, and one story claims his move west was one to "save his skin" from an irate husband.

316

Allegedly, his exit from the community began with an escape through a window in his family's Manor Farm home, and from there he began the trek to the west.

Based on another story from a farm worker who had been employed by the Van Fleets in Fleetville, Galusha stopped in Nebraska on his way to Colorado. This man claimed he met up with "Duke" on the plains of Nebraska, where our errant Van Fleet was "breaking wild colts."

The worker, deathly ill in the Great Plains winter, had been left in a ranch shed to die, but Duke happened across him and then looked after him, nursing the man back to health – with the aid of whiskey.

Although these stories are colorful and not provable, in the latter case sounding like some public relations story to rehabilitate his reputation back home, they do fit in with Galusha's known movement west.

Galusha had a son by his first marriage to Addie Browning Van Fleet, which ended early in her death. At some point, their son Alva Van Fleet relocated to New York City, where presumably he lived the rest of his life, no records about him having been found.

Galusha then married Flora Ann LeSueur, daughter of Martel and Sarah Phleger LeSueur of Floyd County, Virginia. At the time of this marriage on 3 March 1888, he was listed in that county's records as a widower. When he returned from the west and why he came to Virginia is unknown. The sole notation for this marriage is that he adopted a daughter, but it is believed that this was more likely with a third wife, Laura _____, who is noted in Van Fleet family history.

317

FLOYD COUNTY, A HISTORY OF ITS PEOPLE AND PLACES, noted that the Van Fleets relocated from Virginia to Missouri. Other records state that Galusha lived in Salem, and it is presumed that he was returning there after a much earlier stay. He was recorded in the 1900 Federal Census in Missouri, and presumably died there in the 1900s.

Galusha Alva Van Fleet as a Constable

A PORTRAIT OF CALIFORNIA

It is possible that the Chinese sailed along America's west coast a thousand or more years ago, but it was explorers Juan Rodriguez Cabrillo in 1542 and Sir Francis Drake in 1579 who were the first Europeans to see land in California and to record those events. However, it was not until 1769 that the Spanish began settlement of the region, establishing a string of Franciscan and Dominican missions.

Traders and settlers from the United States came to California, then Mexican territory, from the early 1800s onward. In 1846 they staged the abortive "Bear Flag Revolt," which attempted to sever California from Mexico, but such did not occur until 1848 as a result of war between the United States and Mexico.

The discovery of gold near Sacramento in 1849 precipitated a massive movement of peoples to this territory, which then gained statehood when Millard Fillmore was president on 9 September 1850, as the thirty-first in the American Union. Interestingly, its first constitution was written in both Spanish and English, reflecting its earliest ethnic diversity.

With 163,707 square miles of land, third largest in the country, California is bigger than most countries of the world, and its current population also reflects the size of many nations. But population growth was slow initially, due to the state's distance from the densely populated east and difficulty in reaching it across unsettled lands.

California's population went from 92,597 at the time of statehood to just under one and a half million in 1900 half a century later. By the 2000 census, California had around thirty-six million.

What Brought Van Fleets to California?

The first reported Van Fleet in California was Allen, whose lineage is not traced by who arrived in the territory before statehood or the Gold Rush, probably in 1848. He and a brother were ranchers, and lived in El Dorado County, dying in the early 1900s.

However, in the following decades there were various Van Fleets who came to California from different family branches. Charles Graham Van Fleet is noted from the Adrian Gerritsen Van Vliet line, arriving in the post-1890 period, as well as William Carey Van Fleet from the Dirck Jans Van der Vliet line, arriving the decade before as a youth.

In the Twentieth Century, California has beckoned many Van Fleets as a land of opportunity, as it has for millions within the United States and abroad. Today the single largest representation of members of this family can be found in the state.

"Academy Awards: 28th Annual," Jo Van Fleet, Jack Lemmon, Grace Kelly, Ernest Borgnine, and Marisa Pavan.

WILLIAM CAREY VAN FLEET (1852 – 1923)

William Carey Van Fleet was born in Maumee, Lucas County, Ohio in 1852. He was the son of Cornelius and Julia Anna Runyon Van Fleet, and the grandson of Matthias Van Fleet, a descendant of the Dirck Jans Van der Vliet line.

William's family had come to Ohio ostensibly to acquire one of the fine farms to be found in the region. However, this timing coincided with the 1830s financial panic, when Andrew Jackson was President. As a result, they were unable to follow through on this plan.

Nonetheless, his father was not without resources or family support, for this was a time when several members of the Van Fleet family relocated to northwest Ohio, including brothers Jared and John Van Fleet, among others.

Cornelius settled in Monclova Township, which is immediately adjacent to Maumee, and began farming. William Van Fleet attended local schools but at age sixteen, suffereing from malaria, he met with an interesting twist of fate. During an aunt's visit, she persuaded his parents to allow her to take him back to California for his health, and to read law in her husband's office.

Soon after arriving by train on the recently completed (1869) transcontinental railroad, William commenced the study of law in Sacramento. After three years he was admitted to the bar on 21 April 1873. Soon after he went to Elko, Nevada, and practiced there for about two years before returning to Sacramento. He was associated in California's capital city with Judge George A. Blanchard and others. Three years later he became district attorney for Sacramento County, and served in that position until 1879.

Van Fleet was elected to the Assembly of the California Legislature as a Republican in 1881 at age twenty-nine, and in 1883 he was appointed a state prison director, serving as such until elected a judge for the superior court for Sacramento County in 1884. He was reelected in 1890, and served until 1892 when he resigned to relocate to San Francisco, becoming associated with the law practice of Edwin B. and Joseph W. Mastick and William Belcher, in a firm renamed Mastick, Belcher, Van Fleet and Mastick.

In April 1894, William Van Fleet was appointed a justice of the Supreme Court of California, replacing a judge who resigned. In the fall of that year, he was elected to finish out the term that ended in 1899.

He ran for a second full term in 1898 with the endorsement of the Republican and Labor Union Parties, but an 1897 opinion he wrote holding judgement excessive in the negligence death of a six year old boy, was highly unpopular. He was defeated, but as he claimed "...there is not in this country one rule of law for the rich and a different rule for the poor...," reflecting his opinion that the victim's social status should not determine the amount of an award. America could use his opinions today.

Soon after leaving the Supreme Court, Van Fleet was appointed a code commissioner and served in this capacity until 1902. He was a Republican national committeeman from 1900 to 1904, and in 1903 was appointed a trustee of Hastings College of Law, now part of the University of California.

Van Fleet was appointed by President Theodore Roosevelt to be a United States District Court judge for the northern district of California on 2 April 1907, serving as such until his death.

It was in this capacity that for the next sixteen years, Judge William Van Fleet was able to carry on the legal work and philosophy that he had begun as a Supreme Court judge.

William Van Fleet married Isabelle Carey, a daughter of Ransome S. and Mary Ann Gotcher Carey if Sacramento, in 1879. She passed away the following year, leaving a small son Ransome Carey Van Fleet. This son was cared for by his maternal grandmother, and when Van Fleet married again in 1887, he continued in her care.

Van Fleet's second marriage to Juila Crocker was into the famed Crocker family, a prominent and wealthy California pioneering clan with extensive financial interests in railroading and in the Wells Fargo Bank. William's brother was to be employed in that financial institution for some years.

In addition to his son Ransome by his first marriage, there were four more children born to the second.

These were:

01. Alan Crocker Van Fleet;

02. Clark Crocker Van Fleet;

03. William Crocker Van Fleet; and

04. Julia Crocker Van Fleet.

Judge Van Fleet's sons Ransome and Alan followed him into the practice of law, becoming prominent men in their field in San Francisco in the early Twentieth Century.

Aside from his involvement in the Republican Party, William Carey Van Fleet was most interested in the professional progress of young attorneys, and went out of his way to advise them in ways to help their careers. Additionally, he was a member of the Episcopal religion, being a communicant of St. Luke's Church in San Francisco.

323

His funeral was held at that church when he died suddenly of a cerebral hemorrhage on 3 September 1923, at age sixty-one. He was buried at Cyprus Lawn Cemetery.

Judge William Carey Van Fleet of California

A PORTRAIT OF WASHINGTON

In many ways, Washington was one of America's last frontiers. It entered the American Union on 11 November 1889, but its population was just 75,110, slightly more than double Alaska's and less than that in virtually all of the country's remaining territories.

Spain's Bruno Hezeta was the first European to sail along the coast of present-day Washington in 1775. He was followed by American Captain Robert Gray in 1792, who explored part of the coast and sailed up the Columbia River.   Later in 1810, Canadians established Spokane House for fur trading, and the Americans followed suit under John Jacob Astor who built an outpost at Fort Okanogan in the following year.

Permanent settlement was delayed in large part because of a boundary dispute with Great Britain, but in 1846 this issue was amicably settled. Some nine years later in 1855 when gold was discovered in the northeast, new settlers to that part of the territory poured in.

Initially the state's population grew slowly, due in part to the rough topography of the region with the Rockies/Cascades creating a barrier and a distinct north-south division.   It was not until the late Nineteenth Century with technology – specifically the availability of railways and steamships – that that these problems were overcome in populating the area.

Washington has a land mass of 71,302 square miles, making it the eighteenth largest of the fifty states. Its heavy forests west of the North Cascades makes the region a major producer of wood products.

What Brought the Van Fleets to Washington?

As noted elsewhere in this commentary, there is a family relationship between northeast Pennsylvania Van Fleets and Congressman Galusha Grow, who authored the Homestead Act of 1862. That landmark event created the very basis for the dramatic settlement of the west following the American Civil War. What had once been estimated to require five hundred years to settle by the American Government, was accomplished in fifty when the frontier was officially declared closed in 1910. This was due in no small measure to legislation making the acquisition of land easy, as well as to the advances of transportation technology and the elimination of dangers from the Indian population.

The brothers Luther and Emmett Van Fleet took advantage of free or cheap land to homestead in the last years of the 1870s. The sense of adventurism that drove so many of their family beforehand, was present in the blood as well for these two. Such action required at a minimum for them to leave the relatively comfortable lives they had in a prosperous farming community of a civilized eastern Pennsylvania, to make their way to the wilderness of Washington to face an unknown future.

Both lines and others of the Van Fleets prospered in Washington, although those tracing their heritage to this two must do so to Emmett, inasmuch as Luther Van Fleet quit the state for California by the late 1880s.

EMMETT VAN FLEET (1849 - 1916)

George Van Fleet was the ninth child of thirteen born to James and Christiana Gardner Van Fleet. He was born in 1821 around the time his parents were planning a relocation to northern Luzerne County, and in any event lived his life there dying in 1893. George married Lexa Penina Thacher and they had four children, all born in Fleetville. Two of these children were Luther, born in 1853, and Emmett, born 23 January 1849.

The story of these two brothers represents yet another chapter in the pioneering history of the Van Fleet family. At an early age, the departed Pennsylvania for the Skagit Valley of present-day Washington, before that area became a state and even before Seattle was established as a city with that name.

On 23 December 1874 at age twenty-five, Emmett Van Fleet married Eliza Mathilda Farnham of Lackawanna County, a daughter of Granville and Harriet Sprague Farnham. He family was descended from Captain Elias Farnham of the famed Green Mountain Boys, who in turn had been granted lands now occupied by Hawley, Pennsylvania, for his services during the American Revolutionary War.

Eliza came west with her husband. Emmett and Eliza settled one mile east of the Sedro-Woolley Valley (as it is now known), where he and his family "knew no neighbors but themselves and counted the later settlers as one by one they came into that wilderness of trees," according to Eliza.

Emmett had grown to adulthood in Fleetville, attending local schools and working on his father's farm. He also learned carpentry which he followed for five years in nearby Scranton.

327

Emmett began leasing land from his father to engage in maintaining his own farm. Then in 1880, he and his young family began the trek that would take them to Washington Territory.

According to his wife, not a single white woman aside from her or child lived in the vast area from Lyman to Sterling, Washington, which was then called Ball's logging camp. The nearest Van Fleet neighbor was a pilot on the Skagit River. No roads and very few trails existed, and it was reported that Emmett had to clear every inch of land to be cultivated from the thick forest growths.

In all, three children were born to Emmett and Eliza Van Fleet, one in Pennsylvania and the other two in Washington. These were:

01. Eva Van Fleet, born 31 December 1876 in Fleetville;

02. Ethel Van Fleet, born 17 August 1887 in Skagit, Washington; and

03. Earl Van Fleet, born 30 March 1889 in Skagit.

Emmett Van Fleet was a lifelong Democrat, like so many other Van Fleets in Pennsylvania. He was not listed with a religious preference, but undoubtedly attended the Fleetville Universalist Church while living in Pennsylvania. His wife, however, was a Methodist.

The Van Fleets contributed the land and funds for the first school in the Skagit area, and Emmett was a school director for a while. Emmett died on 12 August 1916, followed by his wife on 10 April 1937 (having been born 24 July 1856).

Pioneer life was very colorful, and an account of it, written by Eliza Van Fleet in 1900, was reported both in Seattle papers and back east in Pennsylvania. It is reprinted here as excerpted from a book, SKAGIT COUNTY HISTORY, published in 1906.

On the third day of May, 1880, I, with my husband and little three year old daughter, bade adieu to every familiar face and scene in our native home of Fleetville, Lackawanna County, Pennsylvania, and started West to make us a home in the forest somewhere in the Puget Sound country. I shall never forget that sad morning. Several kind friends and neighbors had called to say good-bye, but I could not say one word. As my husband helped me to get my wraps on and half carried me out to the station more than one suppressed sob reached my ear. A brisk drive to the station and we had started West. The lovely morning and the beautiful scenery drove away all feeling of homesickness. As none of the three northern lines was then built we came via the Central Pacific to San Francisco. There we took passage on the ocean steamer "Oregon" for Portland. After stopping there a day or two we went back down the Columbia River to Kalama, then took the train to Tacoma, then on to Seattle by boat.

As a 'bus drove us to the Occidental Hotel (then a plain wooden structure) I remarked that it was strange that they could call so small a place a city, for it looked to us more like a country village, with the streets not all cleared of the stumps, and such big stumps with notches cut in them, which excited our curiosity. As the last letter we received from Mr. Van Fleet's brother Luther was written from Sterling, on the Skagit River, we took passage on the steamer "Chehalis" for that place. I was a little abashed to find that I was the only woman on board the boat with at least forty men bound for the Ruby Creek gold fields. However, I soon found that they were kindly disposed (and) well bred....

329

One of them gave me a paper which contained glowing accounts of the gold being discovered at Ruby Creek. One day and night on the steamer and we were landed at Ball's logging camp, instead of a village we had expected to find. A man clerking in the little log store at the camp, Mr. Smith by name, soon made himself known and invited me in to meet Mrs. Welch. A daughter of Mr. Ball. She was the only white woman in the camp, in fact, the only white woman anywhere in the vicinity. She was very kind, and as I was quite weary after our twenty days of travel, she soon prevailed upon Mr. Van Fleet to let me stay with her until the next steamer would go up the river. The next morning Mrs. Welch showed me the two large rafts her father had made. There had been four feet of snow on the level that winter and as they knew the snow was very deep on the high mountains they were afraid of an overflow. She also pointed out to me the high water marks that were then plainly discernable on nearly all the trees six feet up from the ground.

We spent the first three months with brother Luther on the place now owned by Ira Brown, then pre-empted the claim we still own and moved in our shanty which was built from split cedar. Several families of Indians were our nearest neighbors. Jerry Benson and his father Stephen Benson were our nearest white neighbors; next came William Woods, William Dunlap, Joseph Hart, and Mr. Bailey. The place where Sedro-Woolley now stands was a vast unbroken forest, owned principally by Scott Jameson. The Woolley portion was still government land.

People settled mainly along the banks of the river first. The voting place for those who lived about the township line...was at Lyman....

330

There were no roads, no schools, no churches – in fact, no white woman except Mrs. Welch in Sterling – and no white children. I lived here for five years before I saw a horse. About the middle of December, 1880, a Chinook wind caused the river to rise very rapidly. As we had never lived near a river before, but had read of the great overflows, we concluded it best to be on the safe side, so Mr. Van Fleet built a platform up about twelve feet in a large hollow of cedar stump, and split cedar boards so we could go up sixty feet if necessary. Some of the neighbors had rafts tied to trees close by, others had a canoe securely fastened to the house. When the water was at its highest point we had a heavy earthquake shock, which was a startling experience.

Our only mode of travel was by canoe or steamer. The Chehalis, Josephene, Daisy and Nellie made regular trips and as the river was high all through the summer of 1880, sometimes they went as far as Portage, above Sauk, with miners and supplies.

A post office had just been established at Mr. Ball's camp, called Sterling, but there was no regular mail carrier. Anyone that happened to be coming up from Mount Vernon brought the mail. Scott Jameson owned the logging camp farthest up the river, it being a mile above Sterling and in charge (was) Charles Harman, foreman.

We felt prepared to work hard and fare poorly a few years and the reality did not fall short of our expectations, but we had not realized how lonely life would be before we had neighbors, schools, etc. Sundays especially were very dreary. When we grew tired of reading there was nothing to do but roam around the forest and listen to the singing of the birds, and the chatter of the squirrels.

We had not lived here very long when an old man, Pawquitzy by name, called to have an understanding with us. As he could (speak) neither English nor Chinook, he brought a young Indian along to interpret for him. After the old man had talked and gesticulated for some time, the young Indian told us that he had said we had no right to be here. That all the land from the head of the Sky-you Slough to the mouth of the Batey Slough belonged to him, had belonged to his father and his grandfather for many years. Mr. Van Fleet quietly remarked, "Oh, tell him the white man cut down trees to raise potatoes to trade to Indian for fish." This pleased the old man and he went away in better humor. We learned afterward that other Indians were afraid to hunt, fish or trap on the old man's ground. The old Indian kept a fish trap in the creek near us and frequently used to bring us a nice mess of fish.

In 1893 Eliza wrote:

The air here is now fresh and cool, and the surrounding country and scenery is to me at least simply grand. Imagine yourself in a level village clearing of about 500 acres surrounded by a vast evergreen forest which extends out and away to the majestic mountains beyond by which we are surrounded on three sides. 'Tis evening. A pleasant time for a pleasant walk, so here we go. In front of the post office we will for a moment pause to drink in the beauty and loveliness of the evening scenery.

The wide planked or gravel streets and sidewalks are decidedly inviting for a promenade or an evening drive. But where are the horses and carriages with which to drive. There are none. Therefore we must fall back upon the natural and original method of locomotion.

332

As we walk up the avenue we notice several nice buildings, the finest of which are the Sedro Hotel, the Methodist Episcopal Church, and the schoolhouse.

A heard of horses are galloping around at their own free will out on the range, as that portion of the Sedro is called. Cowbells are tinkling in the distance and the horses and cattle range at large. Gardens and crops, of course, are fenced.

A steamer that plies the waters of the treacherous Skagit River, lying at our right, gives a warning whistle for the draw bridge...to be opened for her to pass on to the more pretentious town down the river, Mount Vernon.

Before we leave the town site, we will turn back and take a look. Oh! The stumps, in front of us, and to the left of us on which recently rested massive monarchs of the forest....

O ----- O

Emmett Van Fleet lived the remainder of his life among the towering trees and new farmlands of the Skagit River Valley. Many Van Fleet descendants are still living in Washington state trace their origins to this early settler.

Emmett Van Fleet's brother Luther, who arrived about a year earlier in the area – 1879 – however, left Washington for California, where he reportedly died in 1914, some two years before Emmett.

While the stories related here are perhaps not atypical of those of many pioneers even in earlier times, we can be thankful for a literate and caring spouse in Eliza who put her thoughts, feelings and experiences to pen and paper for all posterity to enjoy, somewhat more than a score and a century later.

333

The only son of Emmett and Eliza Van Fleet was Earl Winfred Van Fleet, who was born 30 March 1889. He married Mary Edith Harris, and they had two children, who were:
01.   Virgil Luther Van Fleet, born 10 April 1916 and named for his uncle, married Rosalie Griffith; and
02.   Ray Irwin Van Fleet, born 7 July 1917.
Virgil L. and Rosalie Van Fleet had two children, Blake Walter Van Fleet and Brenda Verlee Van Fleet (born 6 October 1956).
Ray Irwin Van Fleet and his second wife had three children, Earl, Delores and Eldon Van Fleet, as well as a daughter LaRayne Van Fleet, by his first wife.

Correspondent Eliza Van Fleet

A PORTRAIT OF OREGON

The object of much Nineteenth Century attention for pioneer families anxious to settle in the west, Oregon was sighted and sailed along in 1792 by American Captain Robert Gray. The famous landmark Lewis and Clark Expedition reached the region somewhat later and spent the winter of 1805 to 1806 at the mouth of the present-day Columbia River.

Settlers who followed in 1834 located in the Willamette Valley, and by 1843 there were sizable waves of pioneers coming overland on the Oregon Trail that Stewart Van Vliet helped establish and secure as a young United States Army officer.

Oregon grew fairly rapidly through migration, particularly after California was added to the American Union in 1850. Oregon followed in 1859 as the thirty-third state, under President James Buchanan.

Although not densely populated with just about four million inhabitants today, the state is large – the ninth biggest – with 98,386 square miles.

What Brought Van Fleets to Oregon?

Van Fleets began moving to the American northwest in the late 1870s, as noted vis-à-vis Washington, but by the mid-1890s various family members from diverse branches were finding their way to the region.

Oregon is home of the "Dr. Van Fleet Rose," a wonderful addition to the flora of Amerca, developed by the Van Fleet family of Morse Van Fleet.

335

MORSE VAN FLEET (1852 – 1929)

Morse Van Fleet was born 16 June 1852, the son of Dr. Martin Nichols and Mary Louisa Smith Van Fleet, in Illinois where his father was practicing medicine. He was a grandson of Joshua Van Fleet Junior, who had relocated his family from Ohio to Illinois before 1840, and a grandson of Joshua Senior, being himself an eighth generation American.

Dr. Martin and Mary Louisa Van Fleet had seven children, among whom was Morse. Morse did not follow his fasther into medicine, but rather was a farmer. Although he was from Illinois, somewhat later in life he relocated further into the midwestern part of the country; that is, to Iowa by 1875.

On 7 July 1875, Morse married Amanda Margaret Jacoba (or possibly Jacobs) and thereafter they had eight children.

These were:

01. Perry Prescott Van Fleet, born 20 May 1876 in Adair County, Iowa, married Mary Elva Starr and died 9 January 1924;

02. Roscoe William Van Fleet, born 25 March 1878 in Freemont County, Iowa, married Anna Mahalia McQueen, death date unknown;

03. Emma May Van Fleet, born 8 September 1879 in Iowa, married Carl Edison Walker, death date unknown;

04. Jesse Morton Van Fleet, born 7 February 1881, married Genella Oarker, death date unknown;

05. Lulu Pearl Van Fleet, born 11 July 1886, married first Scott Lloyd Coffey and second James Alexander Jamieson, died 9 August 1962;

06. Chester Arthur Van Fleet, born 24 June 1883, married Veda McCracken and died 16 February 1916 before his thirty-third birthday, and is buried in Portland, Oregon;
07. Herschel Carl Van Fleet, born 15 May 1889, married Caroline Virginia Green, date of death unknown; and
08. Lilian Rose Van Fleet, born 9 December 1895 and died 23 January 1896 as an infant, and is buried in Halsey, Oregon.

This Van Fleet family departed Iowa and relocated to Oregon, sometime in the early 1890s, and various descendants live there to this day.

Of these children, Roscoe William Van Fleet who married Anna Mahalia McQueen had a son named LeRoy Eston Van Fleet. He in turn was the father of the contemporary Paul Elliot Van Fleet by his wife, Ruby Schultze Van Fleet.

The Dr. W. Van Fleet Rose

While difficult to obtain, the "Dr. Van Fleet" climbing rose has a medium white bloom with a small pink center. It is hearty for colder climates.

While difficult to find, it can be ordered cheaply from Pickering Nurseries, 670 Kingston Road, Ontario L1V 1A6, phone 905/839-2111 (fax 905-839-4807); or more costly at Heirloom Old Garden Roses, 24062 NE Riverside Drive, St. Paul, Oregon 97137, phone 503/538-1576. Check area codes!

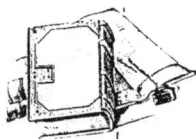

337

A PORTRAIT OF VERMONT

Vermont was first settled by the French under Champlain in 1609. Europeans utilized for fur trade purposes, but it was not until 1724 that the first American – through the English – settlement occurred at Fort Dummer, near present-day Brattleboro.

Vermont was once the western territory of the Province of New Hampshire. However, it became the fourteenth state in the American Union on 4 March 1791, the first outside the original colonies.

George Washington was President of the United States at the time that Vermont became a state. One of his chief lieutenants during the Revolutionary War was Ethan Allen, a furnituremaker who led the famous Green Mountain Boys – still a reference to Vermonters – in their capture of Fort Ticonderoga. In other ways as well, this dimunitive land with a small population played a pivotal role in the War for Independence as well as in the War of 1812.

Vermont with limited growth remains the forty-ninth in population at the present time, and is forty-ninth in size with just 9,615 square miles of territory.

What Brought Van Vliets to Vermont?

Only the family of Christian Van Vliet is known to have moved to Vermont in the 1800s. Although of a farming background, it is believed that general family considerations played the decisive role in this relocation, rather than any special agricultural opportunities. However, Van Vliets of this line still reside in Vermont.

338

GERRIT STEWART VAN VLIET (1815 - 1901)

Gerrit Adrianse Van Vliet, eldest son of Adrian Gerritsen Van Vliet, lived at Marbletown near his parents before relocating to the more easterly reaches of New York sometime around 1709. Specifically, Gerrit and family relocated to the Fishkill area. Among his children putting down roots on this Hudson River shore was Adrian Gerrit Van Vliet – named for his grandfather – who in turn had a son named Petrus Van Vliet.

By the following generation – that is, the fifth in America – a son was born in 1790 to Petrus who was named Christian Van Vliet. A farmer, Christian married Rachael Hough, and after he was widowed, he married twice more.

It was by his first marriage, however, that he had five children, including a son – and a sixth generation American – who was named in something of a family tradition, Gerrit Stewart Van Vliet.

One of three boys, Stewart as he was known throughout his life, and brother Frederick Van Vliet saw service to their country through the military. Both of these Van Vliets served in the Mexican War, but this commentary focuses on the fame of just Stewart.

G. Stweart Van Vliet was born on 21 July 1815 in Ferrisburg, Vermont, where members of his father's family had relocated. He was appointed at age twenty-one to the United States Military Academy at West Point, and graduated ninth in his class in 1840. Thereafter he he was assigned to serve in the Artillary until 1847. He became a captain, and was then transferred to the Army's Quartermaster Corps.

339

Van Vliet volunteered to serve in the Seminole Wars that were raging in Florida in the 1840s, as the following account relates. But his principal military actions early in his career focused on the War with Mexico in the late 1840s, serving as a primer for what would come in the American Civil War. Specifically, in the Mexican War he was present at both Monterrey and at Vera Cruz, being cited for leading the charge at Monterrey that won the day.

Following that war, Van Vliet served the military by building outposts on the Oregon Trail in the late 1840s and 1860s, being a primary architect for the development of Fort Kearney in Nebraska Territory and for Fort Leavenworth in the Kansas Territory. In 1857, he was responsible for fitting out the Utah Expedition in its action vis-à-vis the Mormons in the Great Salt Lake, and was credited with leaving his endangered command behind to proceed alone to negotiate – successfully and peacefully – with their leader, Brigham Young.

At the outbreak of the American Civil War, Van Vliet was stationed at Fort Leavenworth. He was promoted to major in August 1861 and acted as Chief Quartermaster of the Army of the Potomac from 20 August to 10 July 1862, when at his own request he was relieved.

He had been appointed Brigadier General of Volunteers on 23 September 1861, but the commission expired on 17 July 1862, a week after his relief. For the remainder of the Civil War he was on duty in New York City furnishing transportation and supplies. In October 1864 he was brevetted through all ranks to Major General of the United States Army, to rank from 13 March, and brevetted Major General from that same date.

He then served as Deputy Quartermaster General with the rank of lieutenant colonel in 1866 and as Assistant Quartermaster General, with the rank of colonel six years later. Meanwhile, he had served as Chief Quartermaster of various military departments and divisions until his retirement for age in 1881, forty-one years after beginning his military career.

Major General G. Stewart Van Vliet

Stewart Van Vliet remained in Washington, D.C. for the remainder of his life. He was a wealthy man, making a fortune in real estate and then investments, and was exceptionally well connected politically and socially. One obituary noted he was a "friend and confidant of Lincoln, Grant, Sherman, Hallack and all the great men of that day who were prominent either in civil or military life."

Indeed, he was a regular twice-weekly visitor to President U.S. Grant's White House, where the two men reminisced about West Point days when Van Vliet was Captain of Cadets and Grant was a Plebe. A later note from a newspaper article in December 1896 stated that he was busily preparing for the upcoming March 1897 inaugural ball for Republican President William McKinley.

Van Vliet was a member of the Army and Navy Club, among other social institutions of the capital, a frequent host and an early member of the Holland Society of New York. Whern he died 28 March 1901 as the oldest "of Uncle Sam's Living Army Officers" at his beautiful Washington home, he was interred at Arlington National Cemetry. His wife Sarah J. Van Fleet followed him there 17 May 1917.

As a footnote, Major General Van Vliet's distant cousin General James A. Van Fleet also had the distinction of being a distinguished West Pointer who survived to be the oldest living member of the United States Army Officers' Corps – or any American officers' corps – as noted in the chapter on him.

Allison Van Vliet Dunn of Berkeley, California, privately published a monograph on the Gerrit Adrianse Van Vliet line in the early 1970s, which can be found in the Library of Congress and New York Historical and Biographical Library.

A PORTRAIT OF TEXAS

Along with Florida, Texas was the first part of the current United States to be visited by Europeans. Pineda sailed along the coast in 1519, and both Cabeza de Vaca and Coronado landed and explored the region in 1541. By the late 1600s, the Spanish had moved in from Mexico to establish permanent settlements.

Texas attracted American settlers following Mexico's liberation from Spain, to such a degree that in 1836 an independent Republic of Texas was declared. Later in 1845, Texas was annexed to the United States as the twenty-eighth state (and largest) of the American Union.

With a land mass of 268,601 square miles, Texas is the second largest state with the second largest population in the country.

Following the American Civil War in 1865, Texas began to develop rapidly. Its massive territory was viewed as excellent grazing land, and the development of barbed wire and the construction of railroads helped spur this industry.

After oil was discovered more than a century ago at Spindletop, additional revenues and economic opportunities helped the growth that has propelled Texas to its present "nation" size in inhabitants and economy.

What Brought Van Fleets to Texas?

In sum, Van Fleets began coming to Texas in the eaerly 1900s for the myriad economic opportunities that were driving a growing population in an expanding business environment.

DUBOIS VAN FLEET (1806 – 1883)

The Van Fleet family that enjoys a presence in Texas today traces its descent to Adrian Gerritsen Van Vliet mainly through his son Jan Van Vliet Senior, his grandson Frederick Van Fleet Senior, and great grandson Frederick Van Fleet Junior, through New Jersey, then upstate New York and Illinois communities.

Specifically, Frederick Van Fleet Junior was born in 1731 in Readington, Somerset County, New Jersey. A farmer, he married Rebecca Dubois in adulthood, a descendant of one of the many Huguenot families that had intermingled with Dutch settlers. They lived in Somerset County throughout their lives, where many descendants can be found to this day.

Following the American Revolution wherein the Indian tribes of the Iroquois Federation were scattered, word came of the fertility of the lands in the so-called Lake Country of central upstate New York. The attraction of this region was well publicized, and accordingly many farmers from the overcrowded New York and New Jersey regions began moving into the area. Thus it was that William Van Fleet, son of Rebecca Dubois and Frederick Van Fleet Junior, relocated to Cayuga County to establish his family in farming in that region.

Their son Dubois Van Fleet was born 1 June 1806 in Owasco, Cayuga County. He engaged in farming like his father, and on 18 August 1831 at age twenty-five, he married Elizabeth Firkins in Wolcott, in neighboring Wayne County. Between that date and 1846, they had six children, who were:

01. Lydia Van Fleet, born 1832;
02. Luticia Van Fleet, born about 1834;

03. Isabel Van Fleet, born about 1837;
04. Hiram Van Fleet, born 8 September 1838 and died 16 September 1903;
05. Martha Van Fleet, born about 1841; and
06. Mary Van Fleet, born 23 January 1843 and died 5 November 1911.

Sometime around 1846 Dubois and Elizabeth Van Fleet moved their family to Warren County, Illinois. He followed Elizabeth's father, George Firkins, an earlier English immigrant who relocated from Wolcott, New York, to settle in Knox County, close to Warren County, in 1837.

It was in Illinois that Dubois and Elizabeth Van Fleet had two additional children,

07. Marcus Edward Van Fleet, born December 1846 and died 17 September 1847 in near Monmouth in Warren County; and
08. Alice Van Fleet, born February 1849.

By 1860 Dubois and Elizabeth Van Fleet joined her father in Knox County, settling in Altona, Walnut Grove Township. By then, however, several of their children were grown, had married, and relocated elsewhere in Warren County. Lydia married Samuel Chapin, while Isabel married Uriah Redin on 2 October 1856 in Warren County. On 8 December 1859 Mary wedded a German immigrant by the name of George Winebright, in Oquawka, Henderson County. Hiram married Mary N. Little on 21 December 1859 and by the time of the national census in the summer of 1860, was listed as the head of his own household in the census.

When the American Civil War began, Dubois Van Fleet volunteered for service in the Union Cause, although by then he was fifty-five years of age. He accomplished this feat by lying about his age, by some ten years, according to records of his service. He entered into active duty at Altona on 25 September 1861 as a private in Battery E of the First Illinois Artillery, Grand Army of the Republic. He trained at Camp Douglas near Chicago.

On 13 February 1862 Dubois's Battery E was sent to Cairo, Illinois on the Mississippi River, where it procured horses, guns and other equipment for a major encounter with the Confederate Army. On 27 March 1862 they boarded boats and landed on 30 March at Pittsburg Landing in the Tennessee River port of Shiloh.

The Confederates mauled the estimated 77,000 Union troops at the 6 April 1862 Battle of Shiloh. Total northern casualties neared 23,000 wounded or captured. Battery E's losses were light, but the wounded included Dubois Van Fleet who was struck in the side by an exploding shell. The shell fragment broke several ribs, damaged his liver, and caused "abdominal dropsy" – an accumulation of fluid in the tissues. He would never fully recover from his wounds.

Although severely injured, Dubois Van Fleet moved on with the Union Army, which took Corinth, Mississippi on 29 May 1862. From there the Army followed the line of the Memphis and Charleston Railroad, marching, camping, and skirmishing until they reached Memphis.

After further training at Camp Pickering, on 26 November 1862 Battery E joined General William Tecumseh Sherman's expedition to Oxford, Mississippi, and then on to White's Station, where on 31 January 1863 they began an extended encampment.

Dubois continued to suffer from his wounds, and on 28 April 1863 he was declared disabled and recommended for discharge. He was honorably discharged from the Union Army on 1 May 1863 at Memphis, with his papers listing his age as forty-six, though in fact he was really fifty-six.

Dubois Van Fleet returned to Walnut Grove, Illinois, and on 6 October 1863 applied for an "Invalid Pension" with Knox County.

The pension in question was granted and confirmed several times during the next twenty years of his life. Although census records listed his as a constable, in fact he never worked again. By 1882 his disability had worsened to the point that a notations stated "he has become so nervous and trembly that he can not do anything and can not help himself, has to be waited upon even to unbutton his breeches, or button them and it all has arisen from the wound in his left side by a piece of shell."

It was further noted that Dubois could not lie down due to the pain and pressure from fluids accumulating in his side, and that he "took to rest sitting in a chair."

In 1883 Dubois Van Fleet and his wife Elizabeth moved in to their daughter Mary's home, residing there with her husband George Wineright in Hale Township, Warren County. Dubois died there on 19 August 1883, and is buried in that county. Elizabeth stayed on with Mary and George until she moved to Kansas around 1885, joining her son Hiram Van Fleet and daughter Lydia Chapin, who formed the base for the Van Fleet family in Kansas. Elizabeth Van Fleet died in Downs, Kansas, on 4 November 1891.

HIRAM VAN FLEET (1838 - 1903)

Hiram Van Fleet was born in Wayne County, New York, on 8 September 1838, the son of Dubois and Elizabeth Firkins Van Fleet. He was the grandson of William Van Fleet, great grandson of Frederick Van Fleet Junior of Somerset County, New Jersey, and a seventh generation American, descending from Adrian Gerritsen Van Vliet.

As a child of about eight, Hiram moved to Warren County, Illinois from upstate New York, with his parents and siblings. At age twenty-one, he married Mary N. Little of Warren County, on 21 December 1859, having been born 22 November 1840. She had just turned nineteen at the time of the marriage, and had come with her family to Warren County from her birthplace in Jefferson, Illinois.

Their first child was born in October of the following year, but others followed:

01. Alonso Levi Van Fleet, born 23 October 1860 in Warren County;
02. William Dubois Van Fleet;
03. Lillie Van Fleet, married a Lewis;
04. Alma Van Fleet, married a Cross;
05. Cora Belle Van Fleet, born 29 June 1874, married Louis Brumbough, and died 23 April 1901;
06. Luella Van Fleet, married a Frost;
07. Mary Lois Van Fleet, married a Thompson; and
08. Clyde C. Van Fleet.

Hiram was a farmer who like his father served the Union Cause during the American Civil War. He enlisted on his second wedding anniversary, 21 December 1861, joining Company A of the 2nd Missouri Volunteer Cavalry, at Benton Barracks, Missouri.

The regiment, organized by Captain (later Colonel) Lewis Merrill under the authority of General John C. Fremont, became known as Merrill's Horse. Merrill's Horse moved into northern Missouri in January 1862 and spent the next eighteen months pursuing Confederate guerrillas. In July and August 1862, Merrill's Horse pursued Poindexter's guerrillas, engaging in skirmishes in Grand River, Lee's Ford, Chariton River and Walnut Creek, near Stockton, Missouri. Hiram Van Fleet, who rose to the rank of corporal, was the sole survivor of an ambush when guerrillas cut off a detachment of horsemen and teamsters.

Merrill's Horse joined up with Davidson's Cavalry Division at Pilot's Knob in June 1863, and on 1 July rode out on an expedition to Little Rock, Arkansas, which was captured 10 September 1863. Hiram joined in the pursuit of Confederate forces under Major General Sterling Price during September and October 1863. He spent forty-two days in the saddle pursuing troops under the command of Confederate Brigadier General John Marmaduke. Merrill's Horse remained posted near Little Rock through March 1864 and saw extensive duty in Arkansas through October of that year, again meeting up with General Price's remaining forces in September and October.

Merrill's Horse moved into Tennessee at the beginning of 1865, operating near Memphis during February. They moved across state to Chattanooga and spent the spring pursuing guerrillas based in Alabama and Georgia, escorting Union trains going from Chattanooga to Atlanta. Following the Confederate surrender at Appomattox, this celebrated regiment mustered out at Chattanooga in September 1865.

Hiram Van Fleet, however, had reenlisted on 13 May 1864 for another three years of service, and was then assigned to Company L, under Captain Richard Phelans of the 13th Missouri Veterans Volunteer Cavalry. He was sent "to help suppress the Indian uprising" in Kansas and in Colorado.

He spent the harsh winters of 1865 and 1866 in Denver in the Colorado Territory. In the spring of 1866 he recrossed the Plains and was honorably discharged at Fort Leavenworth, Kansas – a military installation built by his distant cousin and fellow Civil War veteran General Stewart Van Vliet – on 13 May 1866.

Hiram Van Fleet must have liked what he had seen in the new state of Kansas during his crossing on horseback, because he moved his family to Miami County there in March 1870. Later, they were to relocate to Osborne County, and still later to Clay County. Within a year of his father Dubois' death in 1883, Hiram's mother Elizabeth moved to Downs, Osborne County, where she joined Hiram's sister Lydia and her husband Samuel Chapin in Kansas. Elizabeth Van Fleet died there on 4 November 1891, and is buried in Downs.

In 1887, Hiram Van Fleet moved his family again, to Twelve Mile, Smith County, Kansas, where he engaged in farming. He spent his last years in Downs, where he was a custodian for the local school. Following an extended illness, he died on 16 September 1903 at age sixty-five.

Mary Van Fleet removed to Aurora and lived with her eldest child, son Alonso Levi Van Fleet, until her death on 20 November 1908, at age sixty-eight.

All of Hiram and Mary Van Fleet's children survived them, save for Cora Belle, who had married William Brumbough on 30 September 1874, dying there on 23 April 1901 at age twenty-six, likely in childbirth in Portis, Kansas.

Some of Hiram Van Fleet's descendants stayed in Kansas well into the present century, essentially as farmers. Other descendants of his have relocated to Texas, California and Alaska, establishing yet additional branches of this family.

ALONZO LEVI VAN FLEET (1860 – 1942)

Alonzo Levi Van Fleet was born to Hiram and Mary Little Van Fleet on 23 October 1860 in Warren County, Illinois. He was an eighth generation American, descended from Adrian Gerritsen Van Fleet via the Frederick Van Fleets of New Jersey, Dubois Van Fleet of Cayuga County, New York, and his father of Warren County, Illinois.

As a child of ten, Alonzo Levi removed to Clay County, Kansas, with his parents in 1870. At age twenty, he married Catherine P. Thomas, who was born 10 February 1861 in Warren County, Illinois, on 31 March 1881. Like so many others who relocated further west to Kansas from Illinois, Catherine's parents settled in Cloud County, Kansas, just after the Civil War in 1866.

The following year, their first child was born, followed by five others. These were:

01. John Albert Van Fleet, born 12 June 1882;
02. Grace May Van Fleet, born 29 November 1883, and died 7 November 1904;
03. William Leroy Van Fleet, born 6 June 1887 and died 4 July 1961;
04. George Frederick Van Fleet, born 14 July 1889 and died 11 April 1945;
05. Effie Ellen Van Fleet, born 5 October 1891 and died 9 July 1958; and
06. Clyde Melvin Van Fleet, born 28 February 1893 and died 13 February 1943.

Alonzo Levi Van Fleet removed to Smith County, Kansas sometime in February 1886. This locale is where his parents and siblings would soon relocate, and it is where the last four of his children would be born.

A farmer by trade, Alonzo Levi was a widower, his wife Catherine dying 19 November 1920. He lived on until 18 May 1942, dying in Concordia, Kansas.

GEORGE FREDERICK VAN FLEET (1889-1946)

George Frederick Van Fleet was born 14 July 1889, the son of Alonzo Levi Van Fleet and a ninth generation descendant of Adrian Gerritsen Van Vliet through the New Jersey lines of the Frederick Van Fleets.

George Van Fleet grew up in Smith County, Kansas where he was born on the family farm. As a young man he was crushed by the death of his would-be wife from smallpox, and enlisted in the United States Army in 1908. A family photograph of the young artillery private shows a handsome countenance sporting a magnificent handlebar moustache, which, in a newspaper interview some thirty years later, was described as "needed for the ladies."

George Frederick van Fleet first saw action in the Philippines, where he was part of the expeditionary force putting down an insurrection of natives in that territory that had so recently been won in the Spanish American War. He was awarded a Silver Star for valor during an engagement with Filipino guerrillas who were holed up in a cave, clearly reflecting a military mindset established in his family.

George Frederick went on to serve in Belgium during World War I. At the end of that conflagration, he was transferred to Fort Sam Houston in San Antonio, Texas, where he married Esther Belle Gill in early 1920. Thereafter, they had two children, to wit:

01. Bernice Ester Van Fleet, born 2 October 1920 and died 6 April 1935; and

02. George Lawson Van Fleet, born 5 November 1922 and died 1 December 1993 in Lubbock, Texas.

Bernice, described as a remarkably attractive girl, was just fifteen when she was killed in a car-train collision in San Antonio on 6 April 1935, to the heartbreak of her parents. Their son George Lawson Van Fleet continued the family name.

According to family lore, George Frederick Van Fleet was offered an opportunity in the 1920s to acquire undeveloped real estate near downtown San Antonio for about four dollars an acre. He turned down the offer, knowing that it was marshy land and therefore worthless. Today, that land is part of the famed San Antonio Riverwalk.

When the attack on Pearl Harbor plunged the United States into the Second World War, George Frederick Van Fleet, who was then a major, remained at Fort Sam Houston in the Quartermaster's Corps. His young son George Lawson Van Fleet, however, saw service in both the European Theater of Operations and later in Japan as part of the Occupation Forces.

In a note of irony, this commentator recalls his father's story of a major mix-up in a billing when then-major George Nelson Van Fleet arrived at Fort Sam Houston during the early days of the War, which could not possibly have been his. That billing was for services rendered to his distant cousin Major George F. Van Fleet.

Some two days before George Lawson married Wilma Ruth Williams, George Frederick Van Fleet died on 11 April 1946.

GEORGE LAWSON VAN FLEET (1922 – 1993)

George Lawson Van Fleet was the second child of Major George Frederick and Esther Van Fleet, born in San Antonio, Texas on 5 November 1922. He was a tenth generation American, descended from Adrian Gerritsen Van Vliet via the Frederick Van Fleet lines in New Jersey, and Dubois Van Fleet of Illinois, among others noted in this commentary.

George Lawson attended local schools and at Jefferson High was an outstanding Cadet in the Reserve Officer Training Corps. This set the stage for a military career.

He entered Texas A&M University and the Corps of Cadets in fall 1940. Following the United States' entry into World War II, however, George L. Van Fleet left college and volunteered for active duty in the Army, on 8 October 1942. He completed Officers' Training School at Camp Walters, California and was commissioned a second lieutenant on 30 November 1943, at age twenty-one. He went to England in April 1944 as part of a general deployment of troops to prepare for the invasion of Nazi-occupied France.

In June 1944, he was assigned as a platoon leader supporting the planned assault in Normandy. His transport ship, however, became disabled in the Channel and was forced to return to England. Later he landed in Normandy on 9 June 1944, and promptly moved to the front lines with his platoon on 13 June.

He was awarded a Bronze Star for meritorious service under combat in France on 24 July 1944. Although he did not discuss the events of what happened on that day, he spent the following month in hospital, suffering from a burst left eardrum and "psychoneurosis, anxiety type," more commonly referred to as shell shock.

355

On 30 July 1944 he was returned to England where he remained for the following nine months. He reentered to France on 3 April 1945 and was in Germany on 10 April. In May he was in Belgium where he was promoted to first lieutenant in June, and then following month he was back in France.

Following the Nazi surrender he returned to Germany where he served as an Occupation Forces company officer September 1945 until January 1946, when he returned to the United States.

Lieutenant Van Fleet was ordered to Camp Robinson, Arkansas, but he had a sufficiently long stay in San Antonio to court and marry Wilma Ruth Williams on 13 April 1946. His father George Frederick Van Fleet had died suddenly on 11 April, but the couple proceeded with a small wedding before George Lawson was sent to Arkansas.

The Army reunited George Van Fleet and his bride and in September 1946 sent them to Japan as part of General Douglas McArthur's Occupation Force. Humorously, those responsible for allocating quarters on the troop transport ship likely confused young Lieutenant Van Fleet for his distant cousin Lieutenant General James A. Van Fleet, and assigned them to a senior officer's suite. Wilma Van Fleet commented that is was as good a honeymoon as they got.

In Japan, Lieutenant Van Fleet commanded an engineering construction company that otherwise comprised black American soldiers.

A photograph from that period in the family shows Wilma standing on the platform of a railroad station, glowing eerily under a sign that reads "Hiroshima."

In July 1947 George and Wilma returned to the United States, and in August he left active duty at Fort Lawton, Washington, remaining in the Army Reserves. George then studied divinity briefly, before returning to active duty on 15 October 1948.

George was sent to Fort Ord, near Monterey, California, and on 13 April 1950, the Van Fleets' seventh anniversary, their first child was born. In October 1950 George Van Fleet was ordered to Korea, where he served as a weapons instructor and advisor to a battalion of Royal Thai troops serving with the United Nations Forces. On 16 November 1950 he was promoted to captain. In an interesting aside, since no captain's insignia were available in the field, an enterprising soldier took two of George's lieutenant bars and joined them with strips cut from a tin can, for the pinning.

Captain George L. Van Fleet was later made an officer of the Most Noble Order of the Crown of Thailand by the king of Thailand, in recognition for his service to that nation's troops.

In February 1952 he returned to Fort Ord, where he remained until 1955, serving as a weapons instructor. He was also a prosecutor in courts marshal although he had no formal legal training, nor for that matter even a college degree. Then in December 1955, George L. was assigned to General Staff Command at Fort Meyer, Virginia. Later, he stayed briefly at Fort Leavenworth, Kansas, where his great grandfather Hiram Van Fleet had been discharged nearly a century earlier. On 28 March 1956, the Van Fleets had a second son, born at Fort Belvoir, Virginia.

In September 1957, Captain Van Fleet was transferred to Vicenza, Italy. In Vicenza, Captain Van Fleet served with the First Missile Command of the Southern Europe Task Force (SETAF), in part working on the Army's early efforts at formulating tactical nuclear and biological warfare tactics.

In April 1958, George L. was promoted to major, at which time a photograph shows a very pregnant Wilma pinning on his first gold leaves. Their third son was born later in July.

In June 1960, Major Van Fleet was transferred to SETAF headquarters in Verona, Italy, where the fourth son of the family was born in 1961. In July of that year, George was transferred back to the United States, and more importantly, to Texas.

In August 1961, the Van Fleets arrived in Huntsville, Texas, where Major Van Fleet headed up the Reserve Officers Training Corps at Sam Houston State Teachers' College (now University). He was promoted to lieutenant colonel in December 1962, and then retired from active duty in July 1965, being awarded his second Army Commendation Medal. He became a popular teacher of history and civics at Huntsville High School, later declining an opportunity to return yet again to active duty to lead a regiment of Rangers in Vietnam.

In 1968, Colonel Van Fleet moved to San Marcos, Texas, becoming Commandant of Cadets at San Marcos Academy. In 1970, he moved to Lubbock, and began the Junior ROTC program at Estacado High School, also teaching civics and history, until final retirement in 1983.

The Van Fleets had five sons who were:

01. Michael Allan Van Fleet, born 13 April 1950, and died the same day;
02. George Allan Van Fleet, born 20 January 1953, in Monterey, California;
03. William Leroy Van Fleet II, born 28 March 1956, in Fort Belvoir, Virginia;
04. Lee Andrew Van Fleet, born 8 July 1958, Vicenza, Italy; and
05. Charles Edward Van Fleet, born 28 January 1961, Vicenza, Italy.

George Lawson Van Fleet died in Lubbock, Texas, on 1 December 1993. His wife Wilma followed on 27 April 2001. They are buried at the Fort Sam Houston National Cemetery in San Antonio. Three of their four surviving sons are attorneys, and all remain as residents of Texas.

358

A PORTRAIT OF UTAH

Spanish Franciscan friars from California were the first Europeans to visit present-day Utah, arriving sometime in 1776. Thereafter fur traders and explorers followed, but permanent settlements did not begin untilthe arrival of the Mormons in 1847. They made this arid land bloom and created a prosperous community and successful economy, based in some part on trade with others following the trails further to the west.

Mormons organized their community as the "State of Deseret" in 1849, the year they sought admission to the American Union. However, controversies over aspects of their faith, most particularly the practice of polygamy, frustrated their effort. Although officially this practice was discontinued in 1890, it was not until 4 January 1898 that Utah was admitted as the forty-fifth state.

With some 84,904 square miles of territory, Utah ranks as the thirteenth largest state. Its population is small with somewhat over two million inhabitants at present. In 1850 shortly after the first pioneers arrived, the Federal Census recorded 11,594 rsidents, and in 1900 there were 276,749 inhabitants, showing remarkable growth in the "Beehive State."

What Brought Van Fleets to Utah?

In 1827, Joseph Smith, who lived near Palmyra, New York, had a vision of the Angel Moroni. Revealed to him were buried Golden Tablets that contained a further testament of Jesus Christ, commonly called the Book of Mormon.

359

Departing from many traditional Christian religious beliefs, the Church of Jesus Christ of Latter Day Saints met with great cynicism and outright persecution in its early years. Nonetheless, in an era akin to the Great Awakening of the Eighteenth Century, that religious phenomenon – revisited in the Nineteenth Century – evoked substantial interest in the new faith.

In the Finger Lakes region of New York, many persons embraced the Mormon religion. But with persecutions continuing, these early adherents began a movement to Ohio, Indiana and finally Illinois, where a new city of enlightenment called Nauvoo was established on the banks of the Missouri River.

Nauvoo was once one of the largest American cities west of the Allegheny Mountains, but its light was not to last long. Attacked and burned by Mormon enemies, the faithful journeyed on westward to a place where they could practice their religion in peace, unbothered by non-believers or persecuters. Thus began the great migration that ultimately led to "the promised land" under Brigham Young, the slain Joseph Smith's successor in the Church of Jesus Christ of Latter Day Saints.

Part of the Van Fleet family from upstate New York joined this movement west to Nauvoo and on to present-day Utah, half a century before statehood. Although they were few in number initially, the descendants of Alanson Van Fleet, grandson of Daniel Van Fleet Junior and a seventh generation American, today they constitute an important group from this family in Utah. They represent the Mormon branch once scorned, but they have been as fruitful as other Van Fleets and Van Vliets who have bloomed and bore fruit in so many other states.

360

ALANSON VAN FLEET (1819 – 1851)

Daniel Van Fleet Junior, a second generation resident of the Minisink Valley, was married and the father of several children before he quit that region and relocated to upstate New York. James, one of his sons, had come to adulthood in the Minisink and married there in 1816, to one Leah Cuykendall, daughter of Martinus and Anna Cool Cuyendall.

In point of fact, all families cited were well established in the Minisink region, and were of Dutch descent. The Cools (or Coles or Koles) were located mainly in the New Jersey portion of that area, and a small Sussex County town is named for them. The Cuyendalls (or Kukendalls) like the Van Fleets were found in both neighboring states in growing numbers.

When Daniel Van Fleet Junior relocated to Cayuga County, his son James followed suit, as did other family members. It was there that James and his children learned of the new religion professed by Prophet Joseph Smith, in the same time frame that James' uncle Joshua, located in not-distant Manchester, was dismissing this faith as fraudulent. The story of James' family, however, was to be different.

James Van Fleet relocated to Ohio, perhaps for religious reasons but certainly economic ones played a role as well. This more, nonetheless, was after all of his children were born in Cayuga County.

Specifically, the children of James Van Fleet were:

01. Alanson Van Fleet, born 28 October 1819 in Wascord, Cayuga County, New York, and died 1851;

361

02. James Van Fleet Junior, born 1824 in Cayuga County;
03. Henry Van Fleet, born in 1826 in Cayuga County;
04. Mary Elizabeth Van Fleet, born 1831 in Cayuga County; and
05. Martha Van Fleet, born in 1836 in Cayuga County.

The Van Fleet family settled in Seneca County in the town of Scipio before 1840, where James and Leah lived the remainder of their lives. The proximity of their Seneca County home and that of Joshua Van Fleet (James' uncle and former 'neighbor" by about twenty-five miles in upstate New York) was perhaps coincidental but highly ironical in the religious context, given Joshua's antagonism toward Mormanism. James died in neighboring Seneca County in 1850 at age sixty, two years after his uncle's death in Marion County.

James was followed in death the next year by his eldest son Alanson Van Fleet. Born in October 1819, he was just shy of age thirty-two when he died of unknown causes in June of that year. However, he left behind a family of some size.

Alanson married Sylvia Chase in 1838 at age nineteen, she being about the same age. This union took place in Sparta, Livingston County, New York. Sylvia was a daughter of Isaac Chase and Phoebe Ogden (her mother's family later playing a major role in Utah history) of Livingston County.

Like his wife, Alanson Van Fleet was an early adherent of the Mormon faith. In the 1840s following the disasters of earlier settlements of their co-religionists including at Nauvoo, Illinois, they joined the movement west under Brigham Young. While wintering in Nebraska in 1847, Alanson married a second time to Jane Turner.

The marriage produced the following children by Sylvia Chase:

01.   Elias Van Fleet, born 17 March 1839 in Sparta, Livingston County, New York and died 13 June 1920 in Farmington, Davis County, Utah;

02.   Helen Maria Van Fleet, born July 1841 in Nauvoo, Illinois and died in September; and

03.   Joseph Smith Van Fleet, born 6 September 1843 in Nauvoo, Illinois, and died in 1900 in Freemont, Utah.

By Jane Turner, his second wife, Alanson sired the following children (twins):

01.   Cyrus Van Fleet, born June 1848 in Nebraska; and

02.   Cyrenus Van Fleet, born June 1848 in Nebraska.

At least one of the twin boys died soon thereafter, and the fate of the second is unknown.

Alanson Van Fleet is known to have died in June 1851, but where remains a question. There is a belief among some family members that he left Nebraska for Canada, never proceeding on to Utah with his substantial family. However, nothing more is known of his life, as this reporting could be in error.

More importantly, the line he established through his Mormon religious affiliation is traced and well documented. Beginning with his eldest child Elias, the story of this Van Fleet line descended from Alanson continues.

ELIAS VAN FLEET (1839 - 1920)

Elias Van Fleet was born in Sparta, New York and died 13 June 1920 in Farmington, Utah. He was descended from Daniel Van Fleet Junior, Jan Van Vliet Junior to Adrian Gerritsen Van Vliet, and was a seventh generation American.

He came to Utah as a very young child in the Brigham Young Company accompanied by his mother and siblings among other extended family members, and as one among the first to enter the Great Salt Valley as Mormon pioneers.

His Mormon faith is a strong characteristic of his life. During his lifetime, he served as Senior President Seventy-Fourth Quorum Seventies, as a missionary to the Dixie area of south Utah in the 1870 and 1871 period, and as a lieutenant in the Black Hawk War. Although a farmer and stock raiser by profession, he also found time to serve as a deputy sheriff in Davis County.

He married twice, first to Lucy Adams, daughter of James and Betsey Leavitt Adams, on 10 May 1860 in Centerville, Utah; and second to Mary Ann Richards, daughter of Willard and Susannah Bayless Richards, on 30 May 1868 in Salt Lake City. With these two wives, he had eighteen children.

His children by Lucy Adams were:
01. Mary Alice Van Fleet, born 13 June 1861 in Farmington, married Hart Udy on 10 January 1877 and died 5 December 1958 in Kaysville, Utah;
02. Elias Judson Van Fleet, born 1 February 1863 and died 18 February 1864 in Utah;
03. Rosebell Van Fleet, born 7 June 1865, married Lemuel Van Rogers 7 February 1884 and died 21 June 1943 in Salt Lake;

04. Sylvia Van Fleet, born 18 July 1867, married Charles Henry Bourne 12 January 1887, and died 10 June 1941 in Salt Lake City;

05. Lucy Van Fleet, born 24 January 1870 and died 11 February 1879 in Farmington;

06. Zina Van Fleet, born 11 October 1871, married Royal Henry Peck 23 May 1890 and died 7 October 1953;

07. Jessie Van Fleet, born 7 June 1873 and died 18 February 1874 in Farmington; and

08. Horace Van Fleet, born 24 August 1878 and died 18 August 1968 in Farmington.

His ten children by Mary Richards were:

01. Willard Richards Van Fleet, born 24 May 1869;

02. Susan Ella Van Fleet, born 5 November 1871;

03. Franklin D. Van Fleet, born 8 March 1874;

04. Elias Chase Van Fleet, born 11 February 1876;

05. Heber John Van Fleet, born 11 January 1879, married Mary Ellen _____ and died in 1938 in Farmington;

06. Hyrum Smith Van Fleet, born 20 February 1882, married Lucy May _____ and died in 1956;

07. Chloe Van Fleet, born 23 August 1864;

08. Mable Hattie Van Fleet, born 23 September 1886;

09. Nina Bayless Van Fleet, born 23 September 1889; and

10. Shirley Irene Van Fleet, born 19 October 1893.

JOSEPH SMITH VAN FLEET (1843 – 1900)

Joseph Smith Van Fleet, a younger brother of Elias, helped establish a sizable Van Fleet presence in Utah as well. He was born 6 September 1843 in Nauvoo, Illinois, after the family had relocated to that new Mormon city on the Missouri.

When those of this faith elected to depart Illinois for the west after the city was largely destroyed by persecuting non-Mormons, he was one of the children to make the long trek that ultimately led to Utah. He died there in 1900 at the young age of fifty-seven.

There is some confusion about his wife's name, and at least one correspondent has reported that it was Jane Turner. In any event, the following are cited as his children:

01. Jospeh Alanson Van Fleet, born 25 December 1865, married Mollie Smith and died 18 January 1912;

02. Henry Van Fleet, born September 1867 and died 1868;

03. Sylvia B. Van Fleet, born December 1868, married Alan Porter and died September 1939;

04. Charles Dewey Van Fleet, born November 1871, married Ruth Edwards and died in 1936;

05. Horace A. Van Fleet, born 1874 and died in 1898;

06. Annie C. Van Fleet, born march 1878, married Myron Richards and died in 1936; and

07. Rhonda Ann Van Fleet, born August 1882, married Hiram Fowler and died January 1934.

HORACE VAN FLEET (1878 – 1968)

The son of James and Lucy Adama Van Fleet, Horace Van Fleet was born 24 August 1878, and at age twenty-three, he married Eva Louise Soule on 17 January 1902, in Hooper, Weber County. She was the daughter of Emory and Mary Secrist Soule.

Horace was a sheriff's deputy for about twenty years, a Farmington city councilman, member of the board of education, and a dairy farmer by profession.

However, Horace was far from prosperous in farming and at one point later in life was forced to sell his property to pay his – and others – bills. While seemingly a simple matter, the division of remaining money caused friction between Horace and his son Horace Junior, an alienation that remained for the rest of their lives.

Horace had a colorful career in law enforcement. In addition to pursuing various bandits and other criminals, he was involved in shoot-outs in which – fortunately – only the law breakers died.

Horace and his wife Eva Soule Van Fleet had just two children, Horace Emerson Van Fleet, born 11 December 1907 and who died 4 August 1977; and Stanford Soule Van Fleet.

Horace Emerson was born in Farmington. As a young man he was a shoe salesman in California, a dress salesman in the Midwest and later, a law enforcement officer like his father. He served in the Farmington city police, the Davis County sheriff's office and also patrolled rail yards. He died of heart problems short of his seventieth birthday.

Horace Emerson had married June Grow on 11 December 1933 in Davis County, daughter of Henry and Ruth Halls Grow. Their children were:

01. Paul Horace Van Fleet, born 22 September 1934 and died 19 June 1975 in Salt Lake City. He had married Renee Lund, and had four children: Michael Van Fleet (born 1 March 1955, died tragically 13 December 1972); Debra Van Fleet; Julie Fleet (married Kevin Dyreng); and Sandra Van Fleet;
02. Janet Van Fleet, born 13 August 1940, married Walter Lester Schofield in 1958 and then Anthony Pinto in 1970; and
03. Scott E. Van Fleet, born 19 November 1947 in Salt Lake City.

Horace's brother Stanford married Josephene _____, and had two children. These were:
01. Bradford A. Van Fleet, born 26 May 1937 and died 7 December 1962; and
02. Kristie Van Fleet.

Scott E. Van Fleet, a son of Horace and June Grow Van Fleet, was born in 1947 in Salt Lake City. He married Dorothy Lynn Whiting, daughter of Oris and Anna Otteson Whiting in Bountiful, Utah, 14 December 1969 at age twenty-one.

Their children are:
01. Tiffany Ann Van Fleet, born 24 July 1969 in Salt Lake, married Darren Keith Richison on 8 April 1987 in Kaysville;
02. Shannon Van Fleet, born 21 December 1971 in Bountiful, married Kevin Brian Blood on 19 January 1991; and
03. Brandon Scott Van Fleet, born 16 April 1978 in Layton, Utah.

PART V.

THE CONCLUSIONS

ARE THE BEGINNINGS

EPILOGUE

There is no "concluding" chapter to this commentary, because there is no end to the story of the Van Fleets/Van Vliets in America. Some three hundred and sixty-eight years after coming to this land, Adrian Gerritsen Van Vliet's and Dirck Jans Van der Vliedt's legacies live on, transformed only by the circumstances of time, new technology and societal evolution.

Whatever the reasons that brought them to America, surely their sense of adventure, desire to be free of political and other restrictions, and an assurance of great futures in the New World had to be among them.

In these things not only was their wish fulfilled, but so too was that for the nation whose roots and eventually foundations they and their fellow Dutchmen helped establish. The benefits of the America that they and their descendants created and have subsequently enjoyed (as well as having shared with countless others) through the centuries remain unique to the American experience.

The Van Vliet/Van Fleet family indeed has been the fulfillment of the American dream. We have been poor and rich, well educated and illiterate, coming from all walks of life. In true American fashion, we are and have been whatever we have sought to be.

Our endeavors that began on the cusp of the American frontier continued in that vein for two centuries, spreading across a continent. In scores of capacities from the humble to the proud, we helped mold America. In this our fourth century, our family is settled in a land devoid of physical frontiers, but it still incorporates the essence of Americanism in new technological frontiers.

Indeed, our longstanding frontier experience helped us evolve in the unique American culture of independence, self-reliance, resourcefulness, pragmatism and inventiveness. As this history clearly relates, we have always been comfortable with change and with the people who make things happen.

Our restlessness reflects this brilliantly. We foster the upstarts and the young, encouraging them to go and make their way in life. We epitomize the ideas that "new" is better than merelt accepting the old; that taking charge is better than playing it safe; that making one's own money is superior to inheriting it; that education and individual merit are to be favored over family connections.

We have also epitomized the idea that class barriers can be eroded by the prospect and achievement of success. This was accomplished by acquiring land in the Seventeenth and Eighteenth Centuries when it was easy to acquire it. Then by education, hard work and merit on which one had to rely for advancement in life in the Nineteenth, Twentieth – and as will come to pass in the Twnety-First – Centuries, the Van Fleet/Van Vliet family progressed as well.

And as I refer to it, our societal evolution reflects that we are no longer part of a small "Hollandized" population of Protestant Dutchmen, French Huguenots and Englishmen in an isolated Sleepy Hollow-like New York Catskills community, but rather an integral part of a larger national one that is multi-ethnic (as Van Fleets/Van Vliets are), religiously diverse, multiculturally comfortable, egalitarian, reasonably well educated, tolerant, future-oriented, and individualistic.

We can take pride in ourselves, our extended family and our country. The values we incorporate and share, outlined in broad brush strokes in our Constitution, are those by which we live. Today, they are emulated by peoples around the world. But our contributions to American society and its founding principles cited in the beginning of this commentary, continue and help make most early documents of our Republic *live*.

For the Life, Liberty and ability to Pursue Happiness that we have inherited, we owe our gratitude to our common ancestors Adrian Gerritsen and Dirck Jans. Now it is up to us to continue their work making America and perhaps the world a continuously better place for all.

SELECTED BIBLIOGRAPHY

Alexander, Robert S., ALBANY'S FIRST CHURCH, Newsgraphics, Delmar, New York, 1988.

Anjou, Gustave, ULSTER COUNTY NEW YORK PROBATE RECORDS, Vol. I, Heritage Press, Bowie, Maryland, 1992.

Braim, Paul F., THE WILL TO WIN, Naval Institute Press, Annapolis, Maryland, 2001.

Broadhead, John Romeyn, comp. And O'Callaghan, Edmund B., and Fernow, Berthold, eds. And trans., DOCUMENTS RELATIVE TO THE COLONIAL HISTORY OF THE STATE OF NEW YORK, 15 volumes, Weed, Parsons, New York, 1856-57.

Budd, Thomas, GOOD ORDER ESTABLISHED IN PENNSYLVANIA 1685, Burt Franklin, New York, 1971 (reissued).

Bushnell, Albert, PROVINCIAL AMERICA 1690-1740, Hart, Greenwood Press, Connecticut, 1905 (reissued 1980).

Condon, Thomas J., NEW YORK BEGINNINGS: THE COMMERCIAL ORIGINS OF NEW NETHERLANDS, New York University Press, New York, 1968.

Christoph, Peter R. and Christoph, Florence A. (editors), THE ANDROS PAPERS 1674-1678, Syracuse University Press, Syracuse, 1989.

Cuddeback, Louis, CAUDEBEC IN AMERICA, Tobias Wright, New York, 1919 (reissued by Amerion House, Mattituck, New York, 1999.

Coleman, Charles C., THE EARLY RECORDS OF THE FIRST PRESBYTERIAN CHURCH AT GOSHEN, NEW YORK 1767-1885, Heritage Books, Bowie, Maryland, 1989.

Davies, K.G., THE NORTH ATLANTIC WORLD IN THE SEVENTEENTH CENTURY, University of Minnesota Press, Minneapolis, Minnesota, 1974.

Delbruck, Hans, THE BARBARIAN INVASIONS, HISTORY OF THE ART OF WAR, Vol. II, University of Nebraska Press, Lincoln, 1989.

Deming, Catherine Meddaugh, GRANDMAS AND GRANDPAS OF YESTERYEAR, Endicott, New York, 1982.

East, W. Gordon, AN HISTORICAL GEOGRAPHY OF EUROPE, Mathuen and Company, London, 1962.

Egle, William Henry, DOCUMENTS RELATING TO THE CONNECTICUT SETTLEMENT IN THE WYOMING VALLEY, Vols. I and II, Meyers, Harrisburg, Pennsylvania, 1893 (reissued by Heritage Press, Bowie, Maryland, 1990).

Galvin, John R., THE MINUTE MEN, Pergamon Brassey, Washington, D.C., 1989.

Gottmann, Jean, A GEOGRAPHY OF EUROPE, Third Edition, Holt, Rinehart and Winston, New York, 1962.

Gumaer, Peter E., A HISTORY OF DEER PARK IN ORANGE COUNTY, NEW YORK, Minisink Valley Historical Society, Port Jervis Print, 1890 (reissued by Heritage Books, Bowie, Maryland, 1894).

Hart, Albert Bushnell (editor), PROVINCIAL AMERICA 1690-1740, Greenwood Press, Connecticut, 1980 (reprint).

Hollister, H., HISTORY OF LACKAWANNA COUNTY, J.B. Lippincott Company, Philadelphia, Pennsylvania, 1885 (reissued by Heritage Books, Bowie, Maryland, 1988).

_____, INDEX: TO BAPTISMAL SURNAMES IN THE REFORMED CHURCH, The Holland Society of New York, New York, 1990.

Jakle, John A., IMAGES OF THE OHIO VALLEY, Oxford University Press, New York, 1977.

Jameson, J. Franklin, NARRATIVES OF NEW NETHERLAND 1609-1664, Scribner, New York, 1909 (reissued by Heritage Books, Bowie, Maryland, 1990).

Leggett, Conaway and Company, THE HISTORY OF MARION COUNTY OHIO, Part I and Part II, Chicago, Illinois, 1883 (reissued by Heritage Books, Bowie, Maryland, 1992).

Lucas, Henry Stephen, THE LOW COUNTRIES AND THE HUNDRED YEARS' WAR, Porcupine Press, Philadelphia, 1976.

Miner, Charles, HISTORY OF WYOMING, J. Crissy, Philadelphia, 1845 (reissued by Heritage Books, Bowie, Maryland, 1991)

Mumford, Mildred, THIS IS WAVERLY, The Waverly Womens' Club, Waverly, Pennsylvania, 1955.

_____, MINISINK VALLEY REFORMED DUTCH CHURCH RECORDS 1716-1830, New York Genealogical and Biographical Society, 1913 (reissued by Heritage Books, Bowie, Maryland, 1992).

O'Callaghan, Edmund B., DOCUMENTARY HISTORY OF THE STATE OF NEW YORK, Vols. I to IV, Weed, Parsons, Albany, New York, 1849-51.

Parker, Geoffrey, THE THIRTY YEARS' WAR, Military Heritage Press, New York, 1897.

Rink, Oliver A., HOLLAND ON THE HUDSON: AN ECONOMIC AND SOCIAL HISTORY OF DUTCH NEW YORK, Cornell University Press, Ithaca, New York, 1986.

Ritchie, Robert K., THE DUKE'S PROVINCE 1664-1691, University of North Carolina Press, Chapel Hill, North Carolina, 1977.

Stickney, Charles E., A HISTORY OF THE MINISINK REGION, Coe, Finch and I.F. Guiwits, Middletown, New York, 1867 (reissued by the Minisink Valley Historical Society, Port Jervis, New York, 1989).

(Unattributed), THE HISTORY OF DUTCHESS COUNTY, NEW YORK, 1880.

(Unattributed), THE MINISINK, Walpack Historical Society, Walpack Center, New Jersey, 1975.

Van de Water, John Ward, CHICHEE'S TRUNK: A TRUE STORY OF ROOTS AND BRANCHES, Jonsalvania Publishers, Canton, New York, 1980.

Wilcoxen, Charlotte, SEVENTEENTH CENTURY ALBANY: A SUTCH PROFILE, Albany Institute of History and Art, Albany, New York, 1981.

INDEX

CHAMPLAIN, 338
CHANG, Xi 277
CHAPIN, Lydia 345 347
350 Samuel 350
CHARLEMAGNE, 11
Emperor Of Germany
12
CHARLES II King Of
England 56 64 65 144
CHASE, Isaac 362
Phoebe 362 Sylvia
362-363
CHATHAM, Earl Of 147
CHEHALIS, Daisey 331
Josephene 331 Nellie
331
CHOWDRY, Oliver 232
CHRISPEL, Marytjen 201
CLARK, 307 335 Carolina
175 Chester 175
Edward 170 Emma
175 Esther 175
Florence 175 George
Rogers 253 257 269
Jasper 175 Marion 175
Mary 170 175
Napoleon 175 Ruth
175 251
CLARKSON, Clarissa
247-248 Nellie G 182
185 189
CLOET, Janneke 81
CLYMER, 168 George 164
167
CODEBEC, Jacob 93 98
107
CODEBECK, Jacob 90
COFFEY, Lulu Pearl 265
336 Scott Lloyd 265
336

COLE, Sarah 133 Teunis
133
COLER, John 213
Rebecca 213
COLL, Jacob Rutsen 127
COLVERT, Reva 310
COLVIN, Israel 164
COOKE, Cardinal 298
COOL, Anna 361
COOLEY, Mary Ann 248
CORNWALLIS, Lord 150
CORONADO, 343
COSBY, Georgia Ann 274
COURTWRIGHT,
Catherine 226
Cornelius 226
COX, Doris 276
CREIGIER, Capt 55
CROCKER, Juila 323
CROM, 128 Gertruyd 73
Gysbert 88 Gysbert
Willemse 73
CROMWELL, Elizabeth
81 Engeltje 81 John 81
Levina 81 Maria 82
CROSS, Alma 348
CUDDEBACK, 107 150
157 Abraham 98 110
116 Benjamin 98
Catherina 98
Catherine 98 Esther
98 Esyntje 98 100
Gerardus Swartout
100 Hester 110
Jacomyntjen 108
Jacques 99 James 98
100 Jane 98 Jesyntje
98 Maria 98 Samuel
108

386

388

390

VAN FLEET (cont.)
Imelda 305 Iredell 273-
274 Isaac 121 309
Isabel 345 Isabella C
314 Isabelle 323 Jack
120 Jacob 206
Jacobus 102 Jacobus
Jr 102 Jacomyntje 105
110 Jacqueline Kay
276 James 102-103
112 117-118 150 156
159-161 164 167-168
170-174 176 186 194
216-217 220-222 230
234 236 238 259-260
270-275 278 285 304
327 361-362 367
James A 166 169 171
173 191 240 287 298
303 356 James Alward
196 286 288-290 295
James Alward III 295
James Alward Jr 295
James Buchanan 213
James Edward 275-
276 James Edward Jr
277 James Franklin
310 James Jr 112 118
295 362 James T 273-
274 Jan 234 Jane 138
362-363 366 Janet
368 Janet Louise 266
Jared 143 208 211
273 321 Jarel 273 Jay
221 275 Jefferson 206
224 Jeremiah 213
Jerimah 207 Jesse 142
310 Jesse Gardner 170
174 179 Jesse
LeGrande 224

VAN FLEET (cont.)
Jesse Morton 265 336
Jessie 365 Jessie Mae
187 191 Jesyntje 105
Jim 274 John 77 85
102 120-121 134 136-
137 139 142-143 207-
211 213 220 229 256
273 276 309 321 John
Albert 352 John
George 186 190 John
Henry 138-139 John II
309 John Jr 120 John
K 237 256 260 270
John Kennedy 204 229
234 237-238 254-255
259-260 270-272 John
Sr 120 John W 213
John Wallace 275-276
Johnny 276 Joseph
137 273 Joseph E 213
Joseph S 142 Joseph
Smith 363 366
Josephene 368
Josephine 285 Joshua
101 105 109 112-113
117-119 145-146 153
155-156 159-160 162
193 204 216 219 222
225-228 230-238 255-
256 260 262 272 361-
362 Joshua Jr 204
229 234 237-238 259-
264 270-272 281 288
336 Joshua Sr 206-
207 237 239 259 261
263 273-277 281 288
336 Jospeh Alanson
366 Judge 323 Judik
77

VAN FLEET (cont.)
Judith 85 133-134 136
141 Judith Gail 275
Juila 323 Julia Anna
209 321 Julia Crocker
323 Julie 368 June
367-368 Karl Frank
310 Kate 221 Kathy
Jean 276 Kristie 368
Kyle Frank Cheng 277
Lamintha 174 Lamitha
179-180 Larayne 334
Larua Lenora 215
Laura 137-139 317
Laura Adelpha 138
Laura Ann 266 Laura
Elizabeth 139 Lavinia
180 182 184-185
Lavinia Lucinda 182
LeRoy Eston 337 Lea
Huff 142 Leah 77 85
117-118 134-135 361-
362 Lee Andrew 358
Lee Frances 191 Lester
138 Lester White 265
Levi 117-119 206 223-
224 234 Levi Jr 207
Levi Sr 207 Lexa
Penina 170 327 Lilian
Rose 337 Lillie 348
Lisa Gayle 276 Lois
Medora 285 Lois Violet
274 Loretta 191
Loretta Rose 187 196
Lori Ann 310 Lozetta
119 Lt 289 356 Lt Gen
292 Lucy 208 211 219
221 364-365 367 Lucy
Ann 238 Lucy E 221
Lucy May 365

VAN FLEET (cont.)
Luella 348 Lula May
139 Lulu E 138 Lulu
Pearl 265 336 Luther
326-327 329 333
Luther G 174 Luticia
344 Lydia 220 344-345
347 350 Lyman
Trumbull 264 Lynnette
276 Mable Hattie 365
Mabry 209 Madeline
310 Magerie 109
Maggie May 139
Marcus Edward 345
Margaret 85 135-136
143 183 208 213
Margaret Ann 213
Maria 98 Maria Ellen
278 Maria Eudocia
263 Maria Louisa 261
263 Marie 77 98 Marie
I 139 Marietta 174
Marilyn 190 Mark
Allan 277 Martha 116-
118 158 170 175 223
345 362 Martha
Jeanne 191 Martha
Melita 285 Martin N
262 Martin Nichols
256 261 263-264 267
336 Mary 77 85 127-
128 133-135 149 155
160-161 169-170 175
208 221 229 256 345
347 350 352 365 Mary
Alice 364 Mary Ann
119-120 223 260-261
263 273 281 364 Mary
E 118 274 Mary Edith
334

AUTHOR BIOGRAPHY

James A. Van Fleet is a thirteenth generation descendant of Adrian Gerrtisen Van Vliet. His career took him to over a hundred countries around the globe, where he worked in international development activities for the United States Government from the early 1960s onward.

In pursuing a second career during the 1980s, Dr. Van Fleet served in several senior academic capacities in international education, retiring in 2000 as professor emeritus from The University of North Carolina. Currently he resided in Naples, Florida, and continues research, writing and occasional projects for the United States Department of State abroad.